On the Development
of a Token Economy
Mental Hospital Treatment
Program

THE SERIES IN CLINICAL AND COMMUNITY PSYCHOLOGY

CONSULTING EDITORS:

CHARLES D. SPIELBERGER and IRWIN G. SARASON

Becker	• Depression: Theory and Research
Endler and Magnusson	• Interactional Psychology and Personality
Friedman and Katz	• The Psychology of Depression: Contemporary Theory and Research
Klopfer and Reed	• Problems in Psychotherapy: An Eclectic Approach
Reitan and Davison	• Clinical Neuropsychology: Current Status and Applications
Spielberger and Sarason	• Stress and Anxiety, volume 1
Sarason and Spielberger	• Stress and Anxiety, volume 2
Ulmer	• On the Development of a Token Economy Mental Hospital Treatment Program

IN PREPARATION

Averill	• Patterns in Psychological Thought: Readings in Historical and Contemporary Texts
Bermant, Kelman, and Warwick	• The Ethics of Social Intervention
Brehm	• The Application of Social Psychology to Clinical Practice
Cattell and Dreger	• Handbook of Modern Personality Theory
Cohen and Mirsky	• Biology and Psychopathology
Janisse	• A Psychological Survey of Pupillometry
Kissen	• From Group Dynamics to Group Psychoanalysis: Therapeutic Application of Group Dynamic Understanding
London	• Strategies of Personality Research
Olweus	• Aggression in the Schools
Sarason and Spielberger	• Stress and Anxiety, volume 3
Spielberger and Sarason	• Stress and Anxiety, volume 4
Spielberger and Diaz-Guerrero	• Crosscultural Research on Anxiety

On the Development of a Token Economy Mental Hospital Treatment Program

RAYMOND A. ULMER
Department of Psychiatry and Human Behavior
Charles R. Drew Postgraduate Medical School

and

Department of Psychiatry and Human Behavior
Martin Luther King, Jr. General Hospital
Los Angeles, California

and

Department of Psychiatry, School of Medicine
University of California at Los Angeles

HEMISPHERE PUBLISHING CORPORATION
Washington   London

A HALSTED PRESS BOOK
JOHN WILEY & SONS
New York   London   Sydney   Toronto

1/1977
Psych.

Hemisphere Publishing Corporation
1025 Vermont Ave., N.W., Washington, D.C. 20005

Distributed solely by Halsted Press, A Division of John Wiley & Sons, Inc., New York.

1 2 3 4 5 6 7 8 9 0   MAMA   7 8 4 3 2 1 0 9 8 7 6

Library of Congress Cataloging in Publication Data

Ulmer, Raymond A
   On the development of a token economy mental hospital treatment program.

   (The Series in clinical and community psychology)
   Includes bibliographies and indexes.
   1. Token economy (Psychology)   2. Psychiatric hospital care.   3. California. State Hospital, Camarillo.
I. Title. [DNLM: 1. Hospitals, Psychiatric.   2. Hospital psychiatric departments.   3. Token economy. WM30
U440]
RC489.B4U38   616.8′91   75-37984
ISBN 0-470-01393-1

Printed in the United States of America

To my wife Carmen and my son George, who are always a source of love, inspiration, and encouragement to me.

Contents

Preface

This book is written as an expression of conviction about the effectiveness of current token economies, and their extremely promising future for the treatment of the short- and long-term patient in a community or state mental hospital. I have been most impressed with the results of token economy mental hospital units, as evidenced by remarkable socially appropriate changes in speech, actions, and appearance in the "untreatable" patient. Sometimes the so-called untreatable patient has a history of many years of continuous hospitalization, and at other times he goes in and out of hospitals frequently. Both varieties of the untreatable patient respond well to token economy treatment, leave the hospital more quickly, and tend to stay out longer than with traditional insight therapy. When token economy approaches are knowledgeably, systematically, and creatively applied, as well as adequately supported by administrators, token economy, in combination with psychoactive drugs, appears to be more successful than any treatment approach now available. And now—as well as in the future—the name of the treatment game is quick results with long-lasting effectiveness.

Token economy is becoming the treatment of choice in many inpatient settings where time, costs, and results are important. The long-term chronic patient is no longer an acceptable burden, because he costs $15,000 or more per year to maintain in any mental hospital. By contrast, token economy social training can be effective after a period of weeks or a few months. Then the patient can be sent to a supervised facility such as a board-and-care home where he can function reasonably well. Dollar savings to the community are substantial, and human suffering costs are reduced greatly, since existence in a mental health facility is not a happy experience for anyone. The effectiveness of token economy treatment is one good argument—among many—for the current reduction in state hospital populations and the setting up of community token economy programs. This is the present strong trend, and it is likely to increase in the future. For these reasons considerable interest is being shown in token economy, and much more will be shown in the future.

This book is written to provide specific answers to questions raised by my colleagues—psychologists, psychiatric social workers, psychiatric technicians, psychiatrists, and rehabilitation counselors—who often ask such questions as: "How can I organize and operate a token economy unit in my hospital?" and

"What problems will I have to face, and how can I handle them?" The problems
are likely to be similar from hospital to hospital. It is my hope that this book
will provide useful answers to questions about the organization and operation of
token economy.

This book, like any token economy program, is the product of team efforts,
and I am indebted to all of the team members. I especially wish to acknowledge
the sensitive and consistent support of my colleagues at Camarillo (California)
State Hospital and Mental Health Center: Hugh Sanford, Head Charge of
Psychiatric Technicians; John Streifel, Staff Psychologist; William Purmort,
Psychiatrist; Marion Sisson, Nursing Coordinator; Irwin Hart, Chief Psychologist;
Roy Jones, Coordinator of Psychiatric Social Work; Lura Stephens, Super-
intendant of Nursing Services; and Charles Allen, Medical Director.

I am indebted to Synanon for a tremendous personal and professional
experience.

Additional thanks are due Linda Reiman for creative and conscientious
editing of the complete manuscript, David Barlow for many scholarly contributions, and Leonard Krasner for the title, recommendations, and, especially,
encouragement.

I am grateful to many students of psychology, psychiatric social work,
psychiatry, and nursing who contributed to this book in addition to the following former students: Allen Hess, Roger Patterson, and William van Doorninck.

I am obligated to token economy for a most gratifying professional and
research experience.

Raymond A. Ulmer, Ph.D.
Former Assistant Program Director
Behavior Modification Program
Camarillo State Hospital
and Mental Health Center
Camarillo, California

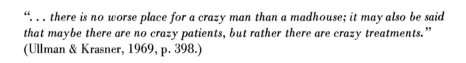
"... there is no worse place for a crazy man than a madhouse; it may also be said that maybe there are no crazy patients, but rather there are crazy treatments."
(Ullman & Krasner, 1969, p. 398.)

On the Development
of a Token Economy
Mental Hospital Treatment
Program

General Background

INTRODUCTION

In all kinds of community and state institutional settings, there is a vast range of potential use for new token economies. (See the Suggested Readings at the end of this chapter for sources of background information on token economy.)

"What could the token economy be?" It *could* facilitate any form of rehabilitation. Because it facilitates the maintenance of behavior at maximal levels of motivation, it *could* be used to help achieve vocational, educational, and therapeutic objectives in prisons, schools, and hospitals. In effect, this system could be a means through which the individuals concerned became responsible for the functioning of their therapeutic, educational, vocational, or training environment. Again, this system *could* be used to assure transfer of the individual's newly acquired behaviors to the outside world. Last but not least, the development and maintenance of complex social behaviors will continue to . . . be a major practical problem to existing institutions. It is here that the methodology of the token economy can help. Indeed, the behavioral methodology can help not only in conceptualizing the social objectives of institutions but also in evaluating the effectiveness of current methods to achieve them. (Ayllon & Roberts, 1972, p. 84.)

Token economy has an exceedingly bright future. For example, the Camarillo Token Economy Program showed that this approach, which was originally applied only to long-term mental hospital patients (Ayllon & Azrin, 1968a), was effective with short-term, frequently returning patients, as well as alcoholics, drug abusers, and sociopaths.[1] This book is a second-generation token economy manual. The first generation (Ayllon & Azrin, 1968a; Schaefer & Martin, 1969) demonstrated clearly the effectiveness of token economy treatment with long-term hospital patients who had previously been declared "untreatable." These were the patients who had generally showed highly deviant behavior as early as childhood or adolescence, had been hospitalized for many years, and had failed to respond to many treatments and formalized programs. The staff gave up on them, and until token economy demonstrated that their behavior could be changed, all concerned usually assumed that these patients would probably spend the rest of their lives in the hospital.

With token economy treatment and psychoactive medication,[2] these patients learned many more socially appropriate behaviors than had ever been expected. As a second-generation token economy manual, this book describes the application of token economy treatment with an entirely different population: short-term patients, the alcoholics, drug abusers, and sociopaths. And broad new vistas of treatment possibilities are opened, because the numbers of these patients are so large—they are far more numerous than chronic mental hospital patients—and, therefore, the usefulness of token economy approaches is increased many times.

The most promising new token economies will probably arise in community-based mental hospitals to care for patients who would previously have been sent to state mental hospitals. This development is particularly important because the decade from 1975 to 1985 is quite likely to be the time of reduction and elimination of many large state mental hospitals, if not entire state hospital systems. (In California, which is typically the trend setter for the nation, the entire state hospital system is slated for liquidation within the next ten years.)

Most chronic and short-term mental hospital patients will probably then live in community mental hospitals, board-and-care homes, and nursing homes. Both chronic and short-term patients are likely to spend shorter and shorter periods in community hospitals, and spend more time in board-and-care and nursing homes. The token economy, introduced first into the community hospital, and

---

[1] Sociopaths (previously called psychopaths) are persons who show no apparent ability or interest in the differences between moral right and wrong. Although they often glibly discuss morality, their behavior shows a clear lack of interest or concern. They have often been labeled "moral imbeciles," although they generally show good intelligence. They have good awareness of reality, but often are committed to mental hospitals for illegal acts, repeated in apparently senseless fashion, so that jail seems unsuitable for them. For a fuller discussion, see Hinsie and Campbell (1970) or Cleckley (1964).

[2] "Psychoactive medication" refers to drugs that have a psychological effect in changing behavior. Sedating medication calms patients, hypnotics tend to produce sleep, and tranquilizing medication acts to soothe the turbulent. (See Hinsie and Campbell, 1970, for a fuller description of the kinds and effects of psychoactive medications.) In a token economy setting, these medications when properly prescribed tend to enable the patient to focus more effectively on the acts of others around him, to respond more suitably to treatment, and to learn more socially appropriate behaviors from the staff's efforts.

then into board-and-care and nursing homes, provides a natural social learning sequence that is likely to enable many patients to make a quick return to effective community living, free of institutionalization. Token economies can easily be tailored for older groups to enable them to function quite well in institutional settings. Many more older patients can learn to live independently (despite serious and frequently irreversible neurological and other physical complications) than is possible with traditional treatment modes.

The majority of the staff are likely to become highly motivated for doing token economy work in all of these settings, and to remain motivated because of fairly rapid changes in patients' behavior as a result of their efforts. (For a fuller discussion of this area, see Chapter 7, the section Staff Selection and Training.) In sum, already established token economies are likely to become larger, and new ones can be expected to proliferate, because of all the treatment approaches now available, the token economy, in combination with psychoactive medication, is the most effective treatment program yet devised, the least costly to the patient in terms of human values, and the least expensive financially to the community.

SOME WORKING DETAILS AND GOALS OF TOKEN ECONOMY PROGRAMS

One of the most effective forms of token economy to date is that developed for working with the long-term mental hospital patient. (An equally effective form of token economy is used with children in classrooms, as reported by O'Leary and Drabman, 1973.) Token economy's ability to change behavior is especially important, because the chronic patient is financially too expensive—some $15,000 per year or more—and emotionally too dear in human suffering endured in 20, 30, and even 40 years of Siberia-like exile in the back wards of hospitals. For these reasons, today's demand is for short-term, effective treatment that maintains an abnormal person in his community or takes him from his social environment for days or weeks, not months or years. As the price of community financial support, each patient must be retained in his community or sent back to it quickly, and token economy, in combination with psychoactive medication, fulfills this requirement far more effectively than any other current approach or one likely to be developed in the near future.

Token economy enables the exact problem behaviors that lead to a patient's exclusion from his community to be focused on, and the scope and frequency of those behaviors to be reduced, so that he becomes more socially acceptable to others. An additional advantage of this program is its suitability to a large range of behaviors of great community interest: drug (Glicksman, Ottomanelli, & Cutler, 1971) and alcohol abuse (Miller, 1972), aggressive antisocial behavior, and other manifestations of inability to get along with others. Some of these uses will be discussed here; many others, such as board-and-care and nursing homes, classroom uses, and applications with children and adolescents, are noted at the end of this book (see Behavioral and Token Economy Bibliographies and Token Economy Manuals).

Recent findings (Roberts & Perry, 1970) suggest that in addition to the advantage of rapidity of treatment, a token economy "graduate" tends to retain his new social skills longer than does a patient discharged from a traditional program. Token economies tend to center on the "nitty-gritty" of teaching specific social skills that a patient can use, be reinforced for, and therefore continue to use in his community. This kind of concrete, specific social teaching is essential to the mental hospital patient who is a poor social learner.

Token economies focus on the techniques and details of social learning in each token transaction. The patient must interact with the staff at that time, and he is given tokens for doing the right things, and tokens are withheld or taken from him for doing the wrong things. Each token transaction is a social learning experience in which the patient is given clear and instructive feedback from the staff on his progress. In some cases the patient can also find out in advance what is expected from him from an orientation form that may be given to him. (On admission to Camarillo State Mental Hospital's Token Economy Program, each patient is given an orientation form, "Welcome to Unit 231," which is reproduced in Chapter 4, the section Patient Orientation. A posted schedule of token rewards is also available—see Chapter 4, Table 4-1.)

In addition to learning from his own experiences, the patient can learn a great deal about what is expected from him and what behavior is not acceptable by observing other patients getting tokens or not getting them from the staff. Modeling—learning from observing—is an extremely useful way for patients to profit from treatment (Bandura, 1969). All of these experiences are used as learning opportunities, on a planned basis, by token economy staff to manage contingencies of reinforcement,[3] so that the patient is rewarded as soon after the desired acts and as appropriately, as possible. Tokens provide an excellent means of rapid, concrete, and meaningful contingency management. It is especially important to note that all token economies, like behavior therapy in

---

[3] In behavior therapy theory, "contingency" is the association of an event—especially a given act by a patient (in a token economy, in this case)—with the kind of reinforcement given to him. A "reinforcement" is anything that may be done or given to the patient to increase the likelihood of his performing the same act again. For example, when a patient in a token economy program makes his bed and is given a token, that token is considered a positive reinforcement, positive because it is considered pleasurable, and a reinforcement if it increases the chances of his making his bed in the future. A negative reinforcement is an unpleasant event whose discontinuance generally leads to an increase in a desired behavior. For example, suppose a patient is given the task of cleaning a bathroom. As soon as he finishes the task, he can leave the bathroom, where he may dislike being, and go to watch TV. In this context, being in the bathroom may be considered a negative reinforcement to cleaning the bathroom.

Punishment is not negative reinforcement, because it is designed to decrease, not increase, the frequency of certain kinds of behavior. For example, fining a patient a given number of tokens for being dirty now is a way of training him to be dirty less often in the future.

general, focus on observable actions such as speech, dress, and bodily movements rather than on attitudes and emotions, which are inferred from what a person does.

At this point, a discussion of some key aspects of three other token economy programs, and of the differences between those programs and Camarillo's, will be useful. The programs are those of Ayllon and Azrin (1968b), Atthowe and Krasner (1968), and Schaefer and Martin (1969).

THREE SAMPLE PROGRAMS

Because token economy is primarily a treatment rather than a research program, the vast majority of token economies, especially unsuccessful ones, are not reported in the literature. Approximately 100 token economies are reported directly in this book (in General References, and Behavioral and Token Economy Bibliographies and Token Economy Manuals.) The two most extensive reports are the classic studies by Ayllon and Azrin (1968b) and Schaefer and Martin (1969). By clearly specifying and empirically defining many basic aspects of treatment, such as use of tokens for contingency management, choice of reinforcers, and roles of various staff members, Ayllon and Azrin set a general pattern for token economies. Their book is a model of behavioral scholarship, effectively focused on the practical problems of changing unacceptable behaviors into socially acceptable ones.

Ayllon and Azrin's subjects were chronic female patients; the reinforcements given them were always part of the normal hospital environment. Reinforcements were usually the opportunity to do things that the patients frequently did, such as serving meals, cleaning floors, sorting laundry, washing dishes, and taking care of their appearance. Other, more glamorous reinforcements were also used, such as passes from the hospital; interviews with the psychologist, physician, or chaplain; permission to watch television; and candy or cigarettes.

Ayllon and Azrin's program differed in many ways from Camarillo's. Ayllon and Azrin had only women patients, and Camarillo had only men. The kinds of reinforcement used by Ayllon and Azrin included preferred work activities as well as interviews with staff members. Camarillo *allowed* patients some choice of work, and used tokens as the reinforcements for satisfactory completion of these tasks. Camarillo patients had interviews with the staff because of the patient's wish to see the staff member, or the staff member's wish to see the patient, but in either case the interview was not used as a reinforcement for any specified behaviors. Ayllon and Azrin's use of television watching as a controlled reinforcement was superior to Camarillo's use of television watching as a noncontingent, desired, and uncontrolled activity. (In sum, Ayllon and Azrin's project seemed more highly controlled than Camarillo's, probably because theirs was a short-term research project with a rich staff/patient ratio. In contrast, because Camarillo's project was a long-term treatment program, its staff/patient ratio was no higher than that of any other treatment program—traditional or behavioral—and it carefully allocated staff time to those activities that were crucial to behavioral change.

Another token economy (Atthowe, 1966b; Atthowe & Krasner, 1968; Krasner, 1965, 1966) consisted of a group of 86 male patients, averaging 65 years of age and 22 years of hospitalization. Most were chronic schizophrenics; the others suffered from organic brain syndromes. In this program, as in all token economies, patients had to earn tokens that could be exchanged for positive reinforcers such as cigarettes, money, passes from the hospital, watching TV, sitting on the ward, or feeding kittens. Patients earned tokens by doing such things as caring for their personal needs, attending scheduled activities, helping on the ward, interacting with other patients, and in general, demonstrating social responsibility for their own and other patients' welfare. Patients who needed immediate reinforcement to strengthen socially responsible behaviors were paid tokens immediately after performing desired behaviors. Patients who demonstrated the ability to wait to be paid, and who still continued with or even increased the frequency of desired behaviors, punched a time card for desired behaviors and were paid tokens once weekly on paydays. The most advanced group of patients were "graduates" of the program, had accumulated 120 tokens, assumed great responsibility in running their ward, and had special 25-hour weekly assignments. (For discussion of token savings see Chapter 4, the section The Token Economy Canteen, and Chapter 7, the section Organizing and Operating a New Canteen.) Graduates did not have to pay tokens for any privileges.

At the beginning of the program, the most apathetic and withdrawn patients were given special attention to teach them how to use a token program. At first these patients seemed to have no particular desires and would not engage in any activity without staff encouragement, nor did they have any interest in purchasing token economy canteen items. These patients were then specially trained to learn the value of tokens in obtaining things that seemed to interest them from the canteen, such as handkerchiefs, coffee, pencils, and ice cream. The staff taught patients to get tokens from an office across the hall from the ward canteen, without working or doing anything socially desirable for them (noncontingently). After patients learned the value of tokens from this procedure, they were taught to do things to earn tokens by engaging in socially desirable activities (contingently). Whenever possible, at the same time that patients were given tokens, the staff gave them verbal, social approval. For example, a staff member might hand a patient a token, and smile and say, "That's very good!" or "You did a fine job!"

Giving tokens with social reinforcements such as smiles and verbal approval is a first step in the process of getting patients to work for social approval alone, without tokens. Patients can then learn to act appropriately in the community, where they will never be given tokens, and often not money, for doing the right things. Linking social approval with tokens helps patients to learn to act appropriately in the community, where *only* social approval may be given.

Krasner and Atthowe's study lasted 31 months and was exceedingly successful. Most patients had become less apathetic and more interested in many activities by the end of the study. Previously, about half of the patients had been too apathetic to even leave the hospital overnight or to go on longer passes. Of those who were discharged, about 40 percent remained in their communities, which was far better than the record for traditional programs. Patients showed greater independence, improved appearance, and took better care of their personal hygiene (in such activities as shaving and showering) than they had previously. An important aspect of this study was its success with bed-wetting patients, who present serious problems in any token economy, and who cannot be discharged, nor can they remain in their communities, often for no other reason than the fact that they are bed-wetters.

There were some significant differences between Krasner and Atthowe's program and Camarillo's. Krasner and Atthowe's program had patients who were substantially older and had spent considerably more time in hospitals than those in Camarillo's program. Camarillo's patients averaged 40 years of age and less than 5 years of hospitalization. It is likely that Krasner and Atthowe specially selected patients for their program—patients who had failed to respond to many other programs, who had been labeled "untreatable," and who were generally much older than the average patient. In contrast, Camarillo's program had patients referred to it who were being admitted to the hospital at that time, and who were randomly selected from that pool of patients for age, length of previous hospitalization, and response to hospitalization. Of course, there were some patients in the Camarillo program who had been there for many years and who were not responsive to this program at a given time; they constituted from 10 to 20 percent of the patient pool at all times.

While Krasner and Atthowe's program was somewhat larger (85 patients) than Camarillo's (60 to 70 patients), it is also likely that it was considerably more richly staffed than Camarillo's. Most token economy programs have a larger number of staff than is usual for a given number of patients in other programs of that institutional setting. Camarillo's program was unusual because it did not have a larger staff/patient ratio than any other program at the hospital (one full-time psychiatrist, one full-time psychologist, one half-time social worker and 20 full-time psychiatric nurses). The greater staff/patient ratio of Krasner and Atthowe's program probably made for substantial ability to modify many behaviors that Camarillo lacked the staff time to observe and respond to appropriately. (Krasner and Atthowe's success with bed-wetters illustrates the kinds of successes that are possible with additional staff and that Camarillo had difficulty achieving.) This difference seemed particularly important in Krasner and Atthowe's staff being able to work closely with patients who were not originally responsive to the token program, and to help them to learn the values of tokens and the ways to earn them. While Krasner and Atthowe's program, lasting only 31 months, demonstrated the effectiveness of token economy training, it probably could have done an even better job with continuance.

Camarillo's program with more than a five-year history was able to utilize a cadre of highly experienced technicians, and many patients who were experienced in the program. "Experienced patients" frequently functioned as effective role models for desired behaviors, or enabled new patients to learn from observation which behaviors were not reinforced or were actually punished.

There were also many similarities in the two programs. Most of the same kinds of privileges were available with tokens, such as cigarettes, care of self and other patients, and passes from the hospital, but money and watching TV were not privileges in Camarillo's program. (Camarillo's program provided selected patients with the opportunity to work in a sheltered workshop setting and to earn money for their work. Watching TV was possible for all patients whenever the TV was on, and was, in effect, a noncontingent reward.) As in Krasner and Atthowe's program, patients at Camarillo who could not wait for their rewards were paid at the time they performed desired acts; others, who could wait, were paid on payday. Camarillo also paid daily as patients applied to the canteen for candies, gum, and cigarettes, and were often paid tokens at the same time. (See Chapter 4, the section The Token Economy Canteen, and Chapter 7, the section Organizing and Operating a New Canteen, for fuller discussions of this point.)

Both programs had a graduate status for patients who had accumulated savings, had regular outside jobs, and had achieved the highest token economy level.

Another program (Schaefer & Martin, 1969) used token economy techniques similar to those of Atthowe and Krasner's and Camarillo's programs. Because of the staff's lack of familiarity with behavioral techniques, Schaefer and Martin spent 18 weeks training all involved personnel: psychiatric technicians, social workers, physicians, janitors, food service employees, and anyone else in the hospital who would have contact with the patients in the program. Psychiatric technicians, for example, were taught which behaviors were considered socially desirable and were therefore to be encouraged, and which were undesirable and were to be discouraged. Each student technician, as well as students and working members of other disciplines, was expected to write a list of desirable behaviors, such as good personal hygiene and appropriate social responses, as reported in Table 1-1.

Throughout the 18-week training period, the staff learned about the work of Pavlov and Skinner, fulfilled assignments in the program, learned to recognize and encourage desirable behaviors with positive reinforcement such as food, bed use, going outdoors, having visitors, smoking, and watching TV, and learned to train patients to use tokens as ways of paying for desired privileges. New staff members were trained each year, and current staff members sometimes attended training sessions to review and renew their knowledge of behavior therapy in general and token economy in particular.

During the first 31 months of operation, there were some 200 patients in the program—about 120 (60%) in the orientation group, 40 (20%) in the therapy group, and 40 (20%) classified as ready-to-leave. *Orientation patients* slept in an

Table 1-1 Desirable Hygienic and Social Behaviors

Hygienic behaviors	Social behaviors
Clean feet	Asking questions
Clean legs or knees	Responding to a greeting
Clean hands or arms	Saying thank you
Clean neck or face	Saying please
No body odor	Speaking during group therapy
Clean navel	Playing card games
Clean fingernails	Watching TV with others
Combed hair	Talking about anything except oneself
Daily underwear change	Walking about the hospital grounds
Clean socks or stockings	
Recent shave (men)	
Suitable makeup (women)	

undecorated bed without a bedspread. They had no locker for their clothing, and ate only after therapy and ready-to-leave group members had finished. They could wear only hospital-provided clothing (instead of their personal clothing), did not attend parties or go to movies, and had only a few visitors. *Therapy group patients* had bedspreads on their beds, draperies on the windows, a dresser for their personal belongings, and a rug on the floor. They were permitted to wear their personal clothing, and could attend parties and movies, entertain visitors, and move freely about the grounds. *Ready-to-leave patients* had private rooms that they were completely free to decorate as they wished. They could leave the hospital grounds during the day, and often did so for community jobs. They entered the dining room first, and ate at the most attractive tables. They spent most of their time off the grounds: working, shopping, at movies or other forms of entertainment, and simply took buses back and forth between the hospital and their various activities.

Whatever their group membership, patients were never summoned, coerced, or even reminded to do anything. They were free to do as they chose: to act appropriately and get tokens, to not act suitably and not receive tokens, or to act inappropriately enough to be fined tokens.

Because the goal of the program was to help patients to function effectively socially without paying them tokens, they were gradually weaned (faded[4]) from tokens, and rewarded with social approval and privileges for suitable actions. Schaefer and Martin's procedures were quite successful, and even exceedingly

---

[4] "Fading" is the process of gradually dropping some aspect of the stimulus situation, in this case tokens as reinforcements, so that learning can be effective without them, and will be shown in the later social situation when the tokens are not present. The behavior therapist in training his subject will often carefully plan to modify the training situation so that it becomes more like a real social situation. As training continues, this often involves dropping artificial reinforcements entirely, or substituting socially suitable stimuli, such as social approval and privileges, in their place.

apathetic patients began to respond suitably to this program. At the end of 31 months, staff efforts seemed justified, and the program was continued. After discharge, only about 16 percent of patients returned, which was well below the 35 to 40 percent return reported in traditional programs. The staff were quite enthusiastically involved in this program.

There are some noteworthy differences and similarities between Schaefer and Martin's and Camarillo's programs.

Since Schaefer and Martin's program was new, considerable preprogram time was spent training the staff. Camarillo's was an ongoing program that, for new staff, used primarily in-service training, which was continuously operative for ongoing staff members. Schaefer and Martin evidently gave thorough training to food service and janitorial staff as well as the program staff. They were more thorough than Camarillo, where attention was paid only to staff members working directly with patients in the program, and not to support staff members outside the program. Schaefer and Martin's three groups, orientation, therapy, and ready-to-leave groups, were parallel to Camarillo's Dorm C, B, and A groups.

Schaefer and Martin avoided pressuring patients in any way to behave appropriately. This contrasted with Camarillo's staff, who carefully explained and influenced patients to behave in ways that would earn them tokens, promotions in the economy hierarchy, and discharge. Schaefer and Martin report "hard data" indicating fewer returns than for traditional programs, and impressions about Camarillo's program (without data) are similar. Camarillo's impressions are less reliable, because at this later reporting, the California mental hospital system has been under great pressure to not admit patients (even those requiring hospitalization), and that can be assumed to reduce readmissions to all programs, regardless of their effectiveness. (For a discussion of legal and financial aspects of discharge and admission factors, see Chapter 5, the sections Discharge Considerations, and Ethical, Moral, and Legal Considerations.

COMMUNITY ASPECTS: BEHAVIOR BEFORE, AFTER, AND INSTEAD OF TOKEN ECONOMY SOCIAL TRAINING

Community living means some degree of conformity of speech, actions, and appearance to those of others living in the community. The person whose ways of not conforming are considered to indicate mental illness may be committed involuntarily to a mental hospital. While the person is in the community, he may be unable to obtain most of the rewards available to the others, such as jobs, money, social status, and prestige. He is then excluded by being sent to a mental hospital. For all practical purposes he may be almost totally lacking in power over his life, as shown by his inability to influence others to give him these rewards; his social strategy for gaining rewards from others is totally inadequate.

Token economy can be considered social training to give the hospital patient the social skills to gain power over others in the hospital—by getting them to discharge him to his community—and power over others in his community to gain the rewards previously denied him, and especially to be able to stay in his community. Thus, token economy is designed to change the patient's inappropriate social strategy to an appropriate and effective one.

This book is designed to help staff members of community and state mental hospitals to understand and to use effectively a particular behavior therapy treatment program—token economy. To this end, it is important to ask and to answer some basic questions about behavior therapy and token economy treatment. These questions are: What does it mean to say that a person is different or abnormal? What is a community? Why is anyone a patient in a community or state mental hospital? The following discussion is an abbreviated answer to these questions (as detailed in Ulmer and Franks, 1973, and reproduced in full in Appendix A).

A community can be thought of as a general area, such as a neighborhood or town, whose residents feel some sense of bond in mutually shared interests. A psychiatric dictionary (Hinsie & Campbell, 1970, defines a community as an aggregation of mutually interdependent individuals residing in a specified area who commonly maintain primary institutions such as churches and schools. A community psychiatrist (Susser, 1968) defines a community as an aggregate of people who have collective social ties by virtue of their shared locale for residence, services, and work. Whatever the definition used, a community is an area in which persons share interests and somewhat similar ways of talking, acting, and dressing. To be accepted in a community, a person must talk, act, and dress somewhat like the others who live there. If a person is somehow different from the others, especially if they are upset by his talking, acting, or appearing physically dangerous, he may be brought involuntarily to the attention of agents of the legal or medical professions. If the deviant person enters the health system, he may be diagnosed as emotionally disturbed or as suffering from a disordered mental state. Only when the person is brought to professional attention and diagnosed by a professional as emotionally disturbed can he be considered abnormal. If the professional believes that the person is seriously disturbed *and* potentially dangerous to himself or to others, the professional may contact the police or the courts. As a result, the person may be committed involuntarily to a community or state mental hospital.

It is important to recognize that a person is *only sent to a mental hospital* if he disturbs others in his community, not simply because he is emotionally disturbed. No one is ever involuntarily committed to a mental hospital for being "psychotic, schizophrenic, insane, or emotionally ill, or for suffering from any other disordered mental state." A person is sent to a mental hospital for speaking or acting in ways that are considered currently or potentially dangerous to himself or to others in his community. Socially unacceptable speech and actions are by themselves sufficient reason for hospitalizing virtually anyone, and, by and large, speech that is quite deviant, even without including physical threats, is sufficient reason for a person to be hospitalized. If the person does not speak or act in ways that disturb those around him, he is not likely to be committed to a psychiatric institution, no matter how inappropriate his thoughts and fantasies.

Studies have shown consistently that about one out of every ten adults living in a community is as socially disturbed as the hospitalized person (Faris & Dunham, 1939; Roe, 1953; Srole, Langner, Michael, Opler & Rennie, 1962). Yet the vast majority of this seriously socially disordered group will never experience hospitalization. Only two out of every hundred of these socially disturbed adults will ever be hospitalized. This is not to belie either the existence or the importance of personal or intrapsychic problems, The emotionally distressed person may be a deeply unhappy human being who feels so heavily burdened that he requests help from a mental health facility, such as a community mental health center. Or he may feel so unbearably burdened that he requests commitment to a mental hospital, but his community will never take the initiative in committing him *solely* because he is distressed.

In parallel fashion, the committed mental hospital patient is not discharged from the hospital because his emotional disturbance is reduced, but *because* the staff see him talking, acting, and dressing as do others in his community, *and* if they believe that he will act in these ways in his community.

These social realities have substantial implications for the diagnosis and treatment of the disturbed and disturbing person in his community. Diagnosis and treatment will be considered in this manual from a behavioristic viewpoint, which implies a focus on observable aspects of the disturbing person's life in his community and in the hospital.

SUMMARY

This chapter details the large number of potential applications of token economy treatment to the learning of simple and complex social behaviors in many institutional settings. Social learning for the long- and short-term mental patient in a state or community mental hospital in token economy programs is discussed. This patient might be an alcoholic, a drug abuser, or a sociopath. The increased usage of token economy is strongly indicated because of the rapidity of its treatment, which saves considerable human suffering by allowing the patient to leave the hospital in weeks or months instead of after many years, which is the current situation for many patients. The taxpayer, too, is saved considerable expense, since it costs at least $15,000 annually to keep a patient in a hospital.

Tokens are used to provide feedback on the staff's perception of the social appropriateness and inappropriateness of a patient's behavior. In effect, tokens specify feedback for the patient on his behavior in the hospital. Using a system of positive and negative contingencies of reinforcement, the tokens are gradually withdrawn to enable the patient to transfer his social learning from the hospital setting to the general society.

Three other token economy programs are described, and compared and contrasted with Camarillo's program.

The meanings of community and of socially appropriate and inappropriate behaviors are discussed as they relate to token economy social training. These social realities are the reasons that a person is involuntarily hospitalized. And they are directly related to token economy treatment, because the goals of treatment are changes in behavior that will enable the patient to return to his community and to remain there, instead of being rehospitalized.

SUGGESTED READINGS

Theory and Practice of Token Economy

Ayllon, T., & Azrin, N. H. *The token economy: A motivational system for therapy and rehabilitation.* New York: Appleton-Century-Crofts, 1968. This is a classic, original, and highly readable work on token economy.

Ball, T. S. *Establishment and administration of operant conditioning programs in a state hospital for the retarded.* Sacramento, Calif.: California State Department of Mental Hygiene, 1969. (Research Monograph) This free manual deals with mentally retarded subjects, not so-called mentally ill ones, but the principles and practices of token economy are so similar for both groups that the person interested in token economy will find it immensely informative. It contains detailed articles on theoretical, administrative, and treatment problems of token economy; and an appendix with charts, tables, and graphs that enable easy recording of most behaviors in a token economy.

Montgomery, J., & McBurney, R. D. *Operant conditioning—token economy.* Sacramento, Calif.: California State Department of Mental Hygiene, 1970. (Research Monograph) This free manual discusses many token economy problems encountered with mentally retarded patients, and contains a short glossary of terms.

Behavior Modification

Bandura, A. *Principles of behavior modification.* New York, Holt, Rinehart and Winston, 1969. This is an excellent, comprehensive, classic text that provides a wealth of information on most aspects of behavior modification, especially in the area of modeling, in which Bandura is the authority.

Behavioral Terminology

Chaplin, J. P. *Dictionary of psychology.* New York, Dell, 1968.

White, O. R. (Ed.). *A glossary of behavioral terminology.* Champaign, Ill.: Research Press, 1971.

Wolman, B. B. (Ed.). *Dictionary of behavioral science.* New York: Van Nostrand Reinhold, 1973.

CHAPTER 2

Camarillo Token Economy Staff: Roles and Coordination

INTRODUCTION

A psychological laboratory tests and applies social learning principles that show how disordered human behaviors can be reduced, and how more appropriate social strategies can be increased. Behavior modification is theoretically and practically sound. Behavioral techniques work easily with a controlled subject in a laboratory setting, especially when relatively simple aspects of the subject's behavior are changed. However, the mental hospital patient is neither a laboratory rat nor a strongly motivated college student. The hospital patient is not likely to be as responsive to behavior therapy as the rat or the student. It is not easy to

15

apply laboratory principles to a subject with a limited and inappropriate social repertoire, and this is particularly true in a far less controlled setting than a laboratory.

To implement changes in the mental hospital patient, a guide is needed. Probably one of the best guides is a behaviorally oriented and trained psychologist, because he is usually familiar with laboratory findings and their limitations, especially for the mental hospital setting. It may well be that a psychiatrist, psychiatric social worker, or psychiatric technician (nurse) is more knowledgeable about behavior therapy than a psychologist in a given mental hospital. If that is the case, then the best-informed person is the behavior therapy leader, because functional ability is far more important than discipline. The reference here is to the psychologist simply because this is the usual case at present, but the situation is changing rapidly.

ROLES OF THE CAMARILLO PSYCHOLOGIST

The Camarillo token economy psychologist guides his fellow staff members in deciding how to apply behavior therapy principles to change the abnormal speech, actions, and appearance of each patient. The psychologist is especially important as a "trouble-shooter" in working with the unusually difficult patient who does not seem to be profiting from token economy treatment. In treating difficult patients, the psychologist works closely with the staff as a consultant, as well as directly with the patient to modify his antisocial and asocial behaviors.

The psychologist also acts in the capacity of clinical consultant when he is asked to help coordinate efforts of other staff members in treating a specific patient. The psychologist may be informed by other staff members of how they evaluate a particular difficult patient. The psychologist will usually read the patient's case record carefully, see the patient, and then objectively assess him (see Chapter 4, the section Patient Assessment). The psychologist will then devise a tentative treatment plan, and communicate it to other staff members, who will then tell the psychologist whether they think that this plan is feasible. For example, the behavior modification plan may call for technicians to work with a patient in ways, and at times, that are simply not possible because of other work demands placed upon them. The psychologist should be most sensitive to technicians' objections, and change his treatment plan accordingly. For if the psychologist is insistent and coercive with technicians, he may lose their good will, and then no treatment plan is likely to be successful.

Technicians spend much more time with any given patient than does a psychologist, and since technicians have far more control over patient's rewards and punishments than does a psychologist, they can deliberately or unwittingly support or sabotage any treatment plan. In effect, the psychologist is responsible for creating a smooth-working and congenial behavior modification team, and his ability to do this will, to a large extent, determine the success or failure of any specific treatment plan for any individual patient. This generalization holds whether the behavior therapy leader is a psychologist, psychiatrist, psychiatric social worker, psychiatric technician, or member of any other discipline.

The psychologist in Camarillo Hospital has responsibilities that he might not have in other settings or, indeed, that might be better handled by another team member in those settings. The Camarillo psychologist has primary responsibility for training student professionals (such as psychiatric residents, and graduate students in social work and psychology) in behavior therapy. The psychologist at Camarillo helps to coordinate training efforts of other staff members. And the psychologist has primary responsibility as a researcher to enlist cooperation from other staff members in developing new behavioral assessment and modification techniques for the continued improvement of token economy treatment. He communicates his research findings in professional books, journals, and manuals, and at professional meetings, for only through formalized professional channels can new research become known and be useful to others.

Direct Patient Treatment

The major role of a token economy psychologist, or whoever is the behavior therapist leader of the token economy team, is that of consultant to other staff members in changing antisocial behaviors of patients into behaviors that are more socially acceptable. There are about 60 patients in Camarillo's program. To be reasonably effective, the psychologist should have short behavior modification sessions with each patient once, and preferably twice, daily. Obviously, the psychologist cannot work with more than a half dozen patients, considering all the other training, research, and administrative responsibilities that he must fulfill. Regardless of which discipline the behavior therapist leader is a member of, he is likely to have limited time for direct treatment of patients. In addition, excessive direct work with patients is likely to be so draining emotionally that he may be less effective than if other kinds of activities take up a substantial part of his working day.

It is reasonable to ask what happens to the other 54 patients, about 90 percent of the population of the program. The psychologist can best help most of the patients by spreading his time and expertise in consulting directly with the staff, especially the psychiatric technicians. He can help the staff to work better and gain greater satisfaction with patients by advising the staff, and especially by acting as a professional role model in demonstrating treatment approaches with patients. It is important to recognize that if a psychologist only gives advice, and does not work with patients, other staff members are likely to not take his words seriously, and even to resent him.

There is a great advantage to a psychologist in working directly with patients. He sees exactly what techniques work best in *that* token economy program. He *learns* which kinds of suggestions are, and are not, acceptable to the staff. And, of course, he tends to improve his skills through direct work with patients.

It is surprising that many of the most vocal opponents and some of the most naive supporters of behavior modification feel that behavior therapy is quite mechanical. Quite the contrary is true, for the individuality of each patient, including his motivation, his moods, and his reactions to a behavior modifier, must be considered if treatment is to be most effective. A patient's emotions are important. An obvious example is the frequent failure of behavior therapy when social reinforcement is used and the patient does not like his therapist. Social reinforcement is the careful use of the therapist himself in saying approving things (positive reinforcement), such as "That's very good," when a patient talks or acts appropriately—to increase the likelihood that the patient will repeat the desirable behavior.

If the patient can be brought to feel positively about his therapist, the time and effort are well invested. If the patient comes to like his therapist, the patient is likely to be motivated to follow through with behavioristic training sessions, and to practice between sessions. If the patient can not be brought to feel more positively about his therapist, the time and effort should be invested in a more promising patient, unless reinforcers other than social ones can be used effectively. Sometimes, dropping a nonresponsive patient for a period of time and then returning to him proves to be a good idea, because the patient works more effectively afterward than he did before. Occasionally a patient is so delusional, unresponsive to psychoactive medication, neurologically impaired, or physically dangerous that behavior therapy is unlikely to be successful and should not be attempted at that time.

Although the behavior therapist will often try to create a pleasant, warm relationship with his patient by being cordial, kind, and obviously interested in the patient's welfare, he will not—as will the traditional insight therapist—depend heavily on his relationship with the patient for therapy to progress. Instead, the behavior therapist will try to use himself as a positive reinforcer, strongly approving of the patient when he talks and acts appropriately, so that these behaviors are likely to be repeated. For example, when a patient begins to speak more appropriately the behavior therapist may say, "That's *very good*, Mr. X! You're doing *fine!*" In contrast, when a patient continues with undesirable behaviors, the behavior therapist may simply ignore the patient by looking away from him.

If at any time a patient does not wish to participate in a session, the behavior therapist accepts the patient's decision. Similarly, when a patient rejects sessions over a period of time, behavior training may be discontinued, but the therapist should seriously consider why the patient does not wish to be involved in treatment. If the therapist can make changes in his approach to the patient, or in some aspects of therapy that may be unpleasant to a patient, these changes should be made to try to make treatment continue. Also, if a patient consistently asks to have sessions ended early, the behavior therapist should examine what is happening in these sessions that is unpleasant to the patient. (The Camarillo psychologist's roles in giving direct treatment to patients, individually and in groups, are detailed in Chapter 5. The overall treatment process is described in Chapter 4, the sections Patient Orientation, Patient Assessment, and Evaluation of Reinforcements. Discharge considerations are discussed in Chapter 5.)

The Psychologist as Consultant
to Individual Staff Members

In Camarillo's program, and probably in most others, there is a great deal of interpersonal involvement between staff and patients, which is not always to the best advantage of either. Staff members and patients have feelings about each other as individuals whom they like or dislike, and these feelings have to be dealt with, especially in the case of troublesome patients, if the program is to be successful. Since many of these problems have a personal component, the staff member involved will often speak privately to the psychologist about a troublesome patient.

These consultations are always initiated by the staff member. (A different situation occurs when the psychologist attempts to coordinate the team's efforts in working with a given patient.) In the case of the technicians, each of whom is specifically responsible for about a dozen patients, one or more patients are usually troublesome, and technicians generally request help with these patients.

The Camarillo psychologist is careful to help the staff with the problem that they present to him, and not try to substitute some other difficulty that he considers to be the real problem. After the staff have been helped with a particular problem, they may report related problems to the psychologist—either new problems or continuing ones—at which point he can deal with them. It is usually best to help the staff to focus on the most important problem as they see it, and then to deal with other problems, after some progress has been made on the primary difficulty. If an approach to handling one patient and one problem at a time is developed, the staff can frequently use some variation of that approach to deal with other problem responses of that same patient or another patient with similar problem behaviors.

There are some exceptions to Camarillo's usual approach of dealing with patients' problems as presented by the staff. Sometimes the staff will discuss aspects of patients' personalities that are not behavioristic, and not directly related to behavioristic treatment. For example, technicians may speak of inner emotional states, such as attitudes, and describe patients as "nice," "hostile," or as "understanding what is said to them, but pretending not to understand." The psychologist often responds to these kinds of complaints about patients by pointing out that these inner states are not directly relevant to either getting into the hospital or getting out, and that it might be better to focus on observable behavior. The staff will often accept this suggestion, because they are more willing to work on behavior, which is more easily changed, than on inner states, which are difficult to change.

Sometimes the staff may complain about patients' behaviors that are not relevant to hospitalization, such as homosexuality. In such a case, the psychologist indicates that he neither approves nor disapproves of patients' sexual contact, but recognizes that human sexual needs are quite strong and that substitute satisfactions can be expected to be sought when more usual ones are not available. In effect, he tells the staff, "If you can't have steak, you take hamburger." The psychologist then tactfully steers discussions back to antisocial and asocial behaviors that can and should be modified into more appropriate forms, because they are essential to leaving the hospital and to living freely in the community.

Typically, the psychologist focuses the staff's attention on the kinds of problems that he works with in direct treatment of individuals or groups of patients. For example, he can suggest to the staff that they use time out and other nonreinforcement techniques (see Chapter 4, the section Evaluation of Reinforcements) for handling patients who speak deviantly. The staff frequently produce and encourage asocial behaviors, especially in long-term patients, because they enjoy patients' peculiarities. When this is tactfully pointed out to them, they are likely to cooperate strongly in changing their responses to patients' inappropriate behaviors.

Cooperation between the staff and the psychologist is quite natural and to be expected in a token economy setting, for they share behavioristic approaches and similar treatment goals for patients. The staff use the psychologist as a consultant who can help the token economy team to work more systematically and effectively so that the team can reach mutually agreed upon goals for their patients. The staff are most willing to cooperate with a psychologist when they consider his suggestions reasonable, and when they consider him knowledgeable, involved, and willing to do his share of the dirty and unpleasant work. The staff are especially willing to cooperate if they find the psychologist receptive to their disagreements with his views, and able to change his suggestions to meet their objections. In sum, the staff tend to work best with a psychologist whom they find professionally competent and personally congenial to their efforts.

An example may help to make concrete the need for cooperation between the staff members. In Chapter 5 treatment of an echolalic patient, who simply repeated everything that was said to him, is discussed. This patient's echolalic speech was considered cute by some technicians who unknowingly reinforced it and thus helped to keep the patient in the hospital, because echolalic speech is unacceptable in the community. Primarily in staff conferences with the psychologist and also in informal discussions with him, the technicians learned it was better to discourage than to encourage Mr. X to speak echolalically. Technicians then began to respond to his repetitious speech with, "That's *dumb talk!* I don't want to hear *dumb talk!*" Technicians also learned to use nonreinforcement techniques such as time-out when Mr. X spoke repetitiously. The technicians probably became more influential in reducing echolalia than the psychologist, who only saw Mr. X twice daily in behavior modification sessions.

The technicians had more intensive contact with Mr. X in stimulating and responding to his speech, than did the psychologist. The psychologist enlisted the technicians' aid by providing them with careful, detailed explanations of what he wished of them, and by letting them know that as members of the treatment team he considered them at least as important as himself. In addition, technicians could see the psychologist working with Mr. X every day, which would naturally encourage them to help the psychologist.

There are two ways then that the psychologist can act as an effective behavioral consultant to other members of the token economy team. He can advise them during staff conferences and other meetings on ways of handling a difficult patient. His advice tends to be trustworthy when he is well acquainted with both a given patient and the staff member raising questions. When the psychologist knows a patient well, he understands that patient's history of positive reinforcements and aversive stimuli that have a role in shaping the patient's current asocial, antisocial, *and* social repertoire. Positive reinforcements that are important behavioral influences on a patient may include cigarettes, attending parties off the unit, and being promoted to a higher dormitory. Nonreinforcing stimuli, such as cigarettes for the nonsmoker, should also be known to the psychologist. Aversive stimuli may include punishments for undesirable behaviors, such as staying in the hospital for arguing with a technician, *provided* that the patient is aware of this contingency and cares about preventing it from happening.

As the behavioral consultant, the psychologist acts as a "trouble-shooter," advising staff and working directly with the patient who is dangerous or disruptive to himself or others. The psychologist tries to understand the contingencies of reinforcement (see Chapter 4, the section Evaluation of Reinforcements) for that patient in terms of the staff's responses to his behavior, and how these contingency links encourage continuance of antisocial and asocial behaviors. Then the psychologist discusses these contingencies with the staff, and helps them to understand how the patient *learns* from the staff to continue these undesirable behaviors. The psychologist does not criticize the staff but explains to them how, if they can change what they are doing with their difficult patient, he can learn to act more appropriately. For example, when a patient talks rudely to the staff, and they punish him, they may be providing him with reinforcement, because punishment is attention, which, if desired by the patient, will tend to maintain and even increase his rude behavior.

Assume that a patient is described as rude or unpleasant. The psychologist tries to help the staff member to consider the patient more objectively, as someone with whom the staff member must work for a period of time, but the patient is not a social friend who must be invited to the staff member's house for dinner. In addition, the psychologist attempts to help the staff member to realize that the patient is responding threateningly or upleasantly to others whom the patient sees as threatening or unpleasant. If the staff can change their responses to the patient, the patient, with time and special training procedures, may begin to behave differently.

If punishment by the staff is a reinforcement, the psychologist may suggest that they try time-out, since this is a nonreinforcement. The patient is unlikely to continue indefinitely his rude speech if he is not reinforced for it with staff attention. The psychologist's suggestion of simply ignoring a patient's obnoxious speech may not be accepted by the staff, because they may feel that unless they actually express their disapproval, the patient is likely to continue and even increase this antisocial behavior. The psychologist should partially accept this argument, because with nonreinforcement the patient's obnoxious speech may well increase at first, but then it may drop below the previous level. The psychologist can point this out to the staff, and request that they try not expressing disapproval for 30 days, and see what happens. After all, he can argue, the patient's history shows that he has been getting punished for years, and that he only continues with this behavior. Why not experiment for one month to see if the psychologist's prediction proves true? The staff may then agree to try this new approach. If they do not, it is usually due to the fact that they are quite hostile to this patient. The staff's hostility may then have to be dealt with by the psychologist. He can explain that he does not blame them for being angry with the patient, but that if they try this approach, they may have less reason to be angry with him in the future.

The psychologist can be most effective as a consultant to the staff in conferences and other settings if he does not consider that behavior therapy is mechanical and can be impersonally applied. Instead, the strong and very real feelings of the staff and the patient must be considered. These feelings must be related to immediate situations, and especially to relationships between the staff and each patient, instead of being seen in the vaguer, more historic way of the traditional insight therapist. In token economy these feelings are handled by accepting them—considering their practical implications for the patient and the staff to live together—and by changing the reality settings of what each expects from the other. Changing reality settings means changing contingencies, considering the emotions of all involved, to improve the effectiveness of working relationships. The psychologist should carefully observe the results of changing contingencies, and be ready to suggest major revisions if they are not working well within a short period of time. For example, if nonreinforcement does not reduce the offensiveness of an obnoxious patient in 30 days, then aversive conditioning, such as withdrawal of candy, cigarettes, or other positive reinforcements, may be necessary.

Alternatively, offering new positive reinforcements, such as going to the movies or swimming, may help to socialize behavior. In trying new positive reinforcements, it is often useful to ask the patient as well as the staff what seems to be important to him. (The Camarillo psychologist's roles are discussed in greater detail in Chapters 5 and 6.)

ROLES OF THE CAMARILLO PSYCHIATRIST

At Camarillo, the psychiatrist as a physician and the acknowledged leader of administrative matters in a medical setting is the final arbiter in such matters as admission and discharge of patients. He functions as leader of the token economy program, unit 238 at Camarillo, which consists of some 60 patients, 20 psychiatric technicians, one psychologist, one psychiatric social worker, and one housekeeper. He is the final authority in such questions as roles and responsibilities of staff members to the program. The psychiatrist acts as a liaison with psychiatrists from other units, and with higher levels of administration, such as the medical director of the hospital.

Patient Transfers from Another Camarillo Program
to Token Economy

A typical example of the psychiatrist's administrative roles is in making the final decision on whether a patient from another program will be accepted into the token economy program. There had been a long history of psychiatrists from other programs freeing themselves of dangerous, obnoxious, or incontinent patients by saying that they needed behavior therapy. This inappropriate transfer process was stopped when the token economy program gained the right to examine fully the prospective transfer patient and his record and to determine his suitability for token economy social training, which is certainly a professionally correct procedure.

Two staff members, usually the psychologist and the Head Psychiatric Technician, go to the unit requesting to transfer one or more of its patients. The inspection team sees the patients, carefully goes over their records, and asks the staff questions about the patients. The team wants answers to such questions as: Are these patients physically dangerous, and is this why the other program wants to transfer them? Do they lack adequate medical and nursing treatment, which staff are evidently reluctant to provide for them? Are they incontinent? Are the records complete and current? Are these patients suited to behavior therapy, as shown in relatively good contact with reality for their ordinary daily lives? Or are they actively hallucinating, showing rapid mood fluctuations, remaining immovably inactive, or showing other behaviors suggesting that they are not getting the right psychoactive medications, and, in any case, that they are unsuited to behavior modification?

After carefully examining these patients and their records, and querying the staff about them, the team notes their findings on one half of a full-sized sheet of paper (Figure 2-1). They also make their recommendations to the unit psychiatrist, who then decides to either follow their suggestions or override them. In any case, he has the full information on the team's findings, is able to make his decision, and defend it with the psychiatrist from the other unit, or the

Proposed Patient Transfer

Patient's Name: Date:

Current Unit:

A. Examination on   B. Condition on Arrival in
   Original Unit   Token Economy Program

Physical and/or
Verbal Aggression:

Continence:

Medical Record:

Evaluation Team:

Evaluation Date:

Recommendations of
Evaluation Team:

Psychiatrist's Decision:

Figure 2-1 Proposed patient transfer form. Part A is filled in during pretransfer examination. Part B is filled in after transfer has been approved and completed, when patient first arrives in token economy program.

medical director of the hospital. The other half of this sheet contains the condition of the patients on arrival in the program, if accepted, so that any differences in the patient when in his original program and when he arrived in the token economy program could be noted.

The patient transfer procedure illustrates both the roles of the psychiatrist and of team cooperation among token economy staff. The psychiatrist is responsible for the overall functioning of the program, but cannot be there to check all details and activities at all times. He must trust and supervise others in order to have the program work effectively in promoting the social learning process of patients suited to the program. And even with the best staff and full authority to choose among patients, 10 to 15 percent of all patients will probably not respond to the program. If the program is saddled with large numbers of patients who are unresponsive, all patients suffer because of inordinate amounts of time spent on just a few patients. And in a token economy staff morale tends to be especially sensitive to feelings of being a "dumping ground" for undesirable patients, with whom the chances of success are practically nonexistent. When staff morale drops, work suffers, and the best and most motivated staff members, especially technicians, tend to request transfers to other programs; and no token economy program can afford to let this happen.

New Admissions to the Hospital

When a new patient comes on the unit, the psychiatrist goes over his records carefully, gives him a physical examination, and writes prescriptions for medication. Prescriptions are for psychoactive drugs and for other needed medications, such as insulin for a diabetic patient. When needed for particular care, the psychiatrist also writes special orders for technicians, such as a high-protein diet for an obese patient. He also requests that the psychologist see the patient to evaluate him for the whole staff. All of these steps are taken whether the patient is new in the hospital or a transfer from another program.

In effect, the psychiatrist's role is to determine if there are any special physical problems, to alert the staff to these problems, and to help the staff to solve them. He also coordinates staff efforts in treating the patient to maximize the chances of the patient changing his antisocial behaviors into socially acceptable ones, so that he can be discharged as quickly as possible from the hospital, and remain as long as possible in the community.

Where the psychiatrist needs expertise in a particular area, he contacts the appropriate staff member, such as the token economy psychologist, to gain information as to what particular procedures should be used with a certain patient. In areas in which he is not proficient and in special situations that call for additional expertise, the psychiatrist consults the appropriate specialist. If the information he needs is available from his own staff, he will obviously get it from them, if not, he will seek out someone in another division of the hospital, and only last will he contact staff members of other institutions. Most consultation occurs in the twice-weekly staff conferences.

ROLES OF THE CAMARILLO PSYCHIATRIC TECHNICIANS (NURSES)

Several important aspects of the psychiatric technicians' (nurses') roles with patients in any mental hospital setting and especially in Camarillo's program need to be discussed. Camarillo's program generally has about 60 patients and about 20 technicians. There is a shift charge for each of the three shifts, and a head technician responsible for all technicians. Technicians are in charge of groups of about 12 patients. Technicians have the usual nursing responsibilities of all mental hospital programs, such as concern for patients' physical welfare, cleanliness, and clothing. Technicians also have to be aware of and concerned about patients' chronic physical problems, such as diabetes, high blood pressure, or cardiac conditions, and are involved with patient's new physical problems, such as colds, pneumonia, and accidents and injuries.

In addition to these physical problems, technicians are heavily involved as behavior therapists in the token economy intensive treatment program. Technicians have to know exactly which antisocial and asocial behaviors brought patients to the hospital and keep them there. And technicians have to be aware at all times of exactly what treatment approaches are being used, and their results.

Because technicians are such a vital part of the token economy program, their suitability and training are of great concern. Technicians usually come to the program after having worked, sometimes for years, in a traditional mental hospital program. Their experience has been in custodial work with patients and in giving them noncontingent rewards. A detailing of these approaches will be useful at this point. Until the mid-1950s most community and state mental hospitals were overloaded with patients, and the overloading increased each year. Typically, patients who remained more than five years never left the institution because they tended not to improve, but to deteriorate with extended residence. Therefore, simple custodial care ("warehousing" of human beings) was frequently the actual "treatment" and "care" given patients. Many technicians are used to custodial care of patients, simply caring for their physical needs and making few efforts to get them discharged. By and large, technicians gave patients noncontingent rewards—meals, a bed, social activities—no matter what their patients did or did not do that was either socially appropriate or inappropriate.

Besides being used to giving custodial care and non-contingent rewards, technicians are often older—late 30s through early 50s—than other members of the staff, have little education, and are resistant to changing their ways of handling patients. For all of these reasons, it is most important to choose technicians who are very motivated to work in a token economy setting, and willing to learn. Since the success of the token economy program is so vitally dependent on technicians, it is necessary to give considerable time and effort to having them function effectively on the token economy treatment team.

Because technicians on the token economy team play such vital roles, professionals have to get along well with them, and this means recognizing some profound differences between the two groups. Typically, technicians are from lower middle class backgrounds, are usually white, and are often quite intolerant of blacks and persons who appear to be hippies because of their dress or general appearance. In contrast, professionals generally come from upper middle class backgrounds, have never had to struggle for financial survival, and did not share the same prejudices as the technicians. Professionals have to recognize their attitudinal differences from the nursing staff, and while not accepting the technicians' values for their own, not try to impose their beliefs on the technicians. It is difficult enough to work with the patients when the whole team like each other or at least can get along well enough to work together; it appears to be counterproductive to bring up political, social, or other issues largely irrelevant to the work situation that can only lead to antagonisms between staff members, and impair the work of the team.

Technicians also provide direct information on patients' functioning for assessment purposes (Chapter 4) and for discharge, as noted below in Staff Conferences (and in Chapter 5). They are key persons in providing information for research projects (Chapter 3), since they know the patients well enough to provide data on their functioning that no one else on the token economy team would know.

It will be useful to detail how the psychologist works with technicians in the Camarillo program, though it should be recognized that these experiences are only a general model and may need considerable modification to apply them to other settings.

The psychologist is the token economy trouble-shooter, helping technicians with difficult patients who are not responding adequately to the program. These patients are sometimes physically aggressive, so that both male and female technicians face constant danger of attack from young, strong, and unpredictably violent patients. Technicians also have to work with totally withdrawn patients, cleaning their soiled beds, changing their clothing when they are enuretic and incontinent, and feeding them when they are totally regressed. Since technicians often have only a high school education (they are not registered nurses, R.N.s), they have little chance for advancement. Promotion to higher levels requires more education than they can acquire easily because of competing pressures of time, work, and family responsibilities. Even the continued existence of their jobs in state mental hospitals has at times been in doubt because the increasing emphasis on community facilities has been leading to declining state mental hospital populations and the closing of many state hospitals.

In Camarillo, the psychologist has to understand clearly and unequivocally the unpleasant and difficult aspects of the psychiatric technician's job in order to be a good consultant to him. The psychologist can hardly expect technicians to be dedicated to such emotionally and financially unrewarding, as well as insecure, work. When the psychologist communicates through his actions, not just superficially with words, his understanding of technicians' job problems, he is likely to be trusted, and his advice sought and accepted. And closer working relationships help the technician and the psychologist, in fact, the entire token economy staff, and especially the patients.

The psychologist tries to be helpful to technicians in their work with the most socially incompetent patients who need almost total care in clothing, feeding, and toileting themselves. These patients have been labeled "babies," which has an unfortunate, self-fulfilling prophecy effect because technicians then treat them like babies, and patients *learn* to be increasingly socially incompetent with this treatment. Patients learn to adapt themselves to passive, helpless roles, and gradually over many years, 20, 30, and 40 or more of continuous hospitalization, develop an ultimate form of passivity and helplessness, called hospitalism. Hospitalism and other social strategies of deterioration are the inevitable products of long-term hospitalization, all resulting from the "training" patients receive to make them easier to handle. And the evidence for the harmful effects of long-term hospitalization seem apparent in the fact that almost invariably patients who have been hospitalized for 10, 20, or 30 consecutive years are shown to have behaved more appropriately on admission than after their long-term hospital stays.

And since hospitalism means total inability to function in the community, it has to be considered as a form of disordered behavior as serious as almost any other set of socially incapacitating speech and actions. Intensive (round-the-clock) and extensive (a year and more of) behavior therapy are required to have hospitalism patients function well enough to cope with community requirements. Hospitalism is an extremely difficult form of antisocial and asocial behavior to treat, and for this reason has received relatively little attention in the Camarillo program.

ROLES OF THE CAMARILLO PSYCHIATRIC SOCIAL WORKER

The social worker has a bachelor's degree representing four years of college, and a master of social work degree (M.S.W.) for two additional years of specialized graduate training in social work. During the last decade a new degree, doctor of social work, (D.S.W.) has been given for approximately three additional years of training. There are relatively few D.S.W. social workers outside of academic and private-practice settings; therefore, this discussion considers only the M.S.W., and not the D.S.W., social worker.

Psychiatric social work has two origins: (1) aiding the poor and physically helpless, primarily with money, but also with assistance in finding jobs, and with medical and other problems; and (2) giving psychoanalytically oriented and other forms of traditional insight psychotherapy. These two origins are unrelated and often quite antagonistic to behavioristic approaches. Nevertheless, it is increasingly common, at least at Camarillo, for a social worker to be interested in behavior therapy and token economy, so that few theoretical or applied arguments arise between the behavioristically oriented social worker, and his like-minded professional colleagues.

The psychiatric social worker is customarily trained almost completely in traditional insight therapy. Since behavior therapy is quite different from insight approaches, the social worker's willingness to learn about behavior therapy, and to use it, rather than insight therapy, as a treatment approach is the most important consideration for determining ability to function effectively on the token economy treatment team.

The psychiatric social worker has many roles in Camarillo's token economy program. Some are routine, as in any mental hospital setting, and others are specific to this program. For example, he is expected to be knowledgeable about the kind of placement that can be made for patients when they leave the hospital—whether this is in their home with their family (wife or parents), or if they have to live by themselves or be placed in a board-and-care or other residency program.

Discharge planning has to be discussed as early as possible, since hospital stays are quite short, averaging between 30 and 60 days for new admissions. Certain patients stay only a week or so, which means that behavior therapy has to focus immediately on the social problems handicapping their ability to survive in their community. Financial and other social aspects of their functioning in the community have to be considered seriously as of the moment treatment is begun. For if these patients do not have enough money to live on, and are unable to compete for and work at jobs, they will almost inevitably have to be rehospitalized. Typically, the social worker obtains Aid to the Totally Disabled (ATD) for patients, which provides them with a subsistence income that enables them to survive in the community. Obviously, with the inflation of the recent years, ATD has proven increasingly inadequate to provide a minimum standard of living for many patients. And the inadequacy of state resources has handicapped California's ability to increase ATD.

The question of financial survival is an important aspect of the social worker's responsibilities because a large percentage of the program's patients are from lower income groups. Neither these patients nor their families have financial reserves under the best of circumstances, and emotional disorder generally makes patients incapable of forming relationships with others who would give them money when they need it.

The social worker also functions as a behavior therapist. He helps to assess patients for therapy and works with them both individually and in the group encounter sessions. Typically, he is a co-leader of the encounter group, working with a technician and the psychologist, in helping to shape behavior into more socially acceptable forms. He negotiates and writes contracts with individual patients, and signs all contracts negotiated by other staff members. (For a fuller discussion of behavioral encounter groups and contracts, see Chapter 6.)

A word about the social worker's coordination with the psychologist is appropriate at this point. The psychologist works closely with the social worker at Camarillo. The psychologist acts as a consultant in helping the social worker to utilize fully the behavioral encounter sessions as social learning experiences for every patient member. Postsession debriefings help to sharpen the focus on overt behavior in later sessions and to avoid the trap of getting into philosophical and insight discussions. The psychologist also consults with the social worker on discharge preparations for each patient. The psychologist suggests discharge when he believes that a given patient has changed his speech and actions as much as he is likely to do, is strongly motivated to return to his community, and is likely to be able to maintain himself there, even living in a board-and-care home or halfway house. Again, as with the technician and the psychiatrist, the psychologist needs to have a warm and cordial relationship for his consultation to be effective and useful to his colleagues.

The social workers serves as a liaison with social workers in other programs, so that the staff can be fully informed on such matters as opportunities to hear outside speakers on subjects relevant to the token economy program. The social worker at Camarillo is responsible for supervision of social work students in some aspects of their training, such as their roles in a token economy program (see Chapter 3, the section Training of Psychiatric Social Work Students).

STAFF CONFERENCES

The following is a description of staff conferences in Camarillo's Token Economy Program. It probably has some similarities, and certainly differences, with other programs in comparable settings.

Purposes

Staff conferences in Camarillo's program are formal, twice-weekly meetings of most token economy staff members to discuss the progress and problems of patients. Those attending are the unit physician (psychiatrist), psychologist, social worker, rehabilitation counselor, and both day- and evening-shift psychiatric technicians who can be spared to attend the meeting. The meeting is held during the period when day and evening nursing shifts overlap. Permanent, dated notes are taken, so that all staff members can find out which patients are discussed and what decisions are made. Sometimes a staff member from another unit or program, or a member of higher administration, will attend to communicate something to the token economy staff. Staff discussions enable each staff member to contribute to the decision-making process, and to feel himself an important member of the team. Each staff member is then more likely to have a sense of involvement in and commitment to both the decisions made for treating patients and the achievement of treatment goals. Token economy staff members should meet at least twice weekly—for frequent and effective communication—instead of following the traditional practice of meeting only once a week.

Informal discussions of patients occur daily, of course, over coffee, in the nursing office, or almost anyplace during working hours. However, informal discussions are not very useful for several reasons. Only a few staff members are present, rather than the whole staff, and cooperation of all persons having contact with patients being discussed is essential. Decisions are not arrived at after a careful airing of views of several staff members; instead, one person generally leads and the few others present follow. Important points of view are likely to be neglected, especially those ideas that are at variance with a leader in an informal discussion. Since notes are not taken at informal discussions, few other staff members ever know which patients have been considered or what decisions have been made.

During formal staff meetings the unit physician usually acts as titular head: that is, he is the final arbiter of decisions, and the psychologist usually acts as technical leader and consultant for token economy psychological treatment problems. The psychologist, or other technical leader of the program, generally makes every effort to be diplomatic, and to avoid giving the impression of ordering other staff members about by being insensitive to their opinions. Instead, the psychologist believes that he can probably be most effective by carefully soliciting opinions of other staff members, and when appropriate, by making feasible suggestions for handling difficult patients and knotty administration problems. The psychologist expects his ideas to be considered seriously if he presents them as suggestions that might be useful in the handling of troublesome patients. The psychologist's ideas tend to be especially well received when the staff feel helpless and at the end of their ropes with an especially difficult, obnoxious, or dangerous patient. His suggestions are most positively considered when he listens carefully and thoughtfully to all objections to them and tries to modify his ideas to meet these objections. The psychologist should not force his ideas on the staff, for if he does, they will not follow through with them, and his plan will fail. Antagonizing the staff at any given time has the additional disadvantage that they will then be less likely to cooperate with him in the future, sometimes even when they agree with his suggestions.

Procedures, and Major Roles of Camarillo Staff Members

Usual procedure is to begin a staff meeting by reading the minutes from the last meeting in the log book. These minutes are in outline form, listing only the topics discussed and the recommendations made. As the minutes are read, for each patient discussed, a given staff member—such as a patient's nursing group leader—may report on his patient's latest speech and actions. All of these comments may be noted in abbreviated form in the record. The staff will then decide whether changes in their approach are needed to reinforce desired behavior in the patient. If he is showing increasingly appropriate behavior, he may be considered for promotion to a higher dorm or even for discharge from the hospital. (Discharge usually takes from 30 to 90 days from the time that discharge planning begins, because of the many arrangements that have to be made for the patient to live in his community.)

Throughout all of these discussions, there is a fairly structured role for each of the staff members present. The psychiatrist is the leader, the final decision maker, and he will usually open and close the meeting. The Head Technician (Chief Nurse) assumes responsibility for his staff and for the patients in his group. The other technicians report on all of their patients, asking for help with the problem ones. The social worker reports on progress in getting patients placed so that they can be discharged, and takes responsibility for processing new patients for discharge. The psychologist consults on problem patients, and accepts responsibility for additional patients to be taken into group or individual therapy. He will also see new patients as they come into the program, and writes them up in the charts. All members of the staff report on meetings they have attended and on other relevant developments throughout the hospital. Psychology and social work students in the program attend staff meetings in order to observe and learn how the staff coordinate their efforts, which is shown clearly in a staff meeting. Guest members may include the staff of any other part of the hospital, especially those working with patients from this program. Typically, the rehabilitation counselor, chaplain, or someone announcing a new program and wishing to have patients sent to it will attend the meeting and answer questions.

Patients and family members of patients never attend staff meetings because of the confidentiality of all discussions.

Roles of Staff Members—In Detail

As noted before, the psychiatrist (unit physician) is the mental hospital unit leader. He opens and closes meetings, and makes all final decisions on the patients' and the staff's activities. (In contrast, the psychologist is the technical leader, focusing on problems of diagnosing patients and implementing behavioral approaches.) After the minutes are read, the psychiatrist invites staff members to bring up any new problems that they wish to discuss. The psychiatrist comments on unusual physical problems presented by each patient that the staff are discussing, such as an obese patient who should be placed on a diet. Or if the psychiatrist considers another patient underweight, he may ask that the patient not miss any meals whether or not he has tokens to pay for them. (No patient is ever kept from a meal because he has not fulfilled token economy program requirements without the explicit approval of the psychiatrist. And no patient can miss more than five meals in a row, by order of the director of the hospital.)

A characteristic discussion is one centering around a patient who is apparently not responding as desired to his tranquilizing medication, and for this reason is evidently not amenable, at this time, to behavior therapy. The staff may request that the psychiatrist reexamine the patient in order to formulate a new tranquilizing prescription. The psychiatrist invariably agrees to do this. All commitments made by staff members are entered into the log book, and at the next staff meeting, three or four days later, each staff member is held accountable for fulfilling that commitment.

The psychiatric social worker is the team member who is responsible for discharge planning. Once the staff decide that a patient should leave the hospital, the social worker begins to work on this task. Discharge planning involves finding a place for the patient to live, either in his home, or in a board-and-care facility. The social worker may also obtain financial support, such as Aid to the Totally Disabled, for a destitute patient who is unable to work (which is generally the case for the long-term patient). The patient then has a subsistence income that enables him to support himself without competing for a job that he is most unlikely to get, or if he does get it, he is not likely to be able to keep it.

Other members present, but rarely participating, may include psychology and social work students who observe and work on the unit as part of their preprofessional training. They are sometimes considered by professional staff as not yet experienced enough to participate in the decision-making processes that comprise the main discussions in any staff meeting. These students often have questions about the process of decision making and are given full answers during supervisorial meetings with the psychologist or the social worker. They are also completely free to talk with other staff members at any time that is convenient for the staff member, outside of the staff meeting.

Usually, the most valuable and detailed information available on patients is presented by technicians (nurses). Technicians "live" with patients in the most comprehensive way, observing them throughout their waking and sleeping hours, and communicating their observations in written and spoken contacts from one shift to another, and from one day to the next. Technician's information is essential to meaningful decision making by the psychiatrist, psychologist, and social worker. No patient could be suitably considered for promotion, demotion, or discharge without full input by the nursing staff. This is especially true in a token economy program, where the core questions are always: How similar is the patient's behavior in the hospital to what would be socially acceptable in his community? And if his behavior is dissimilar, how can it be changed to help him to become acceptable to others in his community?

Professional staff members always ask for technicians' recommendations on a patient, and will generally accept them for changes in a patient's status *if* technicians agree among themselves. When technicians disagree—which is quite common because a patient often behaves differently during one shift than during another, or with one technician than another—professional staff can help by finding and exploring major themes of when, under what contingencies, and in what context a patient behaves appropriately and inappropriately. These major themes enable a fuller and more effective coordination of all staff efforts to modify a patient's behavior into more appropriate forms. The information from technicians is welded into a new treatment plan, and most often this information is brought out by technician's at the staff meeting. Indeed, this aspect takes up most of the meeting time, and is the most important function of the staff meeting.

Throughout the staff meeting, the psychologist acts as a consultant, making specific suggestions on assessment of patients, treatment procedures, and evaluation of readiness for discharge. A behavioristic psychologist is in an especially good position to advise on these questions; because of the highly specific assessment techniques that he uses, he may have definite answers to such crucial questions as: In what kind of social setting are patients likely to show appropriate or inappropriate behaviors? In effect, the psychologist conducts mini-consultations with other staff members whenever they present difficult patients in staff meetings.

SUMMARY

Detailed information on many aspects of the treatment roles of Camarillo staff members, and how they cooperate in the token economy team to change antisocial and asocial behaviors into behaviors that are more acceptable to the patients' communities, are presented in this chapter. Although the experiences and conditions at Camarillo differ from those of other token economies, they are clearly detailed so that readers can decide knowledgeably why, how, and if they will use Camarillo's approaches.

This chapter offers a brief introduction to the need for guidance on the application of laboratory findings—on which Camarillo's token economy is based—to a mental hospital setting.

Camarillo's psychologist has many key roles, since he is technically the best-informed member of the team. He works closely with other staff members in coordinating their efforts to implement consistency in modifying behavior. He works directly with patients in both individual and group sessions, and implements these efforts through consultation with the staff.

The psychiatrist is the administrative leader of the Camarillo program, and in sole charge of most medical decisions. He works closely with all members of the token economy treatment team to lend his authority and medical expertise to the integrated work of the team. He is responsible for the acceptance or rejection of a transfer patient from other Camarillo programs, and for physical examinations when a new patient is admitted to the token economy program.

Technicians (nurses) are key persons in that they spend the most time with each patient and therefore have the greatest influence of all staff members in modifying each patient's behavior into socially acceptable forms. Technicians provide most of the information for determining promotions and demotions within the program, and discharge from the hospital.

The Camarillo psychiatric social worker makes family contacts, and is responsible for discharge planning, placement of the patient, and financial support for him in the community. The social worker also functions as a behavior therapist, working with patients on an individual basis, negotiating contracts with them, and acting as co-leader in group encounter sessions. He trains social work students and serves as a liaison with social workers in other programs.

Twice-weekly staff conferences are used for formal exchange of evaluations of patients, determination of plans for promotion, and demotion within the program, and discharge from the hospital. Written records are kept of each meeting, and staff members are held accountable for commitments made in previous conferences.

SUGGESTED READINGS

Traditional Insight Therapy vs. Behavior Therapy

Eysenck, H. J. *Experiments in behavior therapy.* Elmsford, N.Y.: Pergamon Press, 1964.

Eysenck, H. J. *Fact and fiction in psychology.* New York: Pelican Books, 1955.

Eysenck, H. J. *Sense and nonsense in psychology.* Elmsford, N.Y.: Pergamon Press, 1957.

These three pocketbooks are clear, simple, and most readable discussions of the differences between traditional insight (evocative) psychotherapy and behavior therapy. They are well worth reading for their presentation of the history and some of the basic ideas of both traditional and behavior therapies.

CHAPTER 3

Training and Research in Camarillo's Token Economy Program

PREPROGRAM TRAINING FOR APPLIED AND RESEARCH ROLES

The staff are well aware that although program training in behavior therapy of new staff members is desirable, it is not obtainable. No staff member except the psychologist has ever been formally trained in behavior therapy, or has ever worked in any strictly behavioral setting prior to working at Camarillo. For this reason, new staff members are chosen from any discipline if they express interest in the program and seem personally suited to working in it. Indeed, it has taken considerable effort to discourage higher levels of Camarillo administration from transferring technicians against their will from other programs into the token economy program. It should be noted that although on some occasions the involuntarily transferred technicians have learned to like the program and to work effectively in it, this has not been the rule.

The physician and social worker are assigned to the program, begin working on the unit knowing nothing about behavior therapy, and generally learn to like and trust this treatment approach. When they are not happy with token economy treatment, they go into other hospital programs.

Staff members from other programs can, and often do, choose to come to work and to learn in the token economy program, and they generally become quite satisfactory team members. This section details how they learn while working in the program, and how students are trained who usually do not work in the program after completing their training. These students need exposure to behavior therapy to round out their understanding of their roles in a mental hospital setting, and at that time are often oriented toward traditional insight therapy. Many of these students later change their orientation to behavior therapy, and work in Camarillo's or some other behavioral program.

The only Camarillo staff member who is a trained researcher is the psychologist. New staff are never chosen on the basis of their ability to do research or even their interest. Instead, staff members and especially students who express a willingness to cooperate with the psychologist in his projects, or students who wish to do their own research, are strongly encouraged by the psychologist to work in the program. Indeed, the psychologist is continually involved in research projects, seeks the assistance of others, and encourages others, psychology students in particular, to do research of their choosing.

IN-SERVICE TRAINING FOR PRACTICE, ACADEMIC CREDITS, AND RESEARCH

Introduction

A token economy program offers some admirable opportunities for training the psychiatric resident, psychological intern, psychiatric social work student, and psychiatric technician (nurse) in the combinative use of each discipline's theory and practice as these meld with behavior therapy. All three mental health disciplines have many aspects in common, and these can be focused on the tangible problems presented by the mental hospital patient who is to be trained to be able to leave the hospital *and* to maintain himself in his community. Token economy offers the student many meaningful training-learning problems as presented by the mental hospital patient. The student can learn to specify many of the potentialities and limitations of the token economy approach. It is a rare and rich opportunity for a student to work in one of the relatively few token economy units, by comparison with the large number of traditionally run units, and he is quite likely to work in a token economy program during his later professional career since the number of units is growing rapidly.

The student in Camarillo's program probably learns more about token economy from the psychologist than from members of all the other disciplines combined. The student's best learning usually comes from the psychologist's supervising him and devoting as much time as possible to the student's learning. (When the student with little background in behavior therapy works directly with a patient without supervision, both the student's learning and the patient's progress are usually seriously handicapped.) One way of increasing the effectiveness of supervision is through group rather than individual supervision. The student can then see other students facing and dealing with similar training problems, and learn how to handle them more quickly than if he were alone. The psychologist can usually observe three or four students working on the program at the same time.

The Camarillo psychologist can also help his student to understand and to fit smoothly into the treatment team. When the student attends staff meetings, he has an opportunity to observe directly the workings of the team as it deals with each patient's community and hospital problems. The student also participates in staff discussions of the patient with whom he is working, an excellent preprofessional experience that allows him to appreciate the need for good working relationships with all token economy members, and shows him how to establish these relationships. The psychologist, typically, helps the student to understand that he cannot command or antagonize any technician. The psychologist, of course, has his interest as well as the student's in mind, since the student spends only a few months on the unit, and the psychologist, who remains there, may well have to pay for the student's antagonizing another staff member. In fact, there is little reason for the student to alienate any technician, since both share a working commitment to the patient's welfare and to the behavioral approach in treating him, and generally wish to work amicably together.

Training of Psychiatric Residents

Camarillo's psychiatric residents have many direct and indirect opportunities for learning. They can speak directly with the psychologist, and do so on many occasions. They are able to participate actively in the program, as part of their residency training. They are invited to hear and meet with outside behaviorally-oriented speakers, and, indeed, many of these speakers are paid for with residency training funds.

Perhaps most important, psychiatric residents can work closely with a behaviorally-oriented psychologist, and learn at first hand his usefulness. Sometimes the value of the Camarillo psychologist lies in his exposing psychiatric residents to views quite different from their own. For example, many residents think that psychoactive drugs in the right prescriptive formula can transform the abnormal person into a normal one. In contrast, the Camarillo psychologist believes that no drug can permanently change any disturbed person into a normal one. The psychologist believes that with the right psychoactive drug the patient can show greater motivation to learn to speak and to behave in patterns that are more nearly normal than the disturbed ones that brought him to the hospital and keep him there. Indeed, the psychologist repeatedly suggests to the residents that the most important function of psychoactive medication is to help the patient to profit from treatment, either behavioral or traditional.

Residents profit greatly from their token economy experiences by learning the values and limitations of token economy so that they can begin to understand the kinds of deviant social repertoires that are most and least responsive to the program. It is repeatedly stressed that simply because someone does not respond to traditional insight therapy, electroconvulsive shock treatment, or any other nonbehavioral approach does not mean that he is suited to behavior therapy. And, conversely, that because someone does respond to nonbehavioral approaches does not mean that he would not respond even better to behavior therapy.

For example, the physically aggressive patient who attacks many staff members and other patients over the years and is not responding to traditional therapy is also dangerous to behavioral staff. Even though he may respond to behavior therapy, he poses a physical threat that few behavioral therapists would care to experience, and he is therefore not a good candidate for a token economy program. Similarly, the patient who has serious brain damage, so that his ability to learn from experience is severely hampered, is not a particularly good candidate for a token economy program unless there is enough staff time available to invest a great effort in changing his behavior.

In Camarillo's program, there have been some unusual patients who were quite good candidates, because they were relatively aware of their situations. Camarillo's program emphasizes encounter groups and written contracts, which work well with sociopathic and paranoid patients, who usually have adequate intelligence and tend to be quite unresponsive to traditional treatment approaches.

Specification of exactly the kinds of patients likely to profit from Camarillo's program is of value to the psychiatric resident because in the future he may have to understand and use behavior therapy to a far greater extent than does today's psychiatrist. (The increased psychiatric awareness of the usefulness and acceptance of behavior therapy is demonstrated in the official, trail-blazing report of the American Psychiatric Association (1973), "Behavior Therapy in Psychiatry.")

Only by knowing the values and limitations of behavioristic approaches under the relatively well controlled conditions of token economy is it possible to recognize the far more stringent limitations of behavior therapy's usefulness for outpatient treatment.

The following guidelines are suggestions of what appear to be some promising training approaches for each psychiatric resident. The resident should carry a few cases, all of whom he sees from three to five times a week, if possible. These patients should be behaviorally trained, with continuing consultation from the psychologist or whomever is the behavioral therapy expert, so that the resident understands and uses suitable social learning principles appropriately. The resident's cases should constitute a representative sampling of mental hospital patients, ranging from the bright, young, and relatively aware verbal patient to the older, long-term, chronic, quite deteriorated patient who shows little awareness or appropriate speech.

The young patient makes an excellent training case for the resident because his usual distaste for institutional life of any kind is a strong motivation for him to cooperate with the resident. The patient generally understands that changing his aggressive antisocial behavior can help him to get out of the hospital sooner and to stay out of institutions longer. The young patient frequently imagines what will happen to him with a few more years of hospitalization, and becomes frightened when he sees the older, chronic, deteriorated patient. The young patient may be verbally or even physically abusive to others, is commonly given a choice by a court—of mental hospital or jail. He dislikes being in the hospital, but reasonably enough prefers being there to jail.

Because of the young patient's responsiveness to treatment, the resident often finds him an attractive choice for intensive therapy. The young patient can generally learn to express his hostility in a controlled, socially acceptable, verbal way, rather than with his fists in an uncontrolled, unacceptable way. Care should be taken to select a patient who is not dangerous to the staff. (See Anger Training Sessions in Chapter 6.) Training is often relatively easy, at least within the confines of the hospital, because the patient wishes to learn how to speak and act toward others so that he will not be deprived of his freedom again. The resident can approach the patient on this basis, and with the help of the team's behavioral expert, he can devise suitable techniques for immediately and positively reinforcing desired speech and actions *as* they occur in training sessions. With the help of technicians, the patient can be positively reinforced for socially acceptable speech and actions *whenever and wherever* they occur, throughout his waking hours. This kind of training sequence takes only a few weeks or a few months, so that the psychiatric resident can feel a sense of achievement in completing his work with his young patient, and in seeing him discharged from the hospital. The previously aggressive patient may still be physically combative, but the likelihood is decreased because of his training, and this tends to be most gratifying to the patient, the psychiatric resident, the rest of the staff, and, hopefully, the patient's community.

When the resident treats the older, deteriorated patient, he can follow this same procedure and the one described in Chapter 5 on direct treatment of the patient by the psychologist. Usually six months to a year are needed to prepare a chronic patient for discharge, so that the resident will generally not work long enough with the patient to reach this goal, but he may see considerable movement of the patient toward discharge. In sum, the future psychiatrist's token economy experience may provide him with an unusually rich opportunity to learn at first hand the values of behavior therapy and the usefulness of other team members.

Training of Psychological Interns

The training guidelines discussed here grew out of experiences at Camarillo, and should be considered as merely suggesting that similar conditions may exist in other mental hospital settings. Special adaptations are likely to be necessary, depending on the unique characteristics of every mental hospital setting.

In Camarillo's experience, the psychological intern has generally agreed with the token economy psychologist on the suitability of behavior therapy for the treatment of mental hospital patients. (The psychological intern, unlike the psychiatric resident and the psychiatric social worker, generally has a good background in behavior therapy, prior to serving on the unit.) Generally, the psychological intern prefers working in a behavior therapy program to working in a traditional one. The intern and the psychologist also share a common training background, except that the psychologist's is somewhat longer, and the intern's includes a more recent and comprehensive knowledge of behavioristic writings. The intern generally works three months on the token economy unit, as part of the year that he has to serve in a mental hospital clinic or other American Psychological Association–approved treatment facility before receiving his Ph.D. in clinical psychology. His schooling includes four years of college resulting in a bachelor of arts or bachelor of science degree, a two- to three-year master's degree program, and a three- to four-year doctoral program. The year's internship usually precedes the writing of the doctoral dissertation.

Because of the psychological intern's schooling and background in behavior therapy, the psychologist can trust him to work with patients with less supervision than is needed by the psychiatric resident or the social work student. (Indeed, the psychologist often learns a great deal from the psychological intern about new behavior therapy techniques.) The psychologist often enjoys working with the psychology student much more than with other students because they share many interests. The psychologist usually finds his relationship with the psychology student particularly gratifying when they are working together on research problems (see the section Staff Research Potentials and Roles in this Chapter).

The intern generally works directly with the psychologist, each treating the same case on alternate days, and both working simultaneously in group behavior modification sessions. Typically, the student chooses about ten representative patients ranging from the younger and most aware patients to those with long hospitalization histories and little responsiveness to others. The intern is given considerable leeway in picking cases of interest to him, because he is then most likely to be involved in treatment, creative in devising approaches, and, therefore, successful in modifying inappropriate behaviors. And perhaps most important, the student is then likely to learn from his experience. In contrast, if the supervising psychologist simply assigns patients to the intern, the intern may be only nominally involved in treatment. In addition, the student always has the option to discontinue treatment of patients whom he has come to fear, dislike, or believe will not profit from behavior therapy. The intern's benefits from training and his efforts seem to be greater if his learning is considered more important than improvement in his patients.

Throughout the intern's work in the token economy program, the psychologist observes him closely, watching sample sessions of the intern's work with each of his patients. After each session, the psychologist discusses patients' progress or lack of progress with the intern, and gives the intern an opportunity to talk about some of his problems in working with his patients. The psychologist seems to be most effective when he does not take a critical attitude toward the intern, but instead considers all the intern's efforts to be part of his learning process. Then, when the patient does not make the kind of progress expected, neither the psychologist nor the intern feels threatened. Discussion of patients' progress, or lack of it, remains quite objective, and treatment of patients continues to be—or even increases as—a meaningful and vivid learning process for both the psychologist and the intern. The psychologist generally makes a few suggestions that are designed to improve the intern's understanding of the treatment process, and to increase the effectiveness of behavior therapy. At the end of each month, the intern writes progress notes that provide both the psychologist and the intern with a chance to review the patients' progress, with comparisons with previous months, and with an opportunity to make specific predictions for the following month about all patients' responses to treatment.

At the end of the training period the psychologist writes an evaluative report to the psychologist in charge of training on the intern's efforts in the program, and carefully and completely discusses this report with the intern. If the intern objects to any aspect of the evaluation, it is changed in a way that is acceptable to both the intern and the psychologist. The intern is given a copy of this evaluation, and another copy may be sent, if requested by the intern, to the intern's major professor. (During one year alone, four interns were supervised, and there never was any problem with the evaluation reports, which were, appropriately enough, quite positive.)

A Case Example: Individual Treatment Under Supervision

The following is an example of a patient being treated by a Camarillo psychology intern with supervision by the psychologist. A psychology doctoral intern worked, with the psychologist's help, with a young, aggressive patient with five years of continuous hospitalization. Mr. Z, age 25, had to have his meals alone because when eating in the cafeteria with other patients, he hit and kicked them and grabbed food from them. To avoid fights, the technicians brought Mr. Z's food from the cafeteria to the unit, so that he did not eat with other patients. The technicians justifiably complained about the extra work. The goal of behavior therapy with Mr. Z was to train him to eat cooperatively with other patients in the cafeteria.

The first training sessions were given to Mr. Z each morning at breakfast. He ate alone from a tray, on the unit, and the intern positively reinforced him with candy and social approval for eating properly. Social approval consisted of the intern saying to Mr. Z, "Your're doing fine! That's *very good!*" The intern and the psychologist trained Mr. Z to eat slowly, to use his napkin to wipe his mouth, and to use a fork and spoon instead of his fingers to put food into his mouth. Mr. Z was also given an empty tray and utensils and asked to imagine various foods. He was then reinforced with social approval and candy (a primary reinforcement) for eating fantasized foods properly.

In later sessions, the intern and the psychologist took Mr. Z to the cafeteria. Sitting one on each side of him, they reinforced him there with candy for eating properly. Mr. Z was told that if he did any grabbing of food from other patients, fighting or kicking, he would immediately be taken from the cafeteria, and would not be allowed to finish his meal. On one occasion Mr. Z physically threatened the intern and the psychologist. He was told in no uncertain terms that if he did not quiet down and eat properly, he would be taken from the cafeteria and get nothing more to eat for that meal. He instantly stopped his belligerency, and became cooperative. After about three months of behavioral training on the unit and in the cafeteria, Mr. Z could eat all three meals in the cafeteria without additional, eating-training sessions.

Training of Psychiatric Social Work Students

The Camarillo token economy experience for social work students was arranged by a social worker who acts as liaison training officer between the hospital and the social work program of the University of California at Los Angeles. All the social work students have at least a bachelor's degree, since the social work program is in the graduate school. Their program lasts two years, and leads to a master's degree in psychiatric social work (P.S.W.). They work in a field placement two or three days a week. The mental hospital field placement offers many rich opportunities for students to function as social workers under supervision, and through these experiences to learn from firsthand contact the work of the social worker, as well as that of the psychologist, psychiatrist, and technician.

The social work liaison training officer works closely with the psychologist in order to make the token economy experience as meaningful as possible for students. The liaison officer helps the psychologist to know exactly what is expected of him, and he, in turn, evaluates students for the training officer. There are few differences on training procedures between the training officer and the psychologist, except for problems of students' time commitments.

Students are often called to meetings and lectures that keep them from working directly with patients as much as the psychologist believes is necessary to do in order to gain an adequate understanding of their token economy experiences.

During the three months that the social work student is on the token economy program, he has many opportunities for learning. He can learn to write up patient progress notes, and have the psychologist help him to learn the most effective ways of using these write-ups to understand the progress or lack of progress of his patients. Writing case reports helps the student to learn appropriate professional ways of communicating in writing with his colleagues. The student participates in staff conferences and is able to appreciate the roles of various token economy staff members, as well as the values and limitations of staff conferences. He can observe the social worker, psychologist, and psychiatric technician working together to forge a team effort to train each patient so that he can be discharged as soon as possible, and remain out of the hospital and in his community as long as possible.

The social work student's role is somewhat similar to that of the psychology student, except that the social work student is not expected to be familiar with behavioral writings, nor to be involved in research. Instead, the social work student depends on the psychologist for knowledge of both old and new writings on behavioristic approaches suitable to a token economy program. The psychologist works closely with the student, and directs him toward effective behavioristic techniques.

The social work student, like the psychology intern, works with a representative group of about ten patients, chosen by him, ranging from the youngest and most aware to the oldest and most deteriorated. The kinds of problems presented by his patients varies, so that he has a large variety of training experiences with them. The student works with younger, verbally aggressive patients, and trains them to channel their anger in words rather than deeds, so that they can live in their communities without endangering others. He works with older patients, offering them candy, cookies, or cigarettes as reinforcements, and training them to work and to speak appropriately. He participates in group behavioral training sessions, and observes patients learning social skills from each other.

After each working session the psychologist tries to spend time with the student to discuss his work with his patients. These supervisory sessions help the student to understand appropriate ways of improving his patients' social repertoires. Typically, the psychologist asks the student to change, as often as possible, the tasks and rewards presented to each of his patients so that their interest and motivation is maintained. In this way, patients are most likely to profit from treatment. In addition, the psychologist usually asks leading questions to help the student think through some of his target behavior goals for his patients and the best approaches to reaching them. In sum, the psychologist tries to tailor the token economy training experience to the student's background and interests so that he can learn as much as possible during his three months in the program.

Training of Psychiatric Technicians (Nurses)

Because psychiatric technicians (nurses) are the basic workers in Camarillo's token economy program, providing other staff members with the most comprehensive and detailed information on the daily lives of patients, there is substantial reason to train psychiatric technicians carefully. For all practical working purposes technicians live with patients. They can give the right reinforcements at the right time, and make the program effective in training patients to behave appropriately socially. On the other hand, even one technician alone can easily sabotage much of the work with many patients, and certainly with a single patient. When one person reinforces for an undesirable behavior what other members of the team do not reinforce for, and, indeed, are trying to eliminate, the behavior will tend to continue indefinitely. Technicians are crucial members of the token economy team, for if a technician deliberately or otherwise acts in opposition to the work of the rest of the team, nothing may be accomplished with the patient.

Because the work of technicians tends to be quite similar in all token economy programs, this discussion may be more directly usable in new token economy programs than are the writings on the work of psychologists, psychiatrists, and psychiatric social workers. Camarillo's experiences can thus be viewed as strongly representative of those in most programs.

As was noted earlier, technicians generally have little education, and often are only high school graduates. They have no previous training in nursing or behavior therapy before working as nurses. (Many years ago I worked as a psychiatric technician on a summer's internship to satisfy a work requirement for a master's degree. When it began, I'd had exactly three weeks of on-the-job training!) Camarillo technicians go through six months of training, most of it on the job, and little of it behavioral unless they have a lecture from a behaviorally oriented psychologist. Prior to coming to the program, they generally have no experience working in a behavioral setting. Most come because they are assigned there. (It is correctly rumored that this program makes technicians work much harder than do traditionally oriented ones. Only those who find it more exciting and satisfying than a traditional program stay in it.)

None of the technicians in the token economy program are registered nurses. (Registered nurses have an extensive background in general science and other subjects taught in college, and then attend an intensive nursing program for about two and one-half years.) Most of the technicians are in this field because they are not trained to do anything else, and they feel that it is permanently secure work. During the period covered by this book (late 1960s and early 1970s), the California mental hospital system was under considerable fire, and Camarillo, the largest hospital in the state was often in danger of closing. As

Camarillo's hospital population dropped, morale among technicians dropped, too. Technicians feared for their jobs, as talk of closing the hospital increased.

And the drop in hospital population was quite artificial, for the counties, Los Angeles in particular, tried desperately not to send patients to the state hospital, even when they needed to be there. The counties were given financial bonuses if they sent fewer patients to the hospital one year than the previous one, and the counties were penalized financially if they sent more patients one year than the year before. These and many more aspects of the hospital's battle for survival were known to technicians, were intensively discussed daily, and led some of the best technicians to leave the token economy program. Many potential trainees never got into programs, which were being cut back, and many trainees left the hospital as soon as possible after finishing their training.

To keep up morale and increase effectiveness of technicians, in-service training has been emphasized. The psychologist focuses on helping technicians to learn by holding long discussions with them on individual problem patients, and by helping them to understand how behavior therapy with one patient can be applied to other, similar patients. In-service training rarely requires technicians to read anything, as this would probably not be done, and the request might antagonize them. Instead, the psychologist usually does literature searches in problem areas and solutions of these problems, and discusses his reading at the pragmatic level of how it applies to technicians' patients.

Some of the problem areas include handling of the canteen, and having patients eat properly and keep themselves clean. Discussions of a given patient with any problem are then used by the psychologist to help the technicians to understand how the solutions might apply to patients who behave inappropriately in similar ways.

This kind of practical, in-service training is attractive to technicians. They appear interested, listen attentively, and follow fairly well the suggestions made by the psychologist. The questions and objections that they raise to these suggestions are usually quite sensible. Technicians often point out that many of the psychologist's suggestions, while sounding good, are not useful because they interfere with technicians' other responsibilities, or are too time-consuming. Other suggestions then have to be made and tried, so that a continual trial-and-error process is developed that enables the creation and continuation of a dialogue that seems to be of considerable value to the patients and the technicians. Through dialogue with the technicians, the psychologist learns a great deal about what can and cannot be done with patients.

SPECIALIZED OUTSIDE CONSULTATIONS

A major aspect of in-service training is outside consultations. Some of the outside speakers have been leading behavior therapists brought to the hospital to discuss their work, and to answer questions of technicians, psychologist, psychiatrist, social worker, and students of all disciplines. These leading behaviorists include: Dr. Cyril Franks, Rutgers University (New Jersey); Dr. Perry London, University of Southern California; Dr. Irwin Lublin, California State University at Los Angeles; and Dr. Zev Wanderer, Center for the Study of Behavior Therapy (Los Angeles). They came to Camarillo for in-service training meetings with token economy staff members and members of other programs.

The token economy program has specialized outside speakers consult with its staff. The speakers are hired for a full day's pay, which is about $120. A speaker arrives at Camarillo at about 9:30 A.M. and makes a presentation to the entire staff of the hospital. After the presentation, he has an informal lunch with token economy staff and discusses whatever issues are of interest to them and to him.

At about 1:00 he sees an individual patient, with interested token economy staff present. He is briefed by a staff member who has prepared in advance for this assignment. After seeing the patient, he consults directly with the staff to make suggestions on handling this patient. Generally, he sees a patient who is unusually difficult, dangerous, or both. This open interview enables the staff to see the outside consultant practice the principles that he "preached" in his presentation. They can also question him directly in these relatively small and informal groupings at lunch and after his interview with the patient. The staff has often commented on how valuable and enriching these multifaceted consultations are to them.

STAFF RESEARCH POTENTIALS AND ROLES

The thrust of behavior therapy in general and token economy in particular is to break with past methods of traditional insight therapy. Token economy presents a movement of applying new knowledge and research to human social problems. It is dependent on continuing research to extend the applicability and efficiency of its techniques. For these reasons, there is often a sense of excitement and adventure with token economy staff members, who feel that they are pioneering new techniques. They become involved in research projects easily and are willing to try new approaches in treatment, document their experiences, and prepare their findings for formal presentations in conferences and technical journals. These general statements are representative of the spirit of Camarillo's program, and can be expected to be a part of the basic fabric of almost any good token economy program, almost anywhere.

Every staff member can become a competent researcher if he will learn research skills, read the literature, and if he is motivated to do the necessary work. While psychologists have certain advantages from their training, adequately motivated psychiatrists, technicians, and social workers can develop research expertise. A staff member not trained in school to do research can learn these skills by working on research projects with someone who is academically trained to do research, probably the psychologist.

Psychologist and Psychology Students

In Camarillo's experience with research, the psychologist and his psychology students are the most actively involved researchers in the program. Other members of the staff, especially technicians, are completely cooperative, and, indeed, research would be impossible without their help. (Technicians provide much of the data on the daily living patterns of patients, their placement in the program, and their past histories, which are vital to research, and could not be obtained from any other member of the team.)

The reasons that the psychologist and his students are the most involved researchers are significant. Traditionally, psychology has been primarily a research discipline, and only secondarily a treatment discipline. Clinical psychology in particular has focused on developing new ways of easily, effectively, and quickly changing antisocial and asocial behaviors into behaviors that are more acceptable to others in various social environments. The emphasis in graduate programs has been on developing research skills, such as knowing exactly what are the latest and best approaches to human behavioral problems, and how these techniques might be applied in treatment settings.

The Camarillo research project presented below illustrates the psychologist's role as a research coordinator, which is similar to his work as a treatment coordinator. In order to do good research, he has to develop and maintain good working relationships with the psychology student, technician, and psychiatrist. The psychology students collected data for several papers (Ulmer, 1970b, 1971c) and convention readings (Ulmer, 1970a, 1970c, 1971a, 1971b, 1971c, 1973a, 1973b) and were explicitly credited for these contributions. One student wrote his doctoral dissertation (Van Doorninck, 1972), on data collected in the program, and the opportunity to do this was always offered to all psychology students. Psychology students were helpful in rough drafting such materials as "Welcome to Unit 231" and in criticizing the final version (see Chapter 4).

The psychologist named and thanked each participant in the research project for his contributions to it. He sent copies of these papers to all members of the research project. In sum, research on the token economy could not have been done by the psychologist alone. The psychologist expressed to all research contributors his awareness that they had cooperated far beyond the call of duty.

Camarillo's psychologist illustrates the tendency of token economy psychologists to be continually involved in one research project after another, often planning for the next project before the current one has been finished.

A Camarillo Research Project

In late 1969, data were collected for two papers (Ulmer, 1970b, 1971c), comparing (1) test responses of all patients to the Children's Minimal Social Behavior Scale (CMSBS) (Ulmer & Lieberman, 1968); (2) patients' speech and behaviors and the dorm in which they were currently living, as reported by the technicians, (3) their placement in the program in one of the three token economy levels; and (4) their age, length of time in the hospital, and previous hospitalization.

The psychologist planned and coordinated this research project. A psychology student who had not previously been on the unit tested all subjects (Ss^1) on the CMSBS. The student was not allowed to have any interactions with Ss other than his testing of them, so that his impressions of patients and their impressions of him outside of the testing session would not influence his evaluation of their responses to the CMSBS or their responses to him. To reduce the likelihood of one set of data being effected because of the particular informant's knowledge of another set of data, the psychologist met individually with the head charge, the technicians' representative, and with the psychiatrist, to obtain current information about patient functioning from them. None of them knew any Ss' (patients') CMSBS scores.

The psychologist then took all of these data, coded them into specially designed data sheets, and had them computer analyzed. Next he set up the data in special tables, and discussed their meaning and implications with Dr. Wayne Zimmerman, statistical consultant to the project. He then surveyed the literature in this area, wrote everything up, and submitted these papers for publication and convention readings.

This research project illustrates only one facet of the need for strong and continuing motivation of involved staff members if token economy is to function as an effective treatment, teaching, and research mental hospital unit. When token economy morale is low, the program will fail, and this is most likely to occur when all staff members—or at least representative members of each discipline—are not involved in all projects, or when higher administration does not give the program its full support.

Technicians

In Camarillo's behavior modification program technicians (nurses) have never taken the initiative to do research. Their consistent role is to provide essential treatment and data-collecting services, so that comprehensive information on the patient's life could be obtained at all times—7 days weekly and 24 hours daily. Data supplied by technicians covers patient's experiences (and the staff's with him) beyond the hours and places in which the psychologist or physician is present. This coverage is vital, for any token economy research project that does not include this information is unlikely to be successful.

Technicians at Camarillo and probably in most other settings do not assume leadership roles in research projects for many reasons. They generally do not have extensive education, at most a few years of college. In order to initiate reserch in behavior therapy it has generally been necessary to have research skills, which require years of schooling, and to have read the literature quite

---

[1] Persons used for testing in an experiment.

well. Technicians usually do not have the educational background, the time to read extensively, or the incentives to do the highly abstract work of research. Good behavioral research requires working with numbers, and concern with finding new ways of assessing and treating patients, not just clinical impressions of patients. Often, current patients do not receive the best known treatments, or even those that may appear most suited to them, as means of testing new techniques. And usually only persons with a research background can understand that it is sometimes absolutely necessary to give some patients less than the best known or most effective treatments, if new and better techniques are to be developed.

Psychiatrist

Camarillo's experience with two psychiatrists in research has been that they were supportive and helpful, but were neither research-trained nor research-oriented. The first psychiatrist was totally supportive in encouraging the staff to cooperate with the psychologist in collecting research data. (This was vital, because without his support—as administrative leader of the program—other staff members, especially the technicians, would not have provided the research data on which the projects were based.) This psychiatrist also read through medical charts and provided substantial material that the psychologist was not able to obtain. The material included number and length of previous hospitalizations, which were very difficult to pull out of the charts. This psychiatrist left the program after a few months, and a second one took over.

The second psychiatrist gave the psychologist complete support on all research projects, and directed the staff to assist him in every way. For this reason, there was never any difficulty with technicians in obtaining the needed data on patients' behavior. Like the first psychiatrist, the second was not research-trained nor research-oriented, so that he was not motivated to initiate new research projects.

These have been Camarillo's experiences. However, a growing number of psychiatrists are behaviorally trained and oriented, and quite competent as researchers. Indeed, there is every reason to believe that any psychiatrist who is adequately motivated to be behaviorally rather than traditionally oriented, and who makes the effort to develop research skills, can become a competent behavioral researcher.

Psychiatric Social Worker

Camarillo's token economy social worker has never become involved in any behavioral research project. He has not been called upon to provide data, and has never initiated a research project. He appears to be quite fully committed to direct patient treatment and to training of other social workers. Nevertheless, the generalizations of potential research competence made about the psychiatrist certainly hold for the social worker. Social workers who are adequately motivated can learn research skills, know the behavioral literature, and become good token economy researchers. In fact, social workers are becoming good researchers in many settings.

SUMMARY

In this chapter some of the factors that are important in training Camarillo's staff for practice, academic credits, and research are discussed. Since none of staff, except the psychologist, has ever worked previously in a behavioral program, the token economy staff has to provide in-service training for new staff members. Training involves helping them to learn behavioral principles of therapy as they apply in this setting.

Training at Camarillo focuses on the work of the psychologist in supervising all disciplines in learning about token economy. The psychologist assists students to understand the workings of the whole team, and to fit into it smoothly. Psychiatric residents learn how to treat young, aggressive patients as well as older, more deteriorated ones. Psychology interns are quite knowledgeable about behavior therapy, and work closely with the psychologist almost in a peer-colleague relationship, rather than a student-teacher relationship. Social work students learn to work directly with patients in individual and group behavior modification sessions. Despite the strong emphasis on psychoanalytic techniques in their academic training, their work on the program is confined to the use of behavioral approaches. Technicians' (nurses') training is of considerable interest and value to patients and to the program in general, and focuses on the pragmatic aspects of what can and should be done with problem patients.

Outside consultants, usually leading behavior therapists, are brought into the hospital. They lecture first, then talk to the staff informally over lunch, and then talk with a patient while the staff observes them at work.

Research is of considerable importance in Camarillo's token economy program and is often quite feasible because of the staff's interest in new treatment approaches. The psychologist is a trained researcher, who offers considerable help to other staff members who are learning to do research. Research is coordinated by the psychologist, usually through working closely with psychology students and collecting other data from technicians and from the psychiatrist. A specific research project is described that used the Children's Minimal Social Behavior Scale (CMSBS) to compare current and past functioning, placement in the token economy setting, and responses to a highly structured interview setting. Technicians are essential in providing necessary research data, but are generally not motivated or trained to function as research leaders. Camarillo's two token economy psychiatrists have not been research-oriented, but they have been completely helpful in research projects.

They and other psychiatrists could easily become competent researchers (many psychiatrists have done so) if they wished to develop research skills. Camarillo's social worker has never been involved in a research project in any role, but he, too, could learn these skills if he chose to do so. In fact, social workers are becoming good researchers in many settings.

CHAPTER 4

A Sample Token Economy Program in Camarillo Hospital, Part I

BACKGROUND

Chapters 4 and 5 describe a token economy program for the adult, male, mentally ill, usually chronic (long-term—a year or longer), Camarillo State Hospital patient. In this chapter the canteen, patient orientation, patient assessment, and evaluation of reinforcements are discussed. In the next chapter direct patient treatment, discharge, considerations, and ethical, moral, and legal considerations are taken up. The patients' wishes for food, a bed, nicer living conditions, cigarettes, and the opportunity to walk about the grounds (ground privileges) are only a few of the motivations that the staff use to help the patient to modify his behavior. For example, when the patient does not wish to work and to earn tokens—the money of a token economy program—so that he can pay for his meals, he may (provided the physician does not object) miss as many as five consecutive meals. The choice is always the patient's, for the staff believes not only that he can make good decisions, despite being seriously disturbed, but

55

that he has the right to make these choices about how he is to live. And the patient's experiences in making choices are an essential part of his socialization process.

The average patient is charged nothing during his first week in the program. He is placed on "welfare," which entitles him to free meals and a bed. After the welfare period, he is informed that he is no longer entitled to free meals and a bed, and that he must now pay for his meals and his bed. He is given a job on the unit, such as sweeping, for which he earns tokens. He can also earn tokens for other socially appropriate behaviors, such as getting up promptly in the morning, and making his bed. (The Camarillo token economy program listing of charges, rewards, and fines (Table 4-1) is posted in a prominent position for all patients to see.)

If the patient proves to be dependable enough to have a job off the unit, he can earn enough tokens to be promoted to a higher-level dorm. Whatever the patient's pattern of behavior, after the welfare period, the choice is his, and the staff always make this clear to him. As one patient said, "Even in a mental hospital, you can't be crazy." The patient tends to behave competently, and to learn to behave even more socially effectively with training and time, partially because the staff consider him essentially rational and capable of making decisions. If the staff consider him essentially irrational and incapable of making decisions, which is the case in most nonbehavioral (traditional) hospital treatment programs, the patient tends to continue to function at a socially inadequate level, or to learn to function more inadequately, as is the case of hospitalism.

Table 4-1   Schedules of Token Charges, Rewards, and Fines

Token charges			
Canteen			
Jelly beans—4 for 1 token			
Small animal cookies—4 for 1 token			
Coffee—2 tokens per cup			
Cigarettes—2 tokens per cigarette			
Large chocolate ice cream cookies—2 for 1 token			
Soda—2 tokens per can			
General	*Dorm A*	*Dorm B*	*Dorm C*
Each meal	2	4	6
Bed for 1 night	2	4	6
Daytime sleeping	4	4	4
Writing paper, per sheet	1	1	1
Envelopes	1	1	1
Ground privileges	a	5	5
Attending dances off unit	a	10	10
Attending parties off unit	a	10	10
Home visits	5	10	15

Table 4-1 (*Continued*) Schedules of Token Charges, Rewards, and Fines

Token rewards

Housekeeping chores	Tokens given
Sweeping day room floor	3
Mopping day room floor	3
Washing chairs with vinegar	10
Dusting day room chairs	5
Cleaning day room tables	3
Cleaning bookcases	3
Washing ashtrays	6
Dusting day room windows and sills	3
Sweeping and mopping stairway	10
Sweeping and mopping balcony	7
Sweeping and mopping medication room	4
Cleaning toilets	5
Cleaning sinks	4
Sweeping and mopping nursing office	3
Sweeping and mopping long hall	8
Folding and putting away clean linen	3
Cleaning barber shop sink	4
Making an extra bed	2
Washing medication cups	3
Cleaning floor of one dorm	8
Cleaning a whole dorm	25
Cleaning washing machine room	3
Bringing in or taking out 1 laundry bag	2

Token fines

Behavior	Dorm A	Dorm B	Dorm C
Dropping ashes on floor	7	8	9
Picking up cigarette butts	5	6	7
Spitting	5	6	7
Stealing tokens	10	20	30
Fighting	25	50	75
Missing industrial therapy assignment	b	10	15

[a]Dorm A residents are not offered this activity.
[b]Dorm A residents are not given industrial therapy assignments.

The Camarillo program is probably a better than average token economy program, since it has a history of almost ten years of continuous operation--which is longer than most—and has a highly involved and motivated staff, and substantial support from higher-level administration. The program originally began as an experimental pilot project, and was deliberately moved to separate quarters, away from the general hospital grounds. Highly qualified nursing personnel were selected. The program was headed by a physician, with a psychologist and a social worker—all quite committed to behavioral rather than traditional treatment approaches. The whole project was sponsored by the medical director of the hospital, and his staff provided considerable support for the project. (The significance, indeed necessity, of high-level administrative support for a token economy program can hardly be overestimated, especially at the beginning when retraining of staff is required—see Chapter 7, the section Facilitating and Handicapping Conditions for Success.)

The following discussion will include a general description of the patient dormitories of Camarillo's program, how each patient earns his way from a lower dorm to a higher one, and overall treatment procedures.

There are three levels of living conditions. Each patient usually begins at the lowest level, Dorm C, and is encouraged to work himself up to a higher dorm. As mentioned above, a patient can earn many rewards and privileges (Table 4-1). The two top levels, Dorms B and A, provide increasing comfort, with greater space allotted for each patient, and a more pleasant atmosphere. A new patient is told by the staff, especially psychiatric technicians, what he must do to advance himself in the token economy program. He is given a copy of the orientation material "Welcome to Unit 231" (see pp. 64–68).

The new patient usually lives in Dorm C, the lowest-level dorm, which is stark and has many beds with little space between them. There are no curtains or drapes on the windows and no bedspreads on the beds. A resident of Dorm C eats at long, crowded tables in the cafeteria, and he is not given second helpings of food. He does not have ground privileges, and only leaves the unit for meals or to spend an hour or so in the courtyard next to the unit. A resident of Dorms B or A automatically has ground privileges, and he can go on the grounds almost any time that he wishes to until 5:00 each evening, unless he is working. To be promoted from Dorm C to Dorm B, a patient must pay 200 tokens, and have the permission of his psychiatric technician group leader, as well as approval from the rest of the staff.

Dorm B has a small sitting room, curtains on the windows, and more space for each resident because it has fewer beds than Dorm C. A Dorm B resident can go to movies, dances, and parties on holidays because of his automatic ground privileges. He eats at smaller tables than a resident of Dorm C, and if he wishes, he can often get second helpings of food. Dorm A follows this same pattern of increasingly nicer living conditions, just as the standard of living improves as one moves up the socioeconomic ladder in the general society. Dorm A is even more pleasant than Dorm B, and the cafeteria tables are small and uncrowded. A Dorm A resident lives in a dorm with large, open spaces between relatively few beds, and there are curtains and drapes on the windows. A Dorm A resident is especially privileged, and he can wander freely about the grounds throughout daylight hours. (For a fuller description of the parallels between token economy levels and those of the general society, especially as shown in Camarillo's Program, see Ulmer, 1970b.)

THE TOKEN ECONOMY CANTEEN

Tokens, token cards, bank accounts, and a canteen are vital aspects of Camarillo's program, and are likely to be essential to a program in any other setting. They are vital because they give patients something to work for—they are the motivators for what is essentially a motivational system of social learning.

The Camarillo canteen is on the treatment unit, near the bedrooms, and is open two or three times daily so that each patient can be paid in tokens for the work that he has done. He can exchange these tokens for many things, such as candy, cigarettes, and soda. He can also deposit these tokens in his bank account or withdraw tokens from the account.

Tokens are usually plastic poker chips of various colors, although wooden ones will do perfectly well. The most important consideration is cost; obviously, the less costly the tokens, the better off is the program. About 5 to 10 percent of tokens are likely to be lost each month. All tokens should have the same value, independent of color or material, because the severely deteriorated patient, who is the most common resident of a token economy program, may be unable to recognize different values for different tokens. Because of their vividness, red tokens are especially useful in individual behavior modification sessions with the severely deteriorated patient.

There are many ways of handling the serious problem of a patient stealing tokens from other patients. Sometimes a patient who steals can be placed on special, clearly identified tokens; this way he is no longer reinforced by stealing (Gates, 1972). Or this patient's tokens can have special markings placed on them, such as adhesives or scotch tape with a technician's signature. Only one special procedure works well at Camarillo because it is so common for the relatively aware patient to steal from the relatively unaware one. Sometimes a patient gets up in the middle of the night and steals tokens from the locker of another patient. Camarillo staff eliminate stealing by giving each patient a token carry-around card with his name on it. Then when a patient earns or spends tokens, each transaction can be noted on his card. Because every patient has his own card, no stealing is possible. Figure 4-1 is a reproduction of a sample token carry-around card.

The *token economy bank account* is important because it provides every patient and the staff with considerable leverage to use token economy precedures flexibly. Token economy bank account cards can be kept in a small box in the canteen, so that each patient's bank balance is immediately available to the staff for any transaction.

The patient never has his bank account card; he can find out his balance only by asking in the canteen. His carry-around card is like a wallet for the ordinary person. When there are too many tokens on the carry-around card, some are

Name:	Date:
No. of token given: Reason given:	
No. of tokens charged: Reason charged:	
No. of tokens given Reason given:	
No. of tokens charged: Reason charged:	

Figure 4-1 Unit 231 token carry-around card.

deposited in the bank account and credited to the bank account card. This is similar to the situation in which a person deposits some or all of his weekly salary in his bank account, instead of keeping the cash or check in his wallet. When the person does not have enough money in his wallet, he may withdraw money from the bank. Similarly, the patient short of tokens for his daily token economy living expenses may draw from his bank account.

A patient needs a bank account in which to store accumulated tokens, which he can then use to pay for promotion to a higher dorm. Sometimes a patient will work hard for a while, accumulate hundreds or even thousands of tokens, and then stop working. The staff will then "lock" his account so that he cannot draw tokens, and he must begin working again to pay for his meals and his bed. The staff may decide to promote a patient who does not have enough tokens in his account. After the promotion he will have a negative balance in his account, owing tokens to the bank. He must then pay half the tokens that he earns each day until the debt is paid off. Bank account cards are kept in the token bank (Figure 4-2). As a patient accrues tokens on his token carry-around card, a technician transfers the amounts to the patient's bank account card.

When a patient is promoted to a higher dorm, he is given a special placement slip (Figure 4-3). There is a ceremony associated with his promotion so that his earning and being transferred to a higher dorm is recognized by others in the program, and he tends to feel that it has social meaning.

The canteen costs about 5¢ per day per patient, at 1975 prices, roughly $1.50 per month per patient, or about $100 a month for a 65-bed program. A canteen is necessary in any program (see Chapters 4 and 7). This money is usually provided by higher administration, and should be guaranteed in advance of starting a new program (see Chapter 7).

Name of patient:			
Date	Deposit	Withdrawal	Balance

Figure 4-2 Token economy bank account card.

Congratulations, Mr. _____ .

You are now living in Dormitory _____ .

You will _____ have GROUND PRIVILEGES.

Figure 4-3   Token economy dormitory placement slip.

The $1.50 per day per patient can be used to purchase candy, coffee, cigarettes, or whatever "goodies" will motivate patients to work for tokens. The goodies offered in the canteen should be changed frequently to maintain every patient's interest in earning tokens.

Goodies for a canteen can be bought in a variety of ways, some of which are quite economical. Candies and cookies in bulk packages should be bought instead of the small packages that tend to be quite expensive. Chocolate is especially costly, far more so than broken or out-of-fashion hard candies, which are less attractive, but enable the canteen to provide many goodies for little money. Because it is more expensive to run a token economy program than it is to run a traditional program, stretching funds is worth the extra effort involved. For example, providing roll-your-own papers and tobacco costs only about a fifth as much as ready-made cigarettes. Once a local wholesale outlet is aware of a token economy program's needs, it can put aside these items. It is far more dependable to buy from wholesale outlets than it is to depend on well-intentioned, but frequently unreliable, sources of donations.

If donations do not come through, and the canteen is empty at any time, every patient is likely to lose faith and trust in tokens, just as we would no longer prize dollars if we could not buy things with them. Unfortunately, the canteen faces many financial difficulties due to fiscal problems at all levels of government. Human services activities increasingly have their budgets cut. State mental hospitals in particular are severely short of funds because they rank low in priority for mental health funds. Community mental health centers and community hospitals have high priority ratings and receive increased funding each year, so that token economies in community facilities are less likely than state hospitals to face serious financial problems.

In a state mental hospital a token economy psychologist is often called on to help raise funds for the program. Sometimes funds can be obtained by giving lunches for other staff members, holding raffles, calling on patients' families for donations, or establishing profit-sharing programs with a hospital workshop. (Profit sharing with any hospital facility is often difficult because funds are in short supply, and there are hospital regulations and legal restrictions on use of such funds.) None of these approaches tends to be particularly effective, especially obtaining donations from families of chronic patients. (A family generally stops contacting any family member who spends more than five continuous years in a mental hospital as a mentally ill patient. The situation is different for the mentally retarded patient, because his family will usually maintain a close and involved contact with him throughout his lifetime.) Research support sometimes enables funding of a canteen, but usually for only short periods of time. A continuing source of funds is most easily obtained from monies set aside for purposes such as patients' benefit funds.

PATIENT ORIENTATION

Orientation is an extremely important part of behavior therapy, because only when the patient understands his social environment fairly well can his token economy treatment be expected to have some effect. To expedite therapy it is essential that the patient be oriented to his hospital situation as soon as possible after his entrance into the unit. Rapid orientation is particularly vital today, because a patient may spend only a few days or weeks in a mental hospital, rather than years or a lifetime, which was frequently the case 20 years ago. To expedite orientation, and to enable the patient to know in concrete, specific form what the hospital environment is all about, as soon as he enters the Camarillo program he is give an orientation form that describes the hospital setting to him. Since the patient usually has no experience with a token economy program, he needs to know what is expected of him, and what he can expect from the staff. He may be quite fearful, whether hospitalization is new to him or he is familiar with it.

The Camarillo psychologist assumes responsibility for writing an orientation form. This form is useful to the staff because each discipline can then see clearly its responsibilities to each patient. The staff also learn what special token economy privileges each patient expects from them. All staff members, and especially new ones, should be given a copy of the orientation form, because it will help them to understand the program. Visitors, especially the family of a patient, or professionals from other token or traditional treatment programs, may become well informed about the program by reading the orientation form.

The orientation form tells the patient what the hospital expects of him, and what he can expect from the hospital. It tells him the names of staff members who are most likely to be important to him, and what facilities are available for socializing and having fun.

Camarillo's token economy orientation form, "Welcome to Unit 231," is reprinted in full below (Exhibit 4-1).

EXHIBIT 4-1

Welcome to Unit 231

Raymond A. Ulmer
Assistant Program Director
Behavior Modification Program

This is a *token economy unit* of Camarillo State Hospital, near Camarillo, California. The psychiatrist on the unit is Dr. William Purmort. The Head Charge of the psychiatric technicians is Mr. Hugh Sanford. The psychologist is Dr. Raymond A. Ulmer. And the psychiatric social worker is Mr. Roy Jones.

You will be assigned to a nursing group with a leader for different days, and the day, afternoon, and night shifts. Your group leader will talk with you and tell you about the unit. Your group leader will help you to know what your job is on this token economy unit. Your group leader will arrange for you to have a physical examination from Dr. Purmort.

You will be assigned a bed and a locker in your dormitory. Your locker is the place to keep your clothing and other personal possessions. You will turn over your food, candy, and cigarettes to the technicians who will keep them for you in the canteen. You should keep your bed made and your locker neat, and you will be given tokens for doing this.

The 231 token economy unit is a *special treatment program* that can help you to get out of the hospital sooner, and to stay out of mental hospitals after you leave this one. *A token economy program* is a way of helping you to learn how to be a happier person.

As part of the token economy program you can earn tokens, which are given to you on cards telling how many tokens you have earned, and the kind of work that you have done. *A token economy card* is like a check that you can cash to get the things that tokens buy. With your card you can buy cigarettes, candy, coffee, and cookies from the canteen on the unit. The canteen is open three times a day: once in the morning, once in the afternoon, and once in the evening. You can also earn tokens for your card by working on jobs off the unit. With these token cards you can pay for your meals and your bed. You will need to have a token card to pay for your food, candy, and cigarettes that are kept for you in a box with your name on it in the canteen. It is part of the *treatment program* that you pay for your own food, candy, and cigarettes with your token card.

There are many ways of earning tokens for your token card. A list is posted on the unit telling you the ways that you can earn tokens for doing different jobs and how many tokens you can get for each job. You can also ask the technicians for a job helping them, and then they will add tokens to your token card. When you earn extra tokens, you can put them into your bank account in the canteen, and draw on them later to pay for the things that you want.

You are paid for doing many of the things that are good for you to do so that you will learn to act better, get out of the hospital sooner, and stay out of hospitals after you leave this one. You may be fined for doing things that are bad for you and that you are not supposed to do. You will be told by the technicians any time that you get a fine, and how many tokens you are being fined.

DORMITORIES

There are three dormitories in the *Token Economy Program*, and you can work your way up so that you can live better in one of the higher dorms. You can earn your way up to the top dorm by behaving well, working, and earning your tokens on your token card.

Dorm C

Dorm C is probably the first dorm that you will live in on the unit. It has no bedspreads on the beds or curtains on the windows, and there are a lot of beds that are pretty close together. If you live in Dorm C, you will eat at crowded tables in the cafeteria, and you will not get seconds of the things that you like to eat. You cannot go out on the grounds for a walk, because you do not have ground privileges while you live in this dorm. It is much nicer to live in the other dorms than in Dorm C. You can get a promotion to a nicer dorm, Dorm B, by working, earning tokens on your token card, and getting along well with the technicians. To get promoted, you must have permission from your group leader, and pay 200 tokens to live in Dorm B, which is a much nicer dorm, than Dorm C.

Dorm B

Dorm B has more room for you than Dorm C. Dorm B is decorated, and you can use a nice sitting room, which even has an ironing board for you to iron clothes. There will be bedspreads on the bed, and curtains on the windows. You will be able to go on the grounds for walks, because when you live in this dorm you get ground privileges. You can then visit with your friends on the grounds, see movies, or go to dances off the unit. You can eat much better in Dorm B than in Dorm C because you eat at smaller tables that are not crowded, and you can often get second helpings of things that you like to eat. You may also get to go home for visits if you want to, and if the staff feels that this is good for you.

Dorm A

This is the nicest dorm in the whole *Token Economy Program*, and the best one in which to live. This dorm has the most space for you. There are bedspreads on the beds, and curtains on the windows. You have a nice large sitting room. You will be able to go on the grounds often because you now have ground privileges. You can go on the grounds to see your friends, or to make new friends, to go for walks, to see movies, or to go to dances off the unit. You can also use the pool or the gym when they are open. You will eat at small tables with a tablecloth, and sometimes get seconds on foods that you like to eat. You can also visit the patients' canteen and buy food and beverages there.

There are several things that you must do so that you can stay in Dorm A, and not be demoted to a lower dorm. You must get along well with the technicians. You should shave and shower yourself everyday, and keep yourself looking neat. You must help by working on the unit, and you must also have an off-unit assignment, called *industrial therapy*. Since you are expected to leave the hospital within three months, you usually cannot stay any longer than that in this dorm.

INTERESTING THINGS TO DO WHILE YOU ARE
LIVING IN TOKEN ECONOMY UNIT 231

There are many rehabilitation services that you can attend, such as occupational therapy, music therapy, recreational therapy, and industrial therapy. Rehabilitation therapy is fun, and you can learn something while enjoying yourself. If you want to find out more about rehabilitation things that you can do while you are on the unit, see Dave Freehauf, Esther Hudson, Bruce Hulett, or Gary Angelo.

There are many different things that you can do in rehabilitation throughout the hospital grounds, and they are listed below. You can go there if you have permission from your group leader, or you may be able to go with a group of other patients from the unit.

Music and Art

If you like to *listen to music* see Dave Freehauf, who is the music therapist, on the 2nd floor of Haggerty Auditorium, right above the gym. Besides the Music Room there are many other rooms with interesting things to do from 9:00 to 11:30 in the morning, and from 1:00 to 3:00 every afternoon, Monday through Friday. All of these rooms are on the 2nd floor over the gym.

1. *KCSH Radio Station* presents modern music, contests, interviews, news, and special programs.
2. *The Art Room* is a really nice place for you to paint and to do other interesting things in art.
3. *The Listening Lounge* is a good place to listen to whatever kind of music you like.
4. *The Typing Room* is a good place to type for fun or to learn how to type.
5. *The Instrument Check-Out and Practice Rooms* are good places to learn to play a musical instrument and to practice on one if you like to play a musical instrument.
6. *The Game Room* is a good place to borrow table games and play them. The Game Room is only open on Tuesdays and Thursdays from 1:00 to 3:00 in the afternoon.

You can also join the *Patient's Band* and practice daily from 3:00 to 4:00 in the afternoon. Then you can play for dances and special events here at the hospital.

Gym

If you like to go to the gym and exercise and play games, you can do that too. John Rona will help you to do what you like to do at the gym.

1. There is *Open Play* of different games such as shooting baskets, and playing ping pong and badminton.
2. You can participate in *Group Activities* some afternoons and evenings, but you must then be accompanied by a staff member. Check with John Rona if you are interested in group activities.
3. You can see a *movie* every Sunday afternoon at 2:00 P.M., and then you can go to the gym unescorted. There is also a movie at 8:00 in the evening for the escorted patients. The billboard will tell you which movie will be shown next Sunday, and there is a different movie every Sunday. The same movie is shown every afternoon and evening in the gym.

Swimming Pool

You can swim in the pool on Monday through Thursday from 2:00 to 3:00 in the afternoon. You can also swim on Saturday and Sunday afternoon from 1:00 to 4:00 P.M. There are also swimming classes that you can attend. Ask Linda Fuller about them, because she is in charge of the pool.

Bowling Alley

If you wish to bowl, talk with your group leader, and he can arrange with Bruce Hulett for you to be able to bowl with other patients from the unit.

Patients' Library

You can read in the *Patient's Library* and sometimes borrow books by asking Erma McLemore, the librarian.

Group Encounter Sessions

You can meet with other patients in a group encounter session in Dorm A to discuss your problems and to help you to learn how to handle them better. Mr. Roy Jones, the social worker on the unit, is in charge of the group, and one of the technicians will also be there. Sometimes Dr. Ulmer and other staff members will talk with you then, too. The group meets every Monday, Wednesday, and Friday from 1:30 to 3:00 in the afternoon. You can also join the *Patient's Group Sessions* on Tuesday, Thursday, and Saturday from 1:30 to 3:00. No staff members will ever attend the Patients' Group. Only patients talk to each other in them.

The group sessions are places to learn why you got into the hospital, and what you can do to get out and stay out of hospitals and jails. The group sessions are a good place to talk about your complaints about anything at all that bothers you. You can learn how to handle things better here in the hospital, and back in your community when you return. You won't be able to talk about your childhood or what other people, like your parents, did to you a long time ago. In these sessions you will be expected to be pretty smart, and to learn to talk and act in the hospital so that you can get out sooner. You will be expected to learn how to talk, act, and look in your community, so that you can stay out of the hospital after you leave it.

Obviously, orientation, like all other aspects of behavior therapy, changes throughout the patient's career in the hospital. Orientation is followed by reorientation as the patient becomes more aware of his surroundings, and especially as he becomes more motivated and more competent to fulfill demands placed on him by the staff and the other patients. The staff reorient each patient by talking to him, and making him aware of their changing expectations of him. Reorientation could not be done only by handing out a standardized printed form, because each patient shows individualized variations throughout his hospital stay. For example, as each patient becomes more capable of meeting the requirements of Dorm C, and is promoted to Dorm B, he must complete increasingly demanding work and other social tasks.

Typically, as the patient moves up the token economy social ladder, he is expected to dress more neatly, and to be generally more responsible for himself at all times. The staff deliberately create a programmed hierarchy of pressures beginning with the relatively permissive, laissez-faire requirements of welfare recipient in Dorm C to essentially normal behavior in Dorm A. For if the role of token economy treatment, or of any other mental hospital program, is to prepare the patient to function effectively in his community, then the staff should, and indeed must, increasingly pressure and motivate the patient to make every effort to improve his social strategy with time. The staff must help the patient to learn new social skills well and quickly, so that he can cope far more effectively with the requirements of others in his community after leaving the hospital than he did before. The staff work best as social change agents if they understand how and why they should be social change agents, are committed to these responsibilities, and communicate their awareness and motivation to the patients. Because the Camarillo staff function in these ways, they can be considered a coordinated team.

The token economy treatment team at Camarillo consists of one psychologist, one psychiatrist, one psychiatric social worker, and about 20 technicians. There are about 60 patients on the unit at all times. The team attempts to be like a good football team, well coordinated and dedicated to achieving its goals. Stars and prima donnas are not very helpful, because they hamper the smooth, overall functioning of the team. Instead, fulfillment of appropriate roles requires careful coordination with other staff members' work, and sometimes subordination of one's wishes (see Staff Conferences in Chapter 2).

The following discussion presents the patient's career in the hospital from the *staff's* point of view. When a patient enters the program, the staff read his folder to get a picture of him as a person so that they can understand him and work with him. The folder reports some of his history, telling how many times he has been in mental hospitals, how he got there, and how long he stayed. His physical problems are detailed, if he has any, and the kinds of treatments given him. Staff members then discuss their impressions of him in staff meetings, and a first treatment plan is developed and adopted. The steps in this plan include patient orientation, patient assessment, evaluation of reinforcements, other treatment problems, direct treatment, and preparation for discharge.

The goal of treatment is, of course, to change the patient's social strategy so that he functions well in the hospital, becomes suitable for discharge to his community, *and* has sufficiently improved social skills to be able to remain in his community. This first treatment program will be constantly modified throughout the patient's stay in the hospital, for as staff observe the patient's progress or lack thereof, they must frequently change their approach to him. In effect, an individual treatment plan is created by the staff, who constantly change the behavioral prescription for each patient. Since a particular behavioral prescription often requires special consideration for one patient, the staff often believe that other patients may feel that they are not as well treated as the patient in question. (In fact, other patients never, in Camarillo's experience, complain of being discriminated against for *this reason*, so that this form of the "discrimination problem" is the staff's not the patients'.) The special behavioral prescription may require that when the particular patient is acting appropriately, he be given greater rewards than other patients, and when acting inappropriately, he be given far greater token fines or privilege deprivations than are exacted from other patients.

When there are any changes planned in the reward or fine system, the patient is always notified in advance, so that he has an opportunity to change his behavior to suit the new conditions of the program. Giving notice is also the staff's way of recognizing the rational, responsible aspects of the patient's personality, because in telling the patient that he will be subject to greater rewards and punishments in the future than in the past, they are really saying that he is capable of changing his behavior when the conditions of his life change. The staff's belief in the patient's rationality is communicated directly to him. He is told repeatedly that he is in the hospital to learn how to get out of the hospital as soon as possible, and how to stay out of hospitals and jails as much as possible, and that he *can* learn these things. All staff members are constantly being made aware of where every patient is in the treatment process, and what treatment is being given to him. Usually the patient's treatment is the overall token economy approach, with some combination of an individual behavioral prescription, modeling, role rehearsal, a written contract, and group encountering.

PATIENT ASSESSMENT

Another very important aspect of token economy treatment is the accurate and comprehensive evaluation of the patient's assets and liabilities, which help or hinder him in responding suitably to others. A patient's assets and liabilities are the target behaviors that will help him to form the most feasible and effective social strategy to get him to be discharged from the hospital, and to help him remain in his community.

Typically, the patient has some obvious, if not flagrant, asocial or antisocial ways of speaking to others, which, under the best of circumstances, tend to make others find him unpleasant. More frequently, he is considered by his neighbors and family to be obnoxious, if not potentially or actually dangerous. He may not speak at all, or if he does, he may proclaim his fantasies, instead of being involved in the social realities others share about him in his community. Even if his inappropriate speech is not followed by strange actions, his conversation alone can be considered behavior that is sufficiently offensive to others to provoke them to place him in a mental hospital. Offensive speech by itself is the major precipitant of mental hospitalization. And if a patient's speech disturbs others, it must be changed if he is to leave the hospital, return to his community, and remain there. Similarly, when a patient's actions alone disturb others, his actions, and not his speech, are the targets of token economy attention.

Checklists of potentially useful target behaviors are available that can be reported reliably by different observers. For example, Aumack's checklist (1969) includes target behaviors such as talking to other patients, staring out of a window, and talking to staff members. Aumack's checklist also includes a weighting system and manual (1968), so that observations can be related relatively easily to treatment plans.

The token economy staff generally focus on the patient's current behaviors, including his social assets and liabilities, and how these are shown in his behavior in the program. The patient's attitude is also important, because if he is unhappy with being in the hospital, and wishes to leave, he tends to be more responsive to behavior therapy than if he is relatively content to remain in the hospital. The patient's motivation to leave the hospital is so valuable that the staff can and in fact must use his motivation if treatment is to be maximally effective.

Some Theoretical Issues

Traditional and behavioral approaches, are clearly differentiated with the key area of personality assessment. Traditional clinical psychology and psychiatry use subjective impressions and inferences about a person to diagnose how he is functioning. The person's speech, behavior, and appearance are used as a basis for inferring what is "really" going on inside of him. What is really going on is considered—especially from a psychoanalytic viewpoint—to be his unconscious (unaware) aspects of his personality, and these are related to his past, especially his childhood. This subjective approach, which has been in use for well over 50 years, is directly related to traditional therapy views that these unconscious aspects of personality are the most important parts of personality functioning, with conscious portions being only the result of what is going on unconsciously.

There are several problems with this traditional approach. If persons infer what is going on in another unconsciously, each person making this inference is likely to have a different opinion. Since this lack of consistency seems to indicate that there is no reliability between observers, who is to know who is right and who is wrong? Even the test instruments used to examine unconscious functioning—such as the Rorschach inkblot test—tend to demonstrate little reliability among testers.

The behavior therapist challenges the assumption that only unconscious aspects of personality are important. It is not what a patient does unconsciously that gets him sent to a mental hospital or jail, but what he says and does, and how he looks that may get him into trouble. And focusing on these observable aspects of personality makes for reliability, for different observers can easily agree on what they are observing, not inferring, about a person. The question of what is important leads to the matter of validity—the truthfulness or value of the behavior that is being measured. And that, from a behavioristic viewpoint, is the operational meaningfulness of the behavior in its social context.

For example, if we observe a person brushing his teeth, we can all agree on what he is doing, and so the assessment process is reliable. We might have differences on what it means in a personality sense, especially if he were brushing his teeth while walking down the street, rather than in the bathroom. Traditional diagnostic techniques consider what is observed to be an indication of unconscious functioning. But this definition, confounded by unreliability, differs according to who is doing the observing. So that validity, too, is not at all established in traditional work, indeed, is far more difficult to establish than reliability.

Behavior therapy is often grounded on the view that since traditional therapy has been unable to solve such basic problems as reliability and validity after some 50 years of trying, maybe it would be better to try a totally different approach—especially if this new way of assessing is more relevant to the work of behavior therapy, than are the techniques of traditional therapy. For these reasons, all behavior therapy is founded on watching what a person does, listening to what a person says, observing how he appears, listening to what he says about himself, and to what others say about him. Essentially this material is taken at face value by the behavior therapist; he does not interpret what it "really" means, or who is lying or telling the truth. He looks only for consistency or inconsistencies in reported behaviors, and he generally assumes that only what is shown consistently, and the social settings in which the behaviors occur, are important.

Behavioral assessment is then easier to do, more directly related to the patient's problems, and, most important, is far more useful for behavior therapy than traditional techniques. For these reasons, the discussions in this book are always based on behavioral, rather than traditional diagnostic, approaches.

Specifics of Objective Personality Assessment

Assessment is based on organized, observable data, such as speech, actions, and appearance, and especially the context in which they are shown, such as their association with other events. Observations should be quite reliable, with each person who sees the patient recording the same kinds of behavior in similar ways. Each observer should focus on important target behaviors, such as the kinds of speech, actions, and appearance that brought the patient to the hospital, and tend to keep him there or to make it likely that when he leaves he will be rehospitalized. The observer should not waste attention on behaviors that may be irritating, such as strange interests of a patient. For example, watching TV too much, which has little influence on his being kept in the hospital, or on rehospitalizing him after he leaves. The observer should not look for attitudes or feelings, and thus should not interpret the meaning of the patient's behavior.

The observer should limit himself to what he sees in concrete actions. For example, hostile speech can be defined in a behavioristic (operational) sense as "saying something to someone that results in the other person moving away," or as "responding with loud or abusive speech."

One way of specifying behavior is from the highly structured interview and behavioral rating scales, because this interview is usually objectively scored and is quite appropriate to a behavioristic setting. The highly structured interview is especially useful in a token economy program, where behavioral assessment is the basis for a behavioral treatment prescription. The interview most commonly used at Camarillo Hospital is the Minimal Social Behavior Scale (MSBS). The MSBS is reproduced in full in Appendix B, including administration and scoring instructions. Translated forms are available in Arabic, French, Greek, Hebrew, Italian, Japanese, and Spanish. The MSBS was originated by Farina, Arenberg, and Guskin (1957), and modified by Ulmer and Timmons (1964, 1966).

The MSBS consists of a ten-minute interview in which all of the examiner's behavior is carefully prescribed, and no variations in speech or actions are permitted. For example, the examiner will say to his subject, "Won't you have a seat?" A "+" is given for any appropriate verbal response or movement toward the seat. A total of 32 performance points and 32 time points (for rapid performance) is possible, combining to a maximum of 64 points. The scale is most useful with hospitalized, chronic schizophrenics and severely retarded subjects. The data of the scale are shown to be highly reliable because of the simple success-failure, noninterpretive scoring system. Good validity is shown for severity of social disability and level of intellectual functioning. The scale also seems to be a suitable instrument for comparison of seriously emotionally and intellectually handicapped subjects. A major disadvantage of the MSBS is that subjects who are *not* severaly handicapped almost invariably make quite high scores. Major advantages of the MSBS are that its administration can be learned quickly by persons with little psychological background, and it can be scored easily by them.

The MSBS was modified by Ulmer and Lieberman (1967, 1968) into the Children's Minimal Social Behavior Scale (CMSBS). The CMSBS is reproduced in full in Appendix C, including administration and scoring instructions. The CMSBS retains the high reliability and validity of the MSBS. The CMSBS has also been translated into Arabic, French, Greek, Hebrew, Italian, Japanese, and Spanish. A major advantage of the CMSBS is that it has a much higher ceiling than the MSBS, so that child, adolescent, and adult subjects who are not severely handicapped, or not handicapped at all, can be objectively evaluated.

In addition to the MSBS's time, performance, and total scores, the CMSBS has motor, verbal-motor, and verbal subtest scores that are valid indices of the level of these abilities (Ulmer, 1971c). Typical CMSBS items include the examiner placing a gold-colored box in front of his subject, and saying, "I'll be busy a minute." A "+" is given if the subject touches the box. A time score is given for the number of seconds, decreasing as the time used by the subject increases. A total of 62 points is possible, including 31 for performance and 31 for timed actions. Besides time and total scores, performance, motor, verbal, and verbal-motor scores are easily obtained. The CMSBS floor (smallest possible score) seems low enough for objective personality assessment, because even chronic, deteriorated child, adolescent, and adult mental hospital patients never obtain minimal scores. The ceiling (largest possible score) also seems high enough, because intelligent, relatively aware, and even gifted children, adolescents, and adults never achieve maximal scores. The CMSBS is especially useful in providing fine, objective evaluations of behavior, because of the large potential range of scores from floor to ceiling, with many possible patterns of subtest scores.

There is a high correlation between CMSBS scores and patient characteristics (variables) on a token economy unit (Ulmer, 1970b, 1971c). What the patient does in the highly structured CMSBS interview is an accurate reflection of what he is doing on the token economy unit. Some of the patient variables studied are: his age; current length of hospitalization; placement in Dorm A, B, or C of the program; and length of time on the unit. All variables studied correlate closely with CMSBS scores, which means that the CMSBS is an excellent indicator of the probable level of other patient characteristics. High CMSBS scores are usually shown by the patient who progresses up the token economy ladder. Low scores are usually shown by a patient who stays in Dorm C.

High CMSBS scores also suggest specific patient behaviors, such as taking the initiative in shaving, showering, working either on or off the unit, responding to one's own name, asking for the key to one's locker, answering questions about oneself, and making appropriate requests of the staff. The kind of skills required to get high scores on a particular part of the CMSBS, such as the motor subtest, are generally reflected in good motor abilities on the unit. And this pattern is also followed for CMSBS verbal and verbal-motor scores, where a patient with high or low scores in these subtests tends to show a comparably high or low level of ability. Other reviews of the CMSBS can be found in Marlowe (1971).

Tabulating and Graphing of Behavior and Behavioral Changes

In addition to the highly structured interview, a patient can be objectively assessed according to the specific target behaviors (which are chosen by the behavior therapist) with systematized recording procedures and careful observation of the patient. A patient can be watched prior to treatment, and changes in his behavior with therapy can be noted. Effects of treatment can also be obtained by stopping therapy for a limited period of time. This way of observing and recording a patient's behavior in his hospital environment can be done using Tables 4-2 to 4-6 and Figure 4-4.

Table 4-2 lists some common behaviors of interest. The observer should study the table in order to become sensitized to these or other prescribed behaviors. A table can be set up to record any target behaviors of any patient. And these

Table 4-2 Samples of Target Desirable and Undesirable Behaviors

Desirable behaviors	Undesirable behaviors
Speaking appropriately—greeting someone or asking about the health of another person	Speaking inappropriately—ignoring someone who speaks to the patient or responding hastily to someone's polite greeting
Dressing appropriately—dressing suitably for the time of day, and neatly and properly	Dressing inappropriately—dressing unsuitably for the time of day, or being unkempt or poorly dressed

Adapted from *Behavioral Therapy* by H. H. Schaefer and P. L. Martin. Copyright 1969 by McGraw-Hill, Inc. used with permission of McGraw-Hill Book Company.

behaviors can then be coded by various signs, such as "+," "—," or "*" to enable quick, easy recording of behaviors.

Some behaviors do not permit other behaviors to occur. These are called mutually exclusive behaviors, such as standing, walking, and running. These mutually exclusive behaviors, noted in Table 4-3, can be coded for quick easy recording by using a code letter for the behaviors being described, such as "s" for standing, and "w" for walking. Using Tables 4-2 and 4-3, the observer can describe behaviors quite clearly, so that a reader can quickly gain a good picture of what the patient is doing.

Concomitant behaviors can be done at the same time, as noted in Table 4-4. Typical concomitant behaviors include drinking (A), smoking (J), and watching TV (L), and, as indicated by the letters in parentheses, these can be coded for quick, easy recording. For example, using Tables 4-3 and 4-4, B-3 means eating a meal *while* sitting. It is important to note *where* any behavior occurs, because the setting often has a great influence on the social meaning of that behavior. For example, a behavior done in the bedroom or bathroom may be perfectly appropriate there, but may be considered abnormal if done on the street in front of others. Sample locations where behaviors are observed are reported in Table 4-5.

Table 4-3 Samples of Mutually Exclusive Bodily Actions

1.	Walking	4.	Lying down
2.	Running	5.	Standing
3.	Sitting		

Adapted from *Behavioral Therapy* by H. H. Schaefer and P. L. Martin. Copyright 1969 by McGraw-Hill, Inc. Used with permission of McGraw-Hill Book Company.

Table 4-4 Sample Concomitant Behaviors

A. Drinking	H. Rocking in chair or on feet
B. Eating a meal	I. Pacing
C. Eating between, or instead of, meals	J. Smoking
D. Dressing or grooming self	K. Talking to others or self
E. Taking medicine	L. Watching TV
F. Receiving tokens	M. Working on assigned jobs

Adapted from *Behavioral Therapy* by H. H. Schaefer and P. L. Martin. Copyright 1969 by McGraw-Hill, Inc. Used with permission of McGraw-Hill Book Company.

Another important descriptive aspect of any behavior is the time of day when it occurs. Table 4-6 presents a time-sample description of various behaviors. Using this format an observer can record *when* and *how often* during a particular time period a given behavior occurs.

The observer records the sequence of target behaviors using simple coded numbers and letters to indicate what a patient is doing at any given time. For example, B (from Table 4-4) at 7:30 means eating a meal.

In sum, Table 4-2 to 4-6 describe which target behaviors are occurring, and where and when they take place. Through the use of these five tables a patient can be quite fully described so that enough information is available to write a meaningful behavioral prescription. This behavioral prescription, plus both target and goal behaviors, forms a good beginning for a first treatment approach in helping a patient in the token economy. And all the information contained in the five tables can be quickly and efficiently recorded on legal-size paper with five columns, each representing a given table, so that checking off each column presents all the information from all five tables. At the bottom of each column, there can be a legend for shorthand descriptions of the various behaviors being recorded, and the places where they occur.

Baselines

A baseline is a measure of the frequency of occurrence of some desirable or undesirable target behavior before treatment (Figure 4-4). A baseline is

Table 4-5 Location of Sample Exclusive and Concomitant Behaviors

Cafeteria or dining room	Lavatory
Day room	Hospital grounds
Sleeping quarters	

Adapted from *Behavioral Therapy* by H. H. Schaefer and P. L. Martin. Copyright 1969 by McGraw-Hill Inc. Used with permission of McGraw-Hill Book Company.

Table 4-6 Time Sampling of Behaviors

Instructions:[a]   + = Patient in *prone position only* on own bed
                    — = All other actions of patient

Observer:	6:30 to 12:00 P.M.
Date:	Time-sampling interval: 1/2 hour

6:30	9:30
7:00	10:00
7:30	10:30
8:00	11:00
8:30	11:30
9:00	12:00

Adapted from *Behavioral Therapy* by H. H. Schaefer and P. L. Martin. Copyright 1969 by McGraw-Hill, Inc. Used with permission of McGraw-Hill Book Company.
[a]This time-sampling table can be used to record any single behavior, such as lying in bed. It can also be used for a series of behaviors such as sitting in bed. Each one of these behaviors can easily be recorded by simply establishing a coding system such as "x" for sitting in bed.

constructed by carefully observing a patient, and recording his behavior on whichever of the five tables are relevant. A baseline is necessary for any behavioral prescription, because only by knowing how often an undesirable target behavior occurs before treatment is it possible to know how effective is the behavioral prescription that changes behavior with treatment. Furthermore, a behavioral prescription must be directed toward the location and time of occurrence of target behaviors, and this information, too, is collected for baseline measures.

Once treatment is begun, and changes in target behaviors are expected, these, when shown, will be recorded in "experimental data" (Figure 4-4). Behavior noted with treatment is called experimental data because these data are the results of an experimental trial of behavior therapy with the patient. If the patient responds, the approach is continued. If at any time the patient no longer seems to be responding to the treatment approach being used, a new treatment plan must be instituted. Often it is important to find out whether the treatment is the probable cause of the patient's changed behavior. To do this, treatment is discontinued, and the patient is carefully observed to see if his behavior returns to approximately baseline levels. If treatment is effective in stopping undesirable target behaviors, then with treatment stopped, undesirable target behaviors should reduce to baseline levels. If treatment is effective in producing or

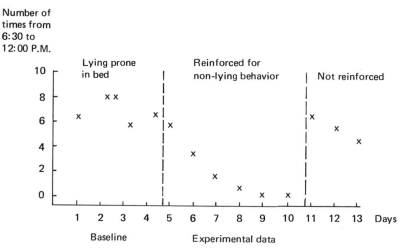

Figure 4-4 Sample graph of behavioral changes.

increasing desirable target behaviors, then with treatment stopped, behavior should decrease to baseline levels. The specifics of this procedure of discontinuing behavior therapy, and checking for its effects are detailed by Ayllon and Azrin (1968a, 1968b).

Often the effects of treatment are indicated more vividly in graphs than in tables, as shown in Figure 4-4. This figure illustrates changes in desirable and undesirable target behaviors, with baseline (pretreatment) and experimental (treatment) conditions.

Camarillo's Behavior Modification Program includes some nontoken economy units that are behaviorally oriented. Because of state of California requirements, a consistent procedure was needed for assessing some 300 patients throughout the program. The state insisted that a procedure be devised for assessing all patients on their level of social functioning on entering the program, the changes to be expected with varying lengths of hospitalization, and their probable level of functioning when discharged. The procedure devised has proven quite useful, and, indeed, has been used throughout Camarillo hospital—interestingly enough, by traditional treatment programs as well as behavioral ones. This procedure, including instructions and scoring guidelines, is reproduced in its entirety in Appendix D.

EVALUATION OF REINFORCEMENTS

Human needs and desires are the motivations that form the driving force and core of behavior therapy in general and token economy in particular. Motivations are used in the token economy program as the means of moving the patient to act to get what he wants, and to reward him for doing what the staff wants him to do. The rewards he gets can be positive, secondary reinforcements, such as tokens, with which he can buy things in the token economy canteen. Only by acting appropriately and getting rewarded for it can the patient learn to live in socially appropriate ways.

A reinforcement is any event occurring after a patient does something that will increase the likelihood of the patient repeating that act. A positive reinforcement is a pleasant event, like getting a token. A negative reinforcement is an event that is not pleasant, and whose withdrawal will increase the likelihood of the behavior that immediately precedes, and brings about, withdrawal of the negative reinforcement. For example, suppose a patient is confined to the unit and not allowed to go on the grounds because of antisocial behavior. Being confined to the unit is a negative reinforcement, so that it increases the likelihood of appropriate behaviors *afterward* when its withdrawal is associated with desirable behaviors on the unit, and being able to go on the grounds. Acting appropriately on the unit then becomes a strengthened desirable behavior.

In contrast, an aversive stimulus, that is, unpleasant stimulation given after a certain kind of undesirable behavior, tends to decrease the probability of the occurrence of that behavior in the future. An example of punishment occurs when a person touches an electric wire marked "Warning. Do not touch." The resulting shock may act as an aversive stimulus, reducing the likelihood of such behavior in the future. (Punishment tends to not be very effective, and has some unpleasant side effects. It is therefore much better to reward desired behaviors than to punish unwanted ones.) Primary reinforcements are those associated with satisfaction of basic, unlearned needs, such as food, water, and sex. Secondary reinforcements are those that can lead to satisfaction of basic learned needs, such as social approval and tokens.

In a token economy it is necessary to utilize many approaches to changing antisocial behaviors. It is quite useful to observe what the patient does on his own most often. It can be assumed (Premack's principle) that because the patient engages in this behavior a great deal, it has reinforcing qualities for him. And when he can be controlled so that he can only engage in that behavior when he performs a behavior that is desired and that he does infrequently, then social learning can occur. For example, suppose a patient watches TV a great deal, but is unwilling to wash his face, rarely does so, and then only when pressured by the token economy staff. His watching TV can be made to be conditional upon his having a clean face. This means linking his frequent behavior to his rarely performed one as part of social training application of Premack's principle. Premack's principle is extremely useful in token economies, and tends to work quite well when all staff members agree to use it in a clearly specified way with a given patient.

If the therapist is unable to find or control motivations for the patient, behavior therapy should not be tried, for it is unlikely to be successful. For example, a chronic, deteriorated patient with 20 or more years in the hospital often seems content to simply sit in a chair. Observing the patient's frequent sitting would be the first step in applying Premack's principle. The patient may not care whether the TV is on or not, and other activities, such as eating, smoking, or socializing, which might interest another patient, do not motivate him. In addition, the behavior therapist does not have the time or the control over technicians to keep the patient from sitting in his chair unless he is being rewarded for performing socially desirable target behaviors. It is useless to begin behavior modification with this kind of patient, because the therapist has little to offer the patient, and the patient knows this. If the therapist can control, through the cooperation of the technicians, the amount of time that the patient can sit in his chair, behavior therapy is off to a promising start. An application of Premack's principle would be to only allow the patient to sit in his chair (the frequently performed behavior) when, for example, he washes his face (the rarely performed, desired behavior).

It is often exceedingly difficult to determine for a given patient which rewards will act as positive reinforcements to encourage desired speech and other behaviors, and which aversive stimuli or withdrawal of which positive reinforcements will reduce unwanted actions. Simple observation of the patient will sometimes provide answers to these questions. At other times trial-and-error testing is necessary to see which rewarding situations and which nonrewarding ones seem to modify his target behaviors. It should be kept clearly in mind that the patient's reward preferences are likely to change frequently and unpredictably. Backup reinforcements are needed when the patient is no longer interested in the "goodies" that his therapist has been offering him. Even when the therapist's current "goodies" seem to be effective, it's often worthwhile to make periodic changes, because the mental hospital patient, like the child, gets bored quickly with almost any routine, even a pleasant one.

Food, candy, cigarettes, and cofee are usually effective positive, primary reinforcements, but they must be individually tested to determine if they will work with a given patient. Tokens, too, are generally useful, but often, especially with a long-term, deteriorated patient, they must be paired, at least at first, with positive, primary reinforcements, such as candy or gum. After the patient learns that tokens can buy the things that he likes, such as candy or gum, he will work for tokens alone. The patient may take months to learn and to cherish the value of tokens, and the behavior therapist often needs great patience. If the patient seems to understand easily and to remember what the therapist says to him, he can often be motivated by offering him prized activities for performing socially appropriate learning tasks. These activities may include ground privileges, watching TV, or playing games in which he interacts with the therapist, such as ball playing.

If a patient cannot be motivated to work and to learn socially appropriate behaviors, or to assume responsibility for his actions, therapy will fail. The therapist must make every effort to find out what will motivate his patient, and then use that motivation as an integral part of treatment. The therapist must offer his patient either primary or secondary reinforcements as a basic part of the treatment process, if change is to occur.

Although the therapist makes every effort to create a warm relationship with his patient, he does not depend on his relationship with the patient to change the patient's behavior. Instead, the therapist uses himself as a positive, secondary reinforcer, strongly approving of the kinds of speech and actions that he wishes the patient to produce. The therapist may disapprove of or ignore undesirable speech and actions of the patient. Aversive stimuli (punishment), such as disapproval, should be used carefully and sparingly, because they often increase the behaviors they are supposed to decrease. A common example of this occurs when a child gets spanked for misbehavior, and the parent's attention, which is an integral part of the spanking, acts to reinforce the punished behavior. In like fashion, the therapist may fail to decrease undesirable target behaviors with aversive stimuli, because he is giving attention to the patient, and the patient prizes this attention.

As an alternative to aversive stimuli, nonreinforcement (ignoring) tends to be a more effective method of reducing unwanted target behaviors. A typical nonreinforcement technique is "time-out," which is shown when a therapist responds immediately to undesired behaviors by turning his head away, staring away from the patient for 10 seconds, and then turning back to look at the patient. The therapist then repeats his original statement, and tries to get a more appropriate response from the patient, while pretending that the patient had not responded inappropriately before.

The goal of time-out is to reduce, and, hopefully, eliminate (extinguish) undesirable behaviors. Time-out does not involve giving positive or negative reinforcements or aversive stimuli to the patient. Instead the patient may be withdrawn from the situation. Sometimes because the patient responds inappropriately to others, he is taken to a quiet room. In doing this, care must be exercised to avoid giving the patient the impression that he is being punished. If the patient considers time-out as punishment, the procedure is not likely to be effective. To avoid giving the impression of punishment, the patient should be taken matter-of-factly to a quiet room, and be given some kind of rather pleasant explanation, such as "I guess it's kind of hard for you to be around other people right now. I feel that way sometimes, too. Maybe it would be good for you to be by yourself for a while." This approach is quite similar to the way to handle a child who is out of control of himself—by not rejecting him, but by helping him to understand that he is mishandling himself, that he needs some time alone to gain control over his behavior, and that he is not being isolated as a punishment.

I once treated a patient with 25 years of continuous hospitalization. When anyone talked to the patient, he responded with an exact repitition of what the person had said to him, which is called echolalia. If I asked the patient, "What day is it?" the patient would answer, "What day is it?" Like an echo, the patient would always answer with what had been said to him. I began treatment by responding to the patient's echolalic speech with an aversive stimulus, saying, "That's *dumb talk!* I don't want to hear *dumb talk!*" The aversive stimulus was not very effective, since there was only a slight reduction of echolalic speech. But when I switched to a time-out technique of ignoring the patient, his echolalic speech rapidly decreased.

Using time-out, I would simply turn my head away from the patient for 10 seconds (counting to myself), and then turn back, asking the same question as before. If the patient again responded echolalically, I would repeat my time-out response. When the patient finally reacted with an appropriate answer, I said "That's very good, Mr. Smith! You're doing fine!" (A full description of treatment of this echolalic patient is given in Chapter 5.)

Reinforcement and treatment of the long-term patient is considerably different from that of the short-term patient. For example, the short-term patient who wishes to leave the hospital can be informed, repeatedly if necessary, of the things that he says and does that are offensive to the staff. (While it may seem unfair and unreasonable, the truth is that when the staff dislike a patient, he is likely to be kept in the hospital. And when they like him, except if the reason is that he is doing hard work that helps the program, he is likely to be discharged quickly.) The aware patient will be helped first to understand what it is that he is saying and doing that is likely to keep him in the hospital and to get him returned after he is discharged. The patient will then be helped to develop a more socially appropriate repertoire so that the staff can discharge him and so that he can remain in his community.

The short-term patient may constantly argue about tokens, resent the staff for making "unreasonable" demands on him, and generally feel hostile toward the whole program. As a first step, the therapist may help the patient to understand that he must get along with the technicians in order to be discharged from the hospital. Then the therapist may help the patient to develop a more socially appropriate repertoire with the rest of the staff. The therapist may say to the patient, "Do you want to get out of here? Then stop arguing with the technicians, and when they ask you to work or pay you with tokens, just go along with them, and you'll get out of here much sooner!"

Next the therapist may help the patient to learn how to talk, act, and dress in ways that are acceptable to the staff. The therapist may use behavioral rehearsal of roles in short, playacting sessions to show the patient how his inappropriate speech, actions, and dress appear to others. Role rehearsal may also be used to demonstrate to the patient the appropriate ways of speaking, acting, and dressing, so that he will be able to learn these behaviors. The therapist may pretend to be the patient, and the patient may act as a technician in a typical argument. Role rehearsal enables the patient to test new ways of acting without the danger of offending others, which could easily happen in a real situation. Modeling and behavioral rehearsal are discussed in detail in Chapter 6, as additional ways of social learning in a token economy program.

Other techniques used to teach the patient to behave in socially acceptable ways are behavioral encounter groups and written contracts, both detailed in Chapter 6. In the encounter group the patient has the opportunity for social learning through hearing how his behavior appears to other patients who live with him and to staff members who work with him. The encounter groups are usually focused on the patient's becoming aware of his inappropriate behaviors and how they must change for him to be discharged from the hospital to return to and remain in his community. The encounter group may also provide the patient with peer pressures to teach him the specific details of changing his inappropriate speech, actions, and appearance. Much of the material for encounter group discussions comes from the written, negotiated contract between the patient and the staff. The contract specifies exactly which behaviors are offensive to the staff, which kinds of substitute behaviors are desired by them, and how the staff will reward the patient for changing himself in socially appropriate ways.

SUMMARY

The Camarillo Token Economy Program is almost ten years old. It includes three levels of dorms, with increasingly higher ones providing more privileges and more pleasant living conditions. A schedule of token rewards and fines for all desirable and undesirable behaviors is posted prominently for all patients to see.

The canteen is an important part of the program because it enables patients to exchange their tokens for many things to eat, drink, or smoke, and therefore gives values to tokens. Much of the Camarillo program is based on the motivating power of the canteen to provide candy, cigarettes, coffee, and soda in exchange for tokens. All tokens have the same value. The amounts are recorded on the token carry-around card held by each patient, to eliminate stealing of tokens. When enough tokens are earned, a record is made in the token economy bank account card. The patient can then take tokens from his account and pay for his promotion to a higher dorm. Financial support for canteens is often difficult to obtain. The canteen costs about 5¢ per day per patient at 1975 figures.

Patients' orientation is particularly important because their understanding of the program and motivation are essential to improving their level of social functioning. An orientation form is given to them on entering the program. This form gives them a general view of the benefits and responsibilities associated with their being part of the program. Token economy team coordination is based on the entire staff's being knowledgeable about all patients, and their working together on changing patient's undesirable behaviors. Objective personality assessment requires careful observation of speech, actions, and appearance and is a useful technique in token economy treatment. The children's and adult's forms of the Minimal Social Behavior Scale enable objective scoring of behaviors directly related to patients' careers in the program.

Observed target behaviors can be recorded in tables and graphs. Tables list what occurs, when, and in what context. Graphs provide a picture of changes that occur with treatment, and when treatment is withdrawn. Only by these careful, quantitative recordings can behavioral changes be related to treatments in the program; otherwise too much guesswork is inevitable, and the result is a less effective program.

Evaluation of reinforcements is extremely important. Reinforcements increase the frequency of behaviors that precede them. Positive reinforcements are rewards that tend to increase the occurrence of the behaviors with which they are linked. Positive primary reinforcements—foods, candy, gum, cigarettes—can satisfy basic physiological, unlearned needs. Positive secondary reinforcements, like tokens and social approval, can satisfy learned needs, such as that they must be earned in order for the patient to be able to get foods, candy, gum, and cigarettes. Negative reinforcements are unpleasant stimuli whose relief, such as no longer restricting the patient to the unit, can lead to increase of behaviors that do not incur restriction. Time-out is a way of reducing undesirable behaviors by giving no reinforcement of any kind. All responses of the staff to a patient's behavior are designed to hasten his leaving the hospital and to prolong his stay in his community. These responses may be presented to him repeatedly, especially if he is a short-term patient, who frequently has good understanding and a strong desire to get out of the hospital. Other planned staff responses include group behavioral encountering and contract writing. All elements of an individual behavioral prescription are designed to maximize the effectiveness of token economy treatment for each patient.

SUGGESTED READINGS

Psychological Terminology

American Psychiatric Association. *A psychiatric glossary*. Washington, D.C.: Author, 1969.

English, H. B., & English, A. C. *A comprehensive dictionary of psychological and psychoanalytical terms*. New York: Longmans, Green, 1958. This is a classic psychological dictionary, although it is somewhat dated by now.

Hinsie, I. E., & Campbell, R. J. *Psychiatric dictionary* (4th ed.). New York: Oxford University Press, 1970. This is an excellent general psychiatric, nonbehavioral dictionary with essays defining terms.

White, O. R. (Ed.). *A glossary of behavioral terminology*. Champaign, Ill.: Research Press, 1971. This is an excellent, fairly comprehensive source of definitions of behavioral terms.

Abnormal Psychology

American Psychiatric Association. *Diagnostic and statistical manual of mental disorders* (2nd ed.). Washington, D.C.: Author, 1968. This somewhat too brief manual is useful and inexpensive. However, its use of technical medical terms make it of limited value to the person without a medical background.

Ulmann, L. P., & Krasner, L. *A psychological approach to abnormal behavior.* Englewood Cliffs, N.J.: Prentice-Hall, 1969. A classic introductory textbook describing abnormal behaviors and their treatment from the behavioral viewpoint. It is well worth reading.

A Sample Token Economy Program in Camarillo Hospital, Part II

INTRODUCTION

Chapters 4 and 5 describe the Camarillo Token Economy Program, its disciplines, the number of staff members, and the number of patients and some things about them. The basic principles of token economy and how they are applied to specific kinds of patient problems and particular patients are presented. Chapter 4 reported on the initial concerns of the program and treatment: the canteen, patient orientation, patient assessment, and evaluation of reinforcements. Chapter 5 describes some of the later aspects of treatment: direct individual or group treatment of patients, and formalized discharge considerations—the "hows" and "whys" of discharge procedures. Most of these approaches are standard in many token economy programs; new Camarillo techniques are described in Chapter 6.

A case history is presented to illustrate the details of working with a single patient in individual behavior modification. Group behavior modification with relatively aware and unaware patients and the effects of modeling are presented. All treatments are designed to make the patient socially competent enough to be discharged from the hospital *and* to remain in his community. The patient's social skills are not the sole reason, or sometimes even the most important reason for his discharge. Financial, legal, and, in a sense, political considerations enter into the staff's weighing of which patient should be discharged and when. These extra-treatment factors, which are important in Camarillo and may well be important in other settings, should be recognized by the staff.

Token economy is often unjustly and inaccurately attacked as inhuman, and even antihuman. For example, token economy may be grouped with psychosurgery and electroconvulsive shock treatment, even though token economy has nothing to do with them. These public slanders of token economy are growing, and the staff should be prepared to deal with them. Token economy is based on legal, moral, and ethical concerns for every patient, and these humane aspects should be explicitly known by all staff members, and by the general public.

DIRECT TREATMENT OF PATIENTS

Individual Behavior Modification

When a behavior therapist works with a single patient, he follows the steps described in Patient Orientation, Patient Assessment, and Evaluation of Reinforcements in Chapter 4. Chapter 5 refers to the course of treatment in these steps in the section Preparation for Discharge.

Example 1

Mr. X was a 54 years old man and had 25 years of continuous hospitalization. At the beginning of treatment he was unable to conduct even the simplest of conversations, such as giving his name, age, name of the hospital, or the date. He had never succeeded in working on the program on any job, nor in learning how to care for himself by dressing, shaving, or showering adequately. His response to most questions was an immediate echoing of exactly the words used by the other person, which was identified as echolalia. About 90 percent of Mr. X's speech was echolalic at the beginning of treatment. He was seen in daily individual sessions for eight months, and simultaneously in daily group sessions for the last six months of his hospitalization. He was then discharged to a board-and-care home.

Treatment consisted of two sessions a day, five days a week, each session lasting from 19 to 30 minutes. The psychologist sat alone with Mr. X at a table in the kitchen of the token economy unit. On the table was a Sears Mail Order Catalog, a magazine with colored advertisements, some cookies and candies, and two red tokens. The psychologist showed Mr. X the two tokens and a few cookies, and said, "Mr. X, if you talk right today, when we finish I will give you these cookies and two tokens." The psychologist then placed the cookies and the tokens on the table clearly in Mr. X's view. Next the psychologist put a line of jelly beans in assorted colors in front of Mr. X, and said to him, "Point to the red candy." When Mr. X did that, the psychologist said with considerable warmth and enthusiasm, "That's very good, Mr. X," and the psychologist immediately placed a piece of candy in Mr. X's mouth. (Behavior therapy is most effective when positive reinforcements are given as soon as possible after the occurrence of desirable behaviors.)

Speech training followed quickly after Mr. X pointed correctly, which he practically always did. The psychologist held two pieces of red candy close to Mr. X's face and said, "What color is the red candy?" At the beginning of training, Mr. X usually answered echolalically with, "What color is the red candy?" The psychologist then repeated his question five or six times, and Mr. X usually continued to echo the question. Then the psychologist said, "Say red only," and Mr. X generally replied, "Say red only." Finally, Mr. X would answer the psychologist's "Say red only" with "Red." At that instant the psychologist would quickly put a piece of candy into Mr. X's mouth, and say, "That's *very good*, Mr. X!"

A similar procedure was followed using a Sears Mail Order Catalog or colored advertisements in a magazine. Typically, the psychologist showed Mr. X two adjoining pages of the catalog with pictures of women wearing different-colored dresses. The psychologist would tell Mr. X, "Point to the lady in the *blue* dress." When Mr. X did this, the psychologist would say, "That's *very good*, Mr. X," and quickly put a piece of candy in the patient's mouth. Then the psychologist would ask, "What color is the *blue* dress?" The psychologist would listen to about five echolalic replies, responding only with, "Say *blue* only." By the end of six months Mr. X's verbal behavior was shaped well enough so that he would answer with the single word "blue" after only a few trials. (Mr. X would in all likelihood have responded appropriately much sooner if it had not been for the interference of a few staff members who were reinforcing his echolalic speech.) For a while the psychologist tried to reduce echolalia more quickly by responding with, "That's *dumb* talk. I don't want to hear dumb talk!" And other staff members also responded in the same way. This approach proved ineffective, and echolalia was reduced more quickly when a time-out technique of ignoring (nonreinforcing) was used relatively consistently by all staff members.

When therapy was first begun, Mr. X was given tokens and sweets whether he spoke appropriately or echolalically. After the first few months, if Mr. X did not speak appropriately, he was not rewarded with tokens and sweets. Instead, the psychologist ended the failed sessions matter-of-factly, telling Mr. X that he had not spoken well that day and that he therefore would not receive tokens and sweets. Mr. X was further told that later that afternoon or the next day there would be another session, and if Mr. X spoke well, he would then be given tokens and sweets. This proceudure worked well, and seemed to motivate Mr. X to make a greater effort in later sessions than in earlier ones. Mr. X learned to respond quickly and appropriately to questions with volitional rather than echolalic speech. By the end of the seventh month, less than half of his speech was echolalic both in and out of behavior therapy sessions. Mr. X began to work on the unit with his echolalia reduced. He showed no other serious problems and was discharged to a board-and-care home in his community, after living some 25 years in the hospital.

Evaluation

Treatment probably would have been more effective in less time (perhaps three months instead of seven) if Mr. X had had three to five sessions daily, seven days a week, rather than two sessions each day, for five days a week. Mr. X's echolalia sometimes increased from one day to the next, and had to be reduced again. His learning losses were most prominent over weekends and holidays, and it often seemed as though after each break, the psychologist had to begin therapy all over again. Despite learning losses, the psychologist found the sessions most interesting because he presented changing tasks to Mr. X. Sometimes Mr. X was asked to identify the colors of objects instead of pictures. Mr. X seemed interested during his sessions and appeared to enjoy them. He showed no concern when other persons were in the room drinking coffee, doing paper work, or even when they watched him. He reduced his echolalic speech by about the same amount throughout a session, whether or not others were observing him. Mr. X proved an excellent model for others observing him to see behavior therapy in practice.

Obviously a great deal of thought, creativity, and effort were needed for a therapist to be reasonably effective in modifying Mr. X's deviant speech and behavior. This was consistent with our findings with similar patients. Whatever was tried with Mr. X usually worked fairly well for a while, and then new approaches had to be tried. New positive reinforcements had to be found to reduce his echolalia. Many rewards appeared at first to be promising reinforcements, but then failed to motivate Mr. X. Typically, cigarettes were not good motivators. Despite the fact that Mr. X smoked occasionally, he would not work for cigarettes in therapy sessions. Candy, cookies, and tokens were good reinforcements fairly consistently, but coffee did not interest Mr. X. Even when motivated to earn rewards, he was only able to work for about 15 minutes in each session. After that he began to respond inappropriately, introduced new bizarre speech patterns, seemed to tire, and generally appeared to lose interest in controlling his speech. He did not show this fatigue effect outside of training sessions, probably because of the shorter periods of demands placed on him in ordinary conversations.

Example 2

The following is an illustration of a general category of individual treatment of a chronic, deteriorated patient, who hardly engages in any speech, not even echolalic, as in Mr. X's case. It also describes some aspects of student learning, independent of his discipline. (More general aspects of supervised learning are detailed in Chapter 3, the section In-Service Training for Practice, Academic Credits, and Research.)

Treatment of the chronic, deteriorated patient often begins when the staff member or the student walks up to the patient. The patient can be expected to be sitting in a chair, where he spends most of his waking or dozing hours, apparently neither watching nor hearing the TV set going continuously in front of him. The behavior therapist may begin by saying to the patient, "Good morning, Mr. A, how are you?"

Assuming that the target behavior is sweeping, and the goal behavior is working alone without supervision, the following is a description of one way of shaping appropriate sweeping behaviors. The behavior therapist hands Mr. A a piece of candy, and says, "If you help me a little bit, I will give you some more candy and two tokens." (This approach is called "priming" of a deteriorated patient with a primary reinforcement of candy, because the word "candy" alone—that is, the promise that he will receive candy later—is often too abstract to motivate the patient to begin to do what is desired of him. Through this process the patient can learn from firsthand experience what the therapist means when he says candy.) If the patient does not leave his chair, but seems somewhat responsive, the therapist may place a broom handle in the patient's hand, *and at the same time* put a small piece of candy in the patient's mouth. When the patient actively grasps the broom handle, the therapist may say, "That's very good, Mr. A, *very good!*" (Saying "very good" is a secondary reinforcement, because it is social, and not directly related to the satisfaction of primary needs, such as eating.)

Step-by-step the behavior therapist will work to have the patient learn to grasp the broom handle on his own initiative, stand up from the chair, and sweep. Directing the patient's behavior in a step-by-step procedure is called behavior shaping. And if good performance of most relatively complex social behaviors is a goal of behavior therapy, shaping is always needed with the deteriorated patient. Behavior shaping can only be effective in small steps, leading eventually to an integrated, complex behavior. Shaping is feasible because the patient is encouraged each step of the way to get more reinforcements, and thus he is encouraged to be motivated to continue to learn. And the therapist—student or staff member—is reinforced by seeing the progressive learning of his patient. As the patient masters the target behaviors, the therapist simultaneously gives him primary and secondary reinforcements, so that the patient learns to associate secondary reinforcements with primary satisfactions. The identification of secondary social reinforcements with primary reinforcement is an exceedingly important new social learning that most chronic patients lack, and is a basic building block of socialization.

After about a month of training, the patient will usually take the initiative in sweeping. The therapist can then promise him extra tokens or candy if he works well that day. And the therapist can walk alongside the patient while he is working, and put a piece of candy in his mouth, starting with 10-second intervals, and gradually extending this period. Simultaneously the therapist should say, "That's *fine*, Mr. A! You're doing *very* well! Keep sweeping." At the end of a training period, at first lasting about 5 minutes, and then lasting 20 or 30 minutes, the therapist may say, "You were *very good*, Mr. A! Here's the two tokens that I promised you. Tomorrow I'll ask you to sweep again, and then I'll give you more candy and tokens. Goodbye."

When the patient can sweep without close supervision, he can be turned over to a technician who can work with him to extend the time period that the patient works, and to increase the kinds of work that he does. This form of behavior therapy often called operant conditioning, has several advantages. Once the patient learns to respond appropriately to one set of stimuli, he can learn more easily than before to respond to other stimuli. He learns to learn, and there is often a positive transfer of specific skills from one task to another, similar one. Mr. A is then in a better position to become an active and effective member of the token economy program. The socialization process is slow and most difficult for him at the beginning. Later, a momentum builds up, and he can learn to progress steadily upward, provided that enough training is given to him so that he acquires new social skills, and is kept from retaining and retrieving old, inappropriate behaviors. Often an exceedingly useful aspect of this training effort is found in the patient's increased conversation, because if the therapist talks to the patient while the patient is working, and the patient responds appropriately, both primary and secondary reinforcements can be given to the patient.

Group Behavior Modification

Introduction

In working with patients in group behavior modification sessions, the psychologist may not have to treat each patient by carefully fulfilling in separate and distinct fashion each of the five steps of behavior therapy: (1) patient orientation, (2) patient assessment, (3) evaluation of reinforcements, (4) token economy team efforts, and (5) preparation for discharge. Instead, these steps can be handled quite informally and relatively freely in the group treatment setting. Group treatment allows for greater flexibility of treatment than does individual behavior modification. For example, individual patient assessment is part of the process of choosing a patient for group treatment, because he is considered to have about the same level of reality awareness, motivation, speech and motor ability as other group members. He may also be about the same age and have a comparable hospitalization history of time spent in hospitals as well as number of admissions as other members of the group. The assumption is made that the patient who is chosen for a given group will respond similarly to other group members when he is offered primary rewards—such as food, candy, or gum—or secondary social rewards of group approval. These assumptions by a behavior therapist are tested in the course of group treatment, and if proven false, the particular patient or patients can be dropped and replacements added.

In addition, the behavior therapist constantly makes changes in the kinds of reinforcements used to increase the motivation and responsiveness to treatment of each member of the group. Changes in reinforcements are necessary because the group member, like a patient in individual treatment, tends to become bored with the same reinforcements. Another factor that makes changing reinforcements necessary is the constantly changing membership of the group. Even the long-term patient will occasionally miss a session, due to physical illness or absence from the unit because of a special hospital appointment, a home visit, or a job, or another reason.

Because of the predictable absence of at least one member of a small group for most sessions, the group should be slightly larger than its optimal size of about three patients with one therapist. (A therapist can carefully observe up to four patients most of the time during a session, but if there are more than that, it is quite difficult for him.) Because of predictable absences, it is wise to start with four patients, and add one whenever one drops out permanently. One therapist alone can work quite effectively for about 30 minutes with three patients. The behavior therapist must concentrate quite hard during this time, because he must try to modify the behavior of at least one patient at a time, while carefully observing the effects of one patient's behavior on the other members of the group. One of the reasons that group behavior modification appears to be more effective than individual treatment is related to the opportunity afforded other members of the group to learn by observing each other. Each group member—and certainly the therapist—acts as a role model for the group, and modeling tends to enhance the effectiveness and speed of behavior therapy. In the group, there is an excellent opportunity for systematic use of controlled modeling.

One relatively aware patient is quite useful in the group. (An aware patient is one who can tell time, knows the day and date, can read a newspaper, and is considered in traditional terms to have some reality contact.) The aware patient can be asked to perform tasks to be learned by less aware patients. The aware patient can also be asked to answer questions of less aware patients, such as the day or date, which helps both patients to learn simple essential social dialogue. And the learning of these responses is often a major achievement in helping the very deteriorated, long-term patient to develop a social repertoire that will enable him to be discharged from the hospital to his community. The patient can then be placed in a board-and-care or nursing home, where he can remain without being returned to the hospital, because he now has sufficient social skills to be able to communicate with others in the home.

These sessions of about 30 minutes each should be given twice daily, and from five to seven days a week. In this way, group members will learn quickly and forget relatively little because of the short intervals between sessions. It is far more effective to work in short sessions more frequently than in longer ones less often, because patients quickly lose interest and concentration lessens as sessions exceed 30 minutes. Other staff members or students can quickly learn the routine training tasks of a given group, in order to be able to take over when the behavior therapist is absent. Substitute therapists are generally just about as effective—and often more so if they are enthusiastic—than the usual therapist.

Example

An actual example of group behavior modification will help to illustrate the theory discussed above. The regressed group included four male schizophrenics, 20 to 60 years of age, with 10 to 40 years of continuous hospitalization. None of them could carry on even the simplest of routine conversations. Most of them could not identify even a few other patients, did not know the location of the hospital, and were unable to name the time of day, day of the week, date, month, or even the year. These patients did not work effectively on jobs, and did not care for their beds or the areas around their beds. They could not dress themselves or shower or shave on their own initiative. Because of their inability to care for themselves and their general social inadequacy, they were called "babies" by the technicians.

This group was of great professional interest to me (the psychologist) because I felt that in working with patients who were so regressed, I could learn a great deal about token economy treatment potentials and limitations. I deliberately chose this highly regressed group in order to test how much their "baby" social strategies could be improved within six months. These patients were similar to those in other token economies, and since those in other programs had responded with considerably improved social repertoires, there was every reason to believe that this group, too, could show better social functioning. In addition this group seemed useful as a demonstration project for the technicians, psychiatrist, and social worker. They might also prove helpful in teaching behavior modification techniques to interns (see Chapter 3, the section Training of Psychological Interns).

Group behavior modification was designed to help this group to change their current, inadequate, "baby" level of social responses into more mature social strategies. Behavior modification was given to them to help them to function at a level of social adequacy that would enable them to leave the mental hospital, and to live permanently in a board-and-care or nursing home. Behavior modification was not expected to, nor did it, enable them to improve their level of social responsiveness to the extent that they could live with their families, or in any setting other than a highly structured one for ex-mental hospital patients. It should be clearly recognized that although behavior modification, in combination with psychoactive medication, is the most powerful treatment approach now available, deeply regressed patients can only be expected to move from one highly structured setting, the mental hospital, to another one, the live-in, special home in his community.

Daily training sessions about 30 minutes in length lasted for about six months. A half-hour was about the limit of patients' attention span for behavioral training. Sessions ended when patients showed lack of concentration, irritation, and impatience. Monday sessions were usually the shortest of the week, because after a weekend without sessions, patients had to be retaught to focus their attention. At the beginning of each session the four patients in the group were asked to sit on two beds facing each other in one of the dormitories on the token economy unit. The psychologist, sometimes with a student, walked between the beds talking to one patient at a time while the other three subjects could see and hear clearly the interchange between whoever was acting as behavior modifier and his subject. The psychologist and his student alternated working with the group, and the one who was not working observed the other one work.

The psychologist started sessions by showing each patient some cookies and two tokens, and saying, "Mr. Y, you see these cookies and the two tokens. If you talk well and you work hard, when we finish talking, I will give them to you! If you don't talk well and don't work hard, when we finish talking, I won't give them to you." During the training sessions the psychologist and his student walked up to each patient, and spoke to him while holding a piece of candy or a cookie in front of the patient. The acting behavior therapist showed great warmth and enthusiasm, and focused his attention on each patient as he spoke to him. The acting therapist would ask one question at a time, such as "What's your name?" or "What's his name?" while pointing to the patient. The therapist might ask the patient to identify by name features of the therapist's face. Each question might be repeated many times, and the patient might be given hints or even the answer if it appeared necessary. When the patient responded correctly, he was immediately given a piece of candy, and great social approval and warmth from the behavior therapist who might say, "That's *very* good, Mr. Y. You're doing *fine!*" The behavior therapist would generally place the candy or cookie right into the patient's mouth, so that the positive reinforcement followed immediately after the right response.

A few tasks were added every day, and older tasks were repeated. Repeated trials of newly learned tasks were necessary in order for a patient to become familiar enough with them to use them outside of training sessions. Indeed, behaviors that were not repeated frequently enough tended to be quickly forgotten by most group patients. A new task might require that the patient look out the window, and tell the therapist whether the day was sunny or cloudy. Another task might be to have a patient ask the name of the therapist, of another patient, or of a visitor. As each patient learned a task, a new one was presented to him.

New tasks were often learned by the patient by the therapist role modeling for him, with such actions as cocking his head from side to side to indicate that at one time he was speaking for himself, and at another time responding for the patient. Role modeling was also used to teach a patient to respond appropriately to such questions as "What color socks are you wearing?" The psychologist or his student acted as himself and then pretended to be the patient, first asking the question with his head to one side, and then answering with his head to the other side. After three or four trials of role modeling both parts, the acting therapist only asked the question, and then looked expectantly at the patient waiting for him to give the answer. The therapist provided the patient with several opportunities to answer the question, and if that did not work, he prompted the patient with the right answer. Or the psychologist asked another patient to tell the patient the right answer. In any case, as soon as the patient did give the right answer, the psychologist quickly rewarded him by putting a candy in his mouth, *and* at the same time said, "That's *fine*, Mr. M! You're doing *very well!*"

Other tasks included naming the color of clothing worn by another patient, such as answering the question, "What color shirt is Mr. P wearing?" Other tasks for a relatively aware, although deteriorated patient included answering omission questions, such as, "Who's not here today?" or "Who's wearing a yellow shirt?" when no member of the group was wearing a yellow shirt. For omission questions, the correct answer may be "Nobody." A deteriorated patient often learned to answer omission questions by answering the question about the yellow shirt for each patient in the group, when none of them were wearing one. In that way the patient learned that no one in the group was wearing a yellow shirt, and he finally learned to answer with, "Nobody." A patient generally learned to answer omission questions correctly by viewing another patient answer correctly an omission question and be rewarded for this answer. Learning from viewing is an example of integrating role modeling techniques into group behavior therapy to speed new social learning.

Obviously, identifying an object or person that is present, or at least has been present, is a far easier task than naming someone or something that is not now present or was not in the past. For this reason, the behavior therapist must expend considerably more thought and effort to train his subjects to answer omission questions than to train them to answer questions referring to existing conditions. It is well worth the effort because recognizing absences is an important part of the patient's socialization process. And the patient who learns to answer omission questions in the group setting will be able to retain this ability *and* generalize it to other settings.

DISCHARGE CONSIDERATIONS

Discharge from the hospital may be based on the staff's belief that the patient is now able to function in his community better than at the time he was hospitalized. This should *not* be interpreted to mean that he is now "cured" or normal, but that he now seems better able to be in his community without getting into trouble than he was prior to token economy treatment (Ulmer & Franks, 1973). There are other reasons for discharging a patient; these are noted below.

Consideration of a relatively aware patient for discharge generally begins when a staff member discusses leaving the hospital with the patient. This may occur after a week, a month, or a year of hospitalization, or even on the first day. Some informal negotiations may occur when the patient expresses some feeling about how long he wishes to remain in the hospital, under what circumstances he wishes to leave, and where he wishes to go when he leaves. A token economy staff, at least Camarillo's, will usually seriously consider a patient for discharge when the technicians believe that he should leave. When the technicians make this suggestion to the psychiatrist, he is quite likely to be receptive to their ideas, and request that the social worker discuss discharge with the patient. The psychiatrist may also ask that the social worker handle the paper work of providing the destitute patient with funds and housing in his community. In California, mental hospital staff have considerable power over the impoverished patient, who is generally only eligible for Aid to the Totally Dependent (ATD) funds and other state services, if he leaves with medical approval.

The patient who leaves with consent of staff is generally one who progresses up the token economy levels. Frequently, he starts in Dorm C and works his way up to Dorm A because he takes care of himself, does his work well, and gets along with staff and other patients. All of these statements apply only to the relatively aware patient who has some motivation to leave the hospital and wishes to cooperate with the staff to be discharged. About one-third of all patients discharged are relatively aware ones.

The process of discharge is quite different for the relatively unaware patient who may have little or no motivation to leave the hospital, or who may even want to stay there. The process of discharge then does not require involving the patient in discharge as a motivating goal for him. Instead, he is told that the staff has decided to discharge him at some time in the future—usually in three to six months—and that he is being taught now how to get along better with others when he leaves the hospital, than he did before he came there. About one-third of all discharges are of this type.

A third category of patient discharges, consisting of about one-third of all discharges, may not involve any changes in behavior. This kind of patient leaves for primarily legal or financial reasons related to the hospitals functioning, rather than treatment reasons. Typically, in a California mental hospital a patient who voluntarily enters the hospital can leave at any time "against medical advice (AMA)" unless the psychiatrist in charge of him considers him too dangerous to himself or to others to be allowed to return to his community. The psychiatrist must then go to court and request permission to hold the patient in the hospital for an additional period of 3 or 14 days longer. The psychiatrist may or *may not* be allowed by a court to hold the patient in the hospital against the patient's will. At the end of some 30 days, for legal reasons reported below, it is most difficult to keep any patient in the hospital any longer against his will, no matter how potentially dangerous he may appear to be to himself or to others.

In California, the Lanterman-Petris-Short (LPS) Acts of 1969 and 1971 prevent the mental hospital from keeping anyone indefinitely unless he is in the hospital while under the control of a conservator, or if he is held on a criminal charge by court order. If he is there while under a conservatorship, the conservator's permission must be obtained before the patient can be released. (The conservator can be a mate, parent, an attorney, the psychiatrist of the hospital unit, a legally constituted conservator's office for the county, city, or state, or anyone appointed as conservator by the appropriate court.)

If a patient in a mental hospital is charged with a crime, he is kept there until the psychiatrist responsible for him certifies that the patient is no longer emotionally ill, and is capable of standing trial for his crime. (The patient is originally sent by the court to a mental hospital because he is judged emotionally ill and emotionally unable to stand trial. He is sent to the hospital for "treatment" of emotional disease, and when "cured," is sent back to court to have his criminal behavior judged. Even from a nonbehavioristic standpoint, this procedure appears quite unjust and inappropriate, Szasz, 1965.)

The patient may also leave the hospital because the funding source (state or county) is short of money, and does not provide enough money for the hospital to care for a full number of needy patients. As the pressure on the hospital increases to take more patients who are disturbing their communities, the hospital may be forced to discharge tranquil patients who would otherwise be retained there. Under the LPS Acts and other California legislation, most California public health monies are given to the counties, and each then decides which patients, and how many, will be sent to the state mental hospital. Frequently, a state mental hospital cannot admit a patient without prior approval from county outpatient mental health services because the county will only pay for hospitalization when *and if* county outpatient staff members send the patient to the hospital. For example, if the patient or his family apply for state mental hospitalization, the patient may not be admitted *unless* a psychiatrist from the county approves his entrance.

There is another way that the county can restrict use of a state or community mental hospital. The county may inform the hospital that it will only pay for a specified number of patient-days for a given fiscal year. For example, Los Angeles County paid Camarillo State Hospital for 700,000 patient-days for fiscal year 1971, but informed the hospital that for fiscal year 1972, it would only pay for 400,000 patient-days. The amount of money being discussed is considerable, since at $30 per patient-day, 700,000 patient-days is $21 million and 400,000 patient-days is $12 million. The difference is $9 million and is a substantial amount of money for almost any county mental health budget.

Of course, each county in California and in many other parts of the country will try to utilize county mental hospital facilities before sending a patient to a state facility. California counties are enjoined by law to use *all* private and public hospital beds for mental patients within each county, *before* sending a patient to the state mental hospital.

It is important to recognize that the impact of these financial, legal, and social aspects of hospitalization is often greater in determining whether, where, when, and for how long a patient will be hospitalized than is the impact of his socially disturbed and disturbing behaviors, and changes made in them by token economy or any other form of treatment.

ETHICAL, MORAL, AND LEGAL CONSIDERATIONS

Applied Aspects

In a real sense, much of token economy treatment is *people training other people to get along better with people in their families and their communities.* And this is not a mechanical process at all, because the feelings of all involved, and sensitivity to their concerns must be a basic part of all treatment. For this reason, this cannot simply be a "how to . . . " book providing x number of easy lessons or instructions on how to work in an ongoing program or how to set up a new one. If the feelings and sensitivities of persons are a basic concern, questions of ethics and morality are quite important to any discussion of token economy. This discussion has become quite well known to the public in recent years, with behavior therapy being severaly criticized in the media (newspapers, journals, TV, magazines, radio, etc.) and the subject of a large number of lawsuits and laws.

To grapple with some of these issues requires some historical perspective of what is being argued about. For 200 years therapy as treatment of the emotionally disturbed person has been based on the view that the person is "ill" rather than sinful, wicked, and somehow guilty of evil deeds, thoughts against God, man, and himself. Treatment is administered to help him, and even if he is not capable of recognizing his needs for treatment, he is entitled to be treated. At the same time, there are serious issues about what treatment means, and who is competent to judge what is proper, helpful, and humane treatment.

In some ways, the most important issues may be what the purposes of treatment are, and who is to judge the purposes of treatment.

In many of these issues, there are some guidelines from traditional insight psychotherapy. But for most situations, insight therapy requires understanding, cooperation, and at least some motivation on the part of the patient to have any effect at all. Therefore, the rights of the patient—for example, to refuse treatment—are fairly well protected, because he can hardly be treated involuntarily. (It should be recognized that behavior therapy is quite different from some treatment forms that are inaccurately grouped with it. Psychosurgery, the use of surgical techniques on the brain itself to change behavior, is totally different from behavior therapy. Electroconvulsive therapy, the use of electric shocks to the brain to change behavior, is also not part of behavior therapy. Furthermore, behavior therapists are often strongly opposed to the use of psychosurgery and electroconvulsive therapy as being inconsistent with the concepts of freedom of choice and human dignity.)

A detailing of "ethics" and "morality" especially relevant to the practice of token economy treatment will be useful here. "Ethical" is defined by Guralnik (1970) as (1) "conforming to moral standards" and (2) "conforming to the conduct of a given profession or group." Stein (1966) defines "ethical" as (1) "pertaining to rights and wrongs in conduct" and (2) "in accordance with the rules or standards for right conduct or practice, [especially] the standards of a profession." Webster's defines "morality" as "moral quality or character of being in accord with the principles or standards of right conduct." Chaplin (1968) defines "ethics" as "the study of moral values and ideals," and "moral" as "characterizing a person or group whose conduct is proper or ethical." And, interestingly enough, neither Hinsie and Campbell's *Psychiatric Dictionary* (1970) nor White's *Glossary of Behavioral Terminology* (1971) defines either ethics or morality.

An underlying issue of ethics and morality is the question of control of human behavior. Who has the right to control others, and for what purposes?

The current concern with the ethics and treatment of behavior therapy is only part of the picture of many inhumanities perpetrated in the name of research and treatment. There are innumerable instances of persons being used as guinea pigs in experimenting with new medical treatments, and this practice is especially prevalent in mental hospitals and in prisons. In each of these instances the human being's inherent rights of dignity and respect or even health and life are ignored. To remedy and especially to prevent these problems, all large human-treatment institutions have human rights committees. These committees review all proposals involving human subjects, whether treatment or research is involved, and their disapproval means that the treatment or research proposal cannot be implemented. Generally there is an ongoing review of all procedures, so that whenever violations occur, these particular practices, or even the program, can be ended.

For example, the King-Drew Medical Complex (Martin Luther King, Jr. General Hospital and Charles R. Drew Postgraduate Medical School) has a Committee for the Protection of Human Rights. This committee reviews all proposals involving humans and determines what hazards are involved, and if the safeguards are adequate. This committee may also enforce the rights of confidentiality of patients, so that all information on them must remain private unless given out with the informed consent of these patients. The American Psychological Association has a manual (1973) that clearly specifies ethical and unethical practices in research. In addition to these guidelines, often strict regulations are proposed at all levels of government—city, state, and federal. The following is a statement from the United States Public Health Service that is probably typical of most federal guidelines in this area.

> Public Health Service policy (Protection of the Individual as a Research Subject, May 1, 1969) requires for each proposal involving human subjects that the grantee institution certify annually that an institutional committee has reviewed and approved the procedures which involve human subjects in accordance with the institutional assurance approved by the Public Health Service. (Instruction Sheet, revised March 1970, for Public Health Service 398).

This kind of statement by a federal funding source means that the institution conducting research must follow carefully all protective guidelines, or it will lose current financial supports and jeopardize future ones.

The situation of research and practice in a treatment program such as token economy is quite similar, and human rights and dignity are of considerable concern. The American Psychological Association (1967) prescribes clear guidelines for ethical practices in token economy and any other form of treatment. The Association (1973) also provides ethical guidelines for research. Violations of these guidelines can lead to censure by the American Psychological Association or even exclusion from it.

These data then represent the larger picture of what constitutes ethical and moral concerns, that is, respect for the rights, feelings, and in general, the dignity of the human being. This includes the psychologist's compliance with the special rules of the American Psychological Association, and compliance of all disciplines working in token economy programs with the ethical guidelines of that discipline, with the regulations of their institution and those of involved levels of the federal government.

The question then arises: Why is there so much controversy on these issues, particularly in regard to token economies? The controversy is based in part on some erroneous views about a supposed difference between traditional therapy and behavior therapy. The popular view is that traditional therapy does not attempt to change persons to have them behave in a more conforming fashion, and that behavior therapy, in contrast, tries to force persons to change their behaviors to conform more with those around them. The truth of the matter is that all forms of therapy try to make their subjects, especially mental hospital patients, conform to the expectations of others in their social environments, their communities (Ulmer & Franks, 1973).

The arguments about free will and the right to make decisions are not particularly valid for mental hospital patients, because our society always reserves the right to hospitalize them involuntarily, and to retain them in the hospital often against their wills. In addition, the reason for hospitalizing a person is that he behaves in ways that offend or endanger others in his community. And the reason for discharging a patient is that he has changed *through treatment,* so that he behaves more similarly and more acceptably to others in his community than he did prior to his hospitalization. Discharge therefore generally suggests that traditional or behavioral treatment has been successful.

In effect, there is a need to clarify the question of whether society has the right to impose unpleasant or even cruel living conditions on patients against their will and whether these are elements of the living conditions of token economies. Neither this society nor any other has the right to impose any cruelties on anyone, whether or not cruelties are for the best long-range interests of the individual or of society, and whether or not these cruelties are called "treatment." For these reasons, all aspects of token economy should be humane, and should demonstrate respect for the dignity of patients.

Here is a concrete example of the severest deprivations given patients at Camarillo. Standard practice is to encourage patients to earn their meals and beds by behaving appropriately and working to earn daily payments of tokens. When patients refuse to work or act appropriately enough to earn these few tokens, they can be deprived of up to five meals, with the attending physician's approval that this deprivation will not be harmful to them in any way. They may also not be allowed to use their beds, and will sleep on a cot. This is not commonly done, but when done, it seems quite effective, and patients do not seem to find it cruel. Indeed, missing one meal or even a few meals has often been considered quite healthy. And no patient with a physical problem is ever deprived of a meal. Other deprivations are restriction to the unit instead of going on the grounds, and missing a movie.

Another argument that is harder to answer is the issue of the right of relatively aware patients to refuse treatment, in this case, token economy behavior therapy. Camarillo patients never have the option of leaving the program for another one, nor can patients from another program transfer to the token economy program. (Transfers that do occur are based on recommendations and examinations by the staff.) However, both kinds of patient-initiated transfers should be allowed as part of the rationale that patients are competent to make decisions in the program, and are therefore entitled to decide to leave or join it.

Electroshock is not given in the program, nor is there any psychosurgery. Patients are not physically mishandled, and they are treated with considerable courtesy. They are commonly called "Mr. ___" and are only called by their first names if they are well known and well liked by staff.

Legal Aspects

There are many legal problems connected with token economies, most of which arise in penal settings and will not be discussed here. Other legal problems are associated with applications of token economy in mental institutions because of the need to use primary reinforcements—for example, food and a bed—as basic motivators of patients.

Many recent court decisions (Wexler, 1973) require that patients be given these primary reinforcements at all times as part of their constitutional rights. If these primary reinforcements are given without their being earned, token economies cannot use these reinforcements to motivate their patients to change their behaviors. In addition, some of these court decisions have ruled that many secondary reinforcements must be given to all patients at all times. These secondary reinforcements include the rights to have visitors, to attend religious services, to wear one's own clothes, to be outdoors regularly and frequently, and to watch TV; privacy with a screen or curtains around one's bed, and a closet or locker.

All of these primary and secondary reinforcements have to be earned in Camarillo's program and in most other token economies. This problem is compounded further by court requirements that patients be paid with money at or above the standard minimum wage for work performed, unless the work is demonstrably therapeutic rather than labor-saving for the institution. None of these court requirements are met by Camarillo's program, or any other program described in Chapter 1. (Indeed, the Patton State Hospital program of Schaefer and Martin occasionally deprived patients of food for up to five consecutive days, and some patients went down to 80 percent of their original body weight. At Camarillo, patients could only miss five consecutive meals, and this was only done with full medical approval.)

To date, these judicial constraints do not seem to forbid traditional token economy operations, but they may do so in the future. If this should happen, this will not mean that token economies can no longer operate, but they will have to creatively change their operations to substitute other reinforcements as motivators for those that they will then have to give noncontingently (without patients earning them). As Wexler (1973) suggests, many reinforcements can be found by simply asking patients what they want, and these can be used as effective motivators.

Research Aspects

The kinds of concerns for the practice of token economy represent the ways in which available knowledge is utilized to help patients. There is no assurance that new knowledge (obtained through research) will be used in the same ways. How that new knowledge may be used in the future should be a concern for today's token economy researcher. Formerly, the researcher did not have to concern himself with how his research would be applied. Prior to World War II, the general belief was that a scientist (often simply and over generally referred to here as a researcher) simply made discoveries of new ways of understanding and controlling nature or man; the subsequent application of his discoveries was not considered to be his business. Politicians, businessmen, administrators, military officers, and others then took that new knowledge and applied it as they saw fit—usually to make money, often to gain power or prestige for themselves or their organizations or countries, or whatever. World War II changed this situation completely. When the Germans set up death camps, murdered millions of persons, and performed cruel experiments, frequently involving torture, on many thousands of others—all in the name of "science"—scientists recognized that something was totally wrong. Humane concerns were completely absent, and torture and murder were being approved and supported as "furthering science."

The second challenge to scientists lay in the atomic bomb. After the Hiroshima and Nagasaki explosions many atomic scientists were conscience-stricken by what they had done. And no one can read very far into the *Bulletin of the Atomic Scientists* without noting the terrible feelings of guilt, penitence, and regret that many atomic scientists have for creating the atomic bomb. Indeed, J. Robert Oppenheimer said, "We did the devil's work" (Kipphardt, 1968).

A very strong parallel argument may be made against behavior therapy in general and token economy in particular. Research findings in these areas can easily be misused. A police state in the United States (in the future), today's Chile, or anywhere else in the world would certainly carefully examine and utilize many behavior therapy and token economy findings to control the behavior of their citizens. The possibilities of control through behavior therapy are indeed very great, particularly if no ethical, moral, or legal constraints are placed on such applications. It may be that behavior therapy is potentially a more powerful weapon of control than the atomic bomb. If behavior therapy were used to harm rather than help persons, it is quite possible that afterward many behaviorist researchers would say that they had done the devil's work.

These questions are being raised not to forbid behavior therapy research, but to make several significant points.

1. Behavior therapy is effective in changing the behavior of human beings.
2. The kinds of changes to be made are to some extent decided by the behavior therapists *as well* as by their patients.
3. New findings on the applications of behavior therapy are likely to make behavior therapy more effective with a wider range of patients in settings now considered suitable, and, in addition, in other settings previously considered unsuitable, for behavior therapy.
4. Controls are needed on the kinds of research findings obtained in order to prevent misuse of the information.

For all of the above reasons, it seems appropriate to ask what safeguards can be built into behavior therapy research to make it less likely that new findings can be used to harm persons, as in a police state, rather than to help them.

Generally, research findings are only applicable in ways that are consistent with the manner in which the research is done. For example, if in a token economy setting, new treatment techniques are tried using ethical and moral safeguards, then the findings of that research are only likely to be effective *when* these same moral and ethical principles are carefully followed.

Therefore, it seems that one of the best ways of preventing the misuse of behavior therapy is to insist that stringent ethical and moral principles be followed in all research. These principles should be constantly revised as new situations arise, and especially when there are misuses of previous findings. Following this guideline would also mean that there would be little likelihood of any harm coming to anyone who is the subject of an experiment.

SUMMARY

This chapter (with Chapter 4) discusses some key aspects of Camarillo's program, how it relates to other programs, and some fundamental issues of all token economy programs.

Direct treatment of patients is discussed, and a detailed description of an echolalic patient and his responses to individual behavior therapy is presented. Some general considerations are outlined for group behavior modification, especially when working with quite regressed patients with long hospitalization histories.

Group behavior modification is described for a group of about four regressed patients. One of these patients may be relatively aware, and he sets up learning-modeling roles for the other patients. Treatment setting, tasks presented to patients, and the roles of the psychologist and his student are described. Group treatment is contrasted with individual treatment, and is found to be generally more effective.

Discharge of patients is generally based on the views of the staff, especially technicians, that patients are now less likely to disturb others in their communities than they were prior to treatment. Another concern may be that the hospital is short of funds and is unable to treat all persons requesting hospitalization; therefore some are denied admission, and others are released sooner than they would be under full financing of the hospital.

Ethical, moral, and legal questions are vexing. These questions are particularly important for token economies because many criticisms are being raised today, and even more will be offered tomorrow. Probably the most important issues are the questions of who is to judge what the purposes of a token economy program are, and what the most ethical, moral, and humane ways to achieve these purposes are.

Rights to treatment are discussed. It is pointed out that psychosurgery and electroconvulsive therapy (ECT or electroshock) are not parts of behavior therapy. Definitions of ethics and morality and their applications in psychology and in institutional settings are given. A specific institution, the King-Drew

Medical Complex, and its human rights concerns are described. There is some discussion of the roles of city, state, and federal governments in the upholding of these human rights in research and applied settings.

Future token economies are likely to have to consider court decisions requiring that all patients be given many of the primary and secondary reinforcements that are currently the major motivators in Camarillo's and other programs. For this reason, some changes will have to be made to follow token economy principles. Fortunately, however, these changes are eminently feasible. There is no reason to believe that token economies will not maintain their current effectiveness despite court-induced changes.

Behavior researchers should emphasize and follow ethical, moral, and legal considerations to reduce the possiblity that their findings will be used for inhumane purposes.

SUGGESTED READINGS

Ethics and Morality and the Control of Human Behaviors

London, P. *Behavior control.* New York: Perennial Library, 1969. This is an excellent book on the issue of who has the right to control others and for what purposes.

London, P. Ethical problems in behavior control. In W. A. Hunt (Ed.), *Human behavior and its control.* Cambridge, Mass.: Schenkman, 1957.

Law and The Control of Human Behavior

Wexler, D. B. Token and taboo: Behavior modification, token economies and the law. *Behaviorism,* 1973, *1*(2), 1-24. An excellent comprehensive survey and commentary on legal problems and decisions of behavior modification in general and token economy in particular.

CHAPTER 6

Creative New Token Economy Techniques

INTRODUCTION

Much of the vitality and viability of behavior therapy lies in the opportunities provided for the behavior therapist to be creative in devising new social-learning techniques to help the disturbed person to cope effectively with others. Behavior therapy tends to be especially effective in a hospital setting, where a patient's reinforcements are controlled. And token economy—as organized, systematic behavior therapy—is able to make efficient use of new techniques for modifying abnormal social strategies. These abnormal social strategies may include standard patient problems or new ones, as society changes and as persons who are ethnically and socially different come into state and community mental hospitals.[1]

Wherever behavior therapy is effective with outpatient subjects, for example, in desensitization, token economy with inpatients tends to be more effective because of its systematized and comprehensive nature. Some techniques discussed in this section originated with insight therapy, and the encounter group is such an example. Other techniques are native to the behavioral movement, such as written negotiated contracts.

It is worthwhile at this point to refer back to Chapter 4, the section Patient Assessment. Patient assessment requires objective, operational definitions, and careful recording of target behaviors during baseline periods prior to treatment. With treatment and the resulting experimental data, the effects of treatment can be evaluated. The effectiveness of any behavioral treatment can also be determined by discontinuing treatment, and noting if deviant behavior returns to the baseline levels shown before treatment. Careful recording of data is essential to the effectiveness of these procedures. Throughout this chapter there will be a detailing of kinds of behavior to be treated, and how they will be recorded. If data are not recorded, the behavior therapist falls into the same trap as the traditionalist; that is, having only the verbal description of deviant and desired behaviors. The lack of "hard data" (numbers) to provide sound information for evaluating and improving the effects of current treatment is one of the major liabilities of traditional therapy.

Changing of deviant behaviors is the goal of all members of the token economy treatment team, and is shown in the use of different treatment approaches. A psychiatric technician may lead a behavioral encounter group. A social worker may be engaged in one-to-one behavior modification with a

---

[1] It is important to recognize that when behavior therapy deals with any human problem area, it does so on an empirical basis of testing which behavioral techniques work, and how well they work under reasonably controlled conditions. Topics dealt with are practically oriented toward modifying behaviors that bother others; sometimes behavior therapy treats behaviors that essentially disturb only one person, the individual who shows them and is under treatment for them. The latter case includes phobias, which primarily handicap the phobic person rather than others in his social environment.

A tremendous variety of human problems can be changed into less troublesome behaviors. The table of contents of one book of behavioral case studies (Ullmann & Krasner, 1965) is a revealing, although dated, sample of the scope of behavior therapy: verbal behavior of psychotics, eating of chronic schizophrenics, systematic desensitization of psychotics, modifying autistic behavior of autistic children, hysterical blindness, anorexia, sexual inadequacies, stuttering, tics, vomiting and speech problems of children, and hyperactivity. A more recent bibliography (Insalaco & Shea, 1970) is even more extensive. Under the heading of "Miscellaneous" the following disorders are listed: anorexia, cerebral dysrhythmia, coreiform movements, chronic crying, enuresis, encopresis, insomnia, marital problems, nailbiting, obesity, postural control, reading, rehabilitation, self-control, self-medication, sleepwalking, study habits, and tics.

regressed patient or even with a group of regressed patients. A rehabilitation counselor may be negotiating a contract between a patient and other staff members. In all of these cases the psychologist may be involved as a consultant to the staff, and as coordinator of various treatment approaches. This is the situation in the Camarillo program. Indeed, a psychologist is often most useful when he spreads his knowledgeability to as many staff members as possible through the consultation process, so that various staff members can work in many different ways, often with the same patient.

NEW TOKEN ECONOMY TREATMENT TECHNIQUES

Role Modeling and Behavioral Rehearsal

Role modeling is a procedure for teaching a patient new social skills with the behavior therapist, other staff members, students, or other patients performing these new social skills. The patient then has a clear demonstration of what is expected of him by others who may know him well from working or living with him for a long time. Role modeling has been shown to be an extremely effective way of changing behavior (Bandura, 1969, 1971).

Role modeling is quite different from role playing, which is a way of acting out a situation in an unstructured way. In contrast, role modeling involves careful, thought-out speech and actions so that someone else can observe and duplicate the speech and actions. Role playing is used in a form of traditional insight therapy, psychodrama, and is described in detail by Moreno (1959), as a way of dealing with unconscious conflicts and problem relationships. Psychodrama can also be modified to be a useful behavioristic treatment by focusing on having a patient learn social skills through playacting behavioral rehearsal sessions. Through this the patient has the opportunity to see himself as he appears to others, *and* to learn to change his ways of responding to others. He can then begin to respond more effectively to other persons by satisfying more of their needs instead of frustrating them. He becomes more predictable to others, because they can guess how he will respond to him, and change their actions to have him respond in ways that they find satisfying.

The increased predictability of this person's responses to others in his community means that he is less likely to disturb others in his social environment. He thus becomes better able to be a more responsible person to others, which will probably make him more socially acceptable, and less likely to be rehospitalized after discharge.

Behavioral rehearsal focuses on suitable ways of behaving now, and unlike psychodrama, it avoids discussion of past problems and disasters. (Behavior therapy generally focuses on the present and the future, on the assumption that the patient can only change and become happier today and tomorrow. Dealing with yesterday, which is over and unchangeable, can be more of a diversion from learning to function better, than dealing for the most part with the present and the future.) Behavioral rehearsal helps to generalize a patient's new appropriate behaviors to many settings so that the social skills he learns and tries out in the token program can be useful to him in other parts of the hospital, and especially in his community. After he tries out these new social skills, he can report back to the group or to the behavior therapist. And he should be able to get help from other staff members and patients in the program in retaining and improving his new social skills to that they can be as useful to him as possible in the hospital, and especially afterward in his community.

Instituting Role Modeling and Behavioral Rehearsal

Role modeling and behavioral rehearsal can be started in any token economy program by having the staff decide exactly which kinds of behaviors they wish to encourage. The staff can begin with each other, demonstrating these behaviors in sessions to show each other what they mean. Then a suitable patient in need of, and motivated for, role rehearsal training can be chosen to observe and practice these behaviors. Whenever the staff begin a new treatment approach, initial successes are important in encouraging them to continue with it. In using this technique, it is therefore best to add one patient at a time until there are four patients in the group—instead of starting out with four patients in the group.

Modeling can also be used in the context of other treatment settings, such as encountering groups and anger training sessions. Modeling can be tried in each of these, perhaps once in a session at first, and then increasing the trials to several during each session. The staff should share their experiences, observe each other, and work together closely, to improve their understanding and ability to use modeling techniques. Modeling should become part of every aspect of token economy treatment, so that the staff is alert to recognize when a patient is performing his daily assignments unusually well and can point him out to other patients as a suitable role model.

ANGER TRAINING SESSIONS

Anger training sessions are a form of behavioral rehearsal designed to help the physically aggressive patient to learn to use words instead of his fists when he is angry with others. Anger training sessions are especially suitable for the young patient who is frequently recommitted to mental hospitals and jail for hitting others. In Camarillo, there are usually two to four patients present with one to two staff members or students. The Camarillo psychologist role models how to express *and accept* verbal nonphysically threatening hostility. The therapist or another patient may call the one who is being talked to a wide and democratic assortment of foul names, the mildest being such words as stupid and ignorant. The one being verbally attacked may be asked to listen only or to respond only verbally. A patient is encouraged to speak as obnoxiously and offensively as possible to another patient or to a staff member.

Throughout each session each patient is frequently reminded of how important it is for him to learn not to hit in order for him to get out of the hospital and stay in his community, but these reminders are only effective if the patient is strongly motivated to get out of the hospital. If the patient is satisfied to remain in the hospital—as is true of many patients—anger training sessions can still be effective, but they must use other rewards than discharge from the hospital. Each session lasts about an hour, and a substantial attempt is made to have each patient become increasingly desensitized to provocation, so that he becomes better able to control himself. With his improved control he becomes better able to respond with words to frustration instead of with his fists. Each patient is constantly given feedback and encouragement on his progress. The patient may be encouraged to attend sessions by giving him tokens or special privileges after each session, for these sessions are not likely to be pleasant or easy experiences for him. It is important to check with the staff to find out how the patient is getting along with other patients and staff members between sessions.

Anger training sessions can easily be combined with other token economy experiences, especially the behavioral encounter group. Progress in one treatment modality should help the patient to profit from other token economy experiences. Anger training sessions can be given once or twice weekly and should continue for months, as the kind of behavior involved may be shown only rarely, and if it is not eliminated, it can cause the patient to be rehospitalized or jailed for a long time. Behavior that is shown rarely and in very different settings is especially hard to change, and because of its serious implications, warrants considerable staff attention and treatment.

Starting New Anger Training Groups

Anger training can be included in any token economy program. The first step is to study the literature carefully to determine the kinds of cases that are usually treated, procedures used, and outcomes found. For example, if experiences in a given institution and case studies in the literature show that males under age 30 with fewer than three hospitalizations respond best to treatment, selection of patients should be made appropriately. The procedures for treatment should be followed carefully in the first trial, and modified from then on, according to experience and results obtained.

If there is no opportunity to search the literature, young males who have been hospitalized for physical aggression against others, who are not dischargeable because they attack others, and who seem suitable to anger training should be selected. Then, each of these patients should be seen individually to determine if each one wishes to be discharged from the hospital, is not delusional, and is motivated to involve himself in anger training sessions. As soon as four such patients are found, the sessions should begin.

The first part of the first session should focus on the group members' perceptions of why they are in the hospital, and how important is it to them to get out of the hospital. Next there should be a general discussion of the procedures that are going to be followed in each session, and the reasons for following them. As soon as the patients understand the procedures and the reasons, one patient should be asked to choose another patient in the group and to say something nasty to him, with the understanding that no one can ever hit anyone else either in the group or outside of it. Having each patient sign a statement in writing to this effect, with a copy given to each patient, tends to make such a commitment more binding.

As soon as one patient has said something nasty to another patient, the behavior therapist, too, should say something obnoxious to that patient. There should then be a discussion by all persons involved about how they feel. The therapist should stress that saying something offensive is often quite as effective, and certainly less dangerous, than hitting. The first sessions should last only about half an hour. The length of sessions should be increased gradually to about an hour, but not longer. Any patient who wishes to leave any session or drop out of training should be allowed to do so without punishment. New patients should be brought in so that there are four members in the group at all times. If a patient hits anyone outside of the group, even a nonmember of the group or someone outside the hospital, this should be brought up and discussed in the group, and behavioral rehearsal as well as desensitization should be done to decrease the possibility of this occurring in the future.

All aspects of anger training sessions should be integrated as carefully as possible into other facets of token economy training, such as working in the program, earning tokens, and activities in the behavioral encounter groups. All staff members should be carefully informed about all patients in anger training sessions, and their progress.

ENCOUNTER GROUPS

The encounter group approach is a development from group psychotherapy, and in ways is both similar to and different from group psychotherapy. Group therapy discussions occur mainly between a leader and other members of a group, rather than between members of a group with little or no participation by the leader. Group therapy discussions are usually relatively gentle, philosophical, and diplomatic, with members hesitant to interrupt each other, or to challenge the truthfulness, appropriateness, or meaningfulness of what anyone says.

Group therapy of the 1960s is the basis of a new approach to group treatment, the encounter group. Encounter groups are founded on the belief that the blunter and more direct a confrontation between group members, the more meaningful is the experience. Encounter groups focus on the here-and-now of emotions, especially hostility and affection of group members for each other. Discussions of members' long past experiences are forbidden. Encounter groups are intense, and act as pressure cookers, almost forcing members to deal directly with their intense feelings as they arise in the group. Tenderness may be shown by touching, and any authentic feeling is accepted, except the use or threat of physical violence. Most encounter groups strongly encourage the expression of verbal violence, such as a member swearing at another member, but forbids physical threats. While encounter groups focus on authentic emotions, this does not mean that one person has license to hurt another person's feelings because he is hostile, justifiably or not. The angry member may be confronted by the group to help him to realize that his hostility is not warranted.

Another cardinal difference between group psychotherapy and encounter groups is the fact that a group therapy leader is important, usually a professional selected in advance, and he acts to direct the group. In encounter groups, the leader may or may not be a professional, he may be designated in advance of a session, or he may arise from the group, as is the case for so-called leaderless groups. Often the leader of an encounter group may have little education—as is the case at Synanon—and lead groups of well-educated professionals, because of his expertise in encountering. In effect, the encounter group is far more democratic than group therapy because the encounter group leader earns his role by demonstrating competence as a leader, not by education or any other background that may not be very important in qualifying him as a leader.

It is worthwhile at this point to discuss why group psychotherapy has little in common with behavior therapy. Encounter groups and behavior therapy have similar assumptions, methods, and goals of treatment. Indeed, the Camarillo program has an extensive history of over five years of melding encountering with standard behavior therapy techniques such as role rehearsal and written contracts. Encountering focuses on the responsible, rational aspects of personality, just as behavior therapy does. Encountering emphasizes such basic aspects of behavior therapy as the here-and-now of learning to handle social situations with others.

Encounter groups do not permit a member to use unhappy experiences of his past as an excuse for being unhappy now, or for making others unhappy with him now. When he talks about the past as a justification for socially inappropriate actions, he is usually told that the group does not want to hear this, but that it does want to know what he is going to do today and tomorrow to make his, his family's, and others' lives happier. For example, the group may suggest that he try to act more maturely by pretending (called an "act as if") that he is adult, and after a while the "act as if" will become a natural way for him to behave with others. An encounter group generally believes that a person learns to behave more appropriately toward others in the group and outside of it, because he assumes responsibility for his improved behavior, and therefore learns to behave more suitably. Typically, an encounter group will emphasize that "today is the first day of the rest of your life," and it will strongly encourage the members to work positively toward their future.

Encounter groups often focus on moral issues, such as phoniness in acting friendly toward someone who is disliked. Encountering often requires that a person be honest with himself and others as part of becoming a moral human being. The encounter groups that focus most directly on moral issues are probably the integrity groups of Mowrer (1964), but Synanon (Yablonsky, 1965; Endore, 1968) and Esalen (as described by Perls, 1969) are also deeply committed to dealing with moral questions.

Honesty in actions, as related to therapy, is quite creatively dealt with by Jourard (1964), who believes that a person must act appropriately with others *before* he can handle his emotions properly. Jourard reverses Shakespeare's dictum: "This above all, to thine own self be true, and it must follow, as the night the day, thou canst not then be false to any man." Jourard believes that only by first acting truthfully and honestly with others, can a person learn to act truthfully and honestly with himself. These moral viewpoints have much in common with social-learning approaches, because they both are based on experience, not insight, as the prerequisite to new and more effective ways of coping with others. These moral viewpoints and behavior therapy both reject traditional insight approaches to behavioral change.

BEHAVIORAL ENCOUNTERING: THE SYNANON GAME IN CAMARILLO

Game Background and Description

The Synanon Game is a special kind of encounter group. It is the most important and most consistently used way in which Synanon members talk to each other. (I have been a member of Synanon for almost six years, and I worked closely with the Camarillo Hospital Behavior Program staff members to help them to adapt the game for use as a regular part of behavior therapy treatment.)

The game has been used extensively to help Synanonists (members of Synanon) to live happily and effectively, and as a forum, to make administrative decisions. (There are three classes of members of the Synanon community: residents, generally ex-addicts and others with severe, socially incapacitating problems; life stylers, who work at jobs outside of Synanon, may never have been addicts, and pay for themselves and their families to live in Synanon; and game players, who work and live outside Synanon, come a few times weekly to play the Synanon Game, and to donate time, work, and money to Synanon. There are about 2,000 members of the Synanon community in several large facilities, mostly in California, and one in Washington, D.C.)

The game developed under the leadership of Charles Dederich, founder of Synanon in 1958, and leader since then. Dederich had considerable experience as a business executive, and was an alcoholic before he began Synanon. In 1958 he began trying to rehabilitate himself and other alcoholics and drug addicts by using confrontational meetings, which developed into the game. He found that game players tended to keep free of any addictions. He called his confrontational meeting a game in order to indicate that there were rules, and that playing the game was supposed to be fun, with no one getting hurt. The game rules are presented in Exhibit 6-1.

EXHIBIT 6-1

Synanon's 1972 Description of Its Game

The physical setup of the game is 7 to 11 persons sitting in a circle. The people in the circle talk to one person within that circle at a time. The person they are talking to is in what is called the "hot seat," and everything about him may be called into question. He may be called about his appearance, behavior, emotions, and so on, usually starting with outside appearances and then going inside the person. Everything is called into question, both good and bad, positive and negative. You are called upon to answer to *ALL* your behavior. The game is not therapeutic, but it does have therapeutic values inasmuch as a person is allowed to see himself as he really is, thus enabling a person to make the changes he himself desires. The basic philosophy is "to struggle to tell the *truth* and hear the *truth*."

Communication is direct in a game. The game is the safest place in the world, as people may say anything they wish so long as there is no violence or threat of physical violence. There are as many reasons for playing the game as there are people. Games are played for fun. Of course, as in most games, there are rules that must be followed and policies that make for better game playing.

RULES

No chemicals (taking in of drugs for pleasure purposes).
No violence or threats of violence.

POLICIES

1. Talk to one person at a time.
2. Support the role if you can; if you can't, keep quiet. Follow the line of questioning, don't defend the person on the hot seat, because you stop him from thinking for himself.

Thanks are due Charles E. Dederich, Chairman of Synanon Foundation, Tomales Bay, Marshall, California, for permission to quote the 1972 version of the Synanon Game Rules. The Game Rules have been edited to clarify a few points but the basic content remains unchanged.

3. Spend only about 20 minutes per person. Move the game around.
4. Break all contracts, conscious or unconscious agreements, to cover up for each other. Don't agree to not examine each other's behavior.
5. Don't leave your chair without telling the person on both sides of you that you are getting up.
6. Don't get too close or point your finger in anyone's face. Don't touch anybody.

MODES

Catharsis: Verbal garbage, valid and invalid indictments. Done to make a person react.

Projection: Telling a person something about himself that you also see in yourself. Projections are true 90 percent of the time.

Indictments: A well thought out observation of a person's negative behavior.

Data Running: Giving information from a personal place. Telling a person how you solved the same problem they are voicing.

TECHNIQUES

Engrossment: Blowing a small incident to gigantic proportions so a person can see the consequences of his smallest actions.

Belittlement: Making a situation smaller than it is. This is done to let a person know that he has done nothing worse than anyone else has done.

Humor: Humor is used to make a person laugh at himself.

Righteous Indignation: Getting on your high horse. Example: "You did what? How could you do such a thing? No one has ever done that!"

Carom Shots: Telling about the actions of a person to another. Talking to someone through another person. A talks to B about C, while C is present.

WHAT YOU CAN DO IN THE "HOT SEAT"

1. Remain silent; say nothing.
2. Lie. But why do this, when you're being given help in order to help youself?
3. Go crazy: Screaming, yelling, etc.
4. Defend yourself: Give excuses for why you do the things you do. Defending can keep you from hearing or seeing the truth.
5. Cop out: To admit to an indictment to get out of the Hot Seat in a hurry. To admit that a change is needed and you see that it is needed.
6. Dump: When you tell the game what you are uptight, angry, or hurt

about. This is a very good way to use your game to get the help you need.

7. Listen: When you really try to hear what your game is saying to you. Listening to the information people are giving to you.

8. Give it the barest: Looking honestly at what is being said. Sifting your information to see what applies and what does not. Deep soul-searching.

9. Tell the truth.

Always label a game as just that—a game. Never let a person leave a game with his or her feelings hurt. Remind him or her that it is a game and that games are played for fun. Don't carry grudges out of the game. *Leave it all in the game*; don't continue it later on the floor.

The game began as a combination of kinds of encounter groups with a strong influence of Alcoholics Anonymous, which Dederich had attended before he founded Synanon. Camarillo patients were given copies of the game orientation form "Your Encounter Group" (Exhibit 6-2) in order to acquaint them with the game rules and procedures.

EXHIBIT 6-2

Your Encounter Group

This introduction to the encounter group belongs to_____.

INTRODUCTION

Welcome to your encounter group. Your encounter group leaders are

_____ .

What you are about to read is important to getting the most out of your group experience. There are only two reasons we meet in this group: (1) to get out of the hospital as soon as possible; (2) to stay out of the hospitals and jails after we get out.

BEHAVIOR MODIFICATION ENCOUNTER GROUPS

People enter mental hospitals because they talk and act and appear crazy to other people. People can think crazy thoughts as much as they want. People don't know what anyone else thinks. Neither you nor anyone else ever got put in a mental hospital or jail for thinking crazy, but only for talking, acting, and dressing crazy. Thinking crazy is not your problem. Your problem is talking, acting, or dressing crazy. This is why we are not interested in what you think. We are interested only in what you say, do, and how you dress.

What Goes On in Our Group

In this group we will discuss what you did or said that got you into the hospital. We will not discuss why you did what you did, or whether it was your fault or not. The past is past, and we don't expect you to do the things again that you did to get yourself into the hospital. We will help you by talking about what you did or said that brought you to this hospital so that you will not do these dumb, crazy things again.

You can get out of this hospital when you no longer talk, act, or dress crazy. When you no longer talk, act, or dress crazy, the staff of your unit will say that you have recovered, and you will leave this hospital. And we will help you so that when you are out of the hospital, you can continue to talk, act, and dress like others in your neighborhood, so that you can stay out of mental hospitals and jails. All members of the group are expected to help each other by giving advice in the group, and then we really help ourselves. We always give advice on how to talk, act, and dress so that we can get out of the hospital as soon as possible and then stay out of hospitals and jails. We help ourselves and others best when we tell the truth about how dumb and crazy they talk, act, or appear to others. This is understandable. No matter how mad you may get, you must not hit anyone or threaten anyone in the group or afterward, when we leave the group. We must forget about being mad, and we must act nicely to everyone after the group meeting. We must also think about the truths that were told to us in the group, and try to change our behavior accordingly.

CONTRACTS

Contracts are agreements that you will behave in a particular way for a promised reward. Contracts are usually written agreements, but they are sometimes informal, spoken promises. Contracts are promises that you make to your fellow patients, the staff, and especially to yourself to change how you talk, act, and appear so that you can get out of the hospital sooner. Contracts can be a useful tool to help you get on and stay on the right track toward reaching your goal of getting out of the hospital. Contracts can also help you to understand and remember what you must do and say to convince the staff that you should be leaving the hospital.

ATTENDANCE

Every time you come to the group, you will improve at least a little bit. You can improve if you listen hard to what is said to other patients. Everything that is said to anyone has something to do with you and your problems. You are also helped when you talk to others to help them. You must listen hard and try to understand *and* remember whatever is said to you. Don't talk when the group is talking to you, but listen instead, because you learn more when you listen than when you talk. Time alone is not going to get you out of the hosptal. Your behavior, which others in your community did not like, got you in here. Your behavior, which others such as the staff and other patients like, will get you out of the hospital. So if you spend 5, 10, or even 20 years in the hospital, it is your fault, because you are acting, talking, and dressing crazy, and that is keeping you here.

Try to Remember

1. Attend as many group meetings as you can.
2. In the meetings, try hard to listen and remember what everyone says to you, and to other patients.
3. Try to help yourself and other patients by giving them advice.
4. *And most of all,* try to change yourself by remembering what you were told is keeping you in the hospital, so that you can get out as soon as possible.

If you do these things regularly and seriously, you will get a lot of help from the group, and the group will help you to be able to stay out of hospitals and jails after you leave the hospital.

The Synanon Game emphasizes direct confrontation much more than any other encounter group, and for this reason it is often called attack therapy. ("Attack" is an inaccurate description for the emotional tone of a game, because it implies aggressiveness and disinterest in the welfare of the person being "attacked." Considerable compassion and concern are usually shown throughout a game, and anyone not showing some warm and humane feelings is likely to be severely criticized.) In the game it is necessary to talk to someone, usually in the form of an indictment, and each indictment is expected to—and generally does—include substantial humane concern by the person doing the indicting for the person being indicted. Indictments may be criticisms of a member's inappropriate speech, actions, or appearance in the group, in any other Synanon activity, or, indeed, in any part of his personal life. As in most encounter groups, the usual indictment is for immoral actions, and the goal of these indictments is to help each member, the one being indicted as well as everyone else present, to recognize those aspects of his speech, actions, and appearance that are distasteful to others.

In addition, each indictment usually includes explicit and specific practical suggestions to each member on how he can change himself to eliminate his moral deficiencies and to make himself more acceptable to others. Every member of a game is expected to help the member who is being indicted. Valid game indictments are called "feeding information or data to the indicted person." Invalid game indictments are called "game noise."

Much of Synanon is closely related to the moral teachings of the distinguished nineteenth-century American philosopher, Ralph Waldo Emerson (van Doren, 1946). The Synanon Philosophy (Exhibit 6-3), a close adaptation of Emerson's words, is read verbatim before every Synanon group meeting. The philosophy is the guiding spirit for all games.

EXHIBIT 6-3

The Synanon Philosophy

The Synanon Philosophy is based on the belief that there comes a time in everyone's life when he arrives at the conviction that envy is ignorance, that imitation is suicide; that he must accept himself for better or worse as his portion; that though the wide universe is full of good, no kernel of nourishing corn can come to him but through his toil bestowed on that plot of ground which is given to him to till. The power which resides in him is new in nature, and none but he knows what it is that he can do, nor does he know until he has tried. Bravely let him speak the utmost syllable of his conviction. God will not have his work made manifest by cowards.

A man is relieved and gay when he has put his heart into his work and done his best: but what he has said or done otherwise shall give him no peace. As long as he willingly accepts himself, he will continue to grow and develop his potentialities. As long as he does not accept himself, much of his energies will be used to defend rather than to explore and actualize himself.

No one can force a person towards permanent and creative learning. He will learn only if he wills to. Any other type of learning is temporary and inconsistent with the self and will disappear as soon as the threat is removed. Learning is possible in an environment that provides information, the setting, materials, resources, and by his being there. God helps those who help themselves.

Thanks are due Charles Dederich, Chairman of Synanon Foundation, Tomales Bay, Marshall, California, for permission to quote the Synanon Philosophy.

The rules for playing the game (Exhibit 6-1) are few and simple. A member can and often does call another member any and all foul names, but no physical violence or threat of violence is permitted. A person who is being indicted can not defend himself, but is expected to listen attentively to game data, to learn about himself, and to make changes in the directions suggested to him by game indictments. The reason a person is not allowed to defend himself in a game is that when he is talking he is believed not to be learning, and therefore he cannot profit from information being given to him in the game. Frequently a person is told during the game that the Synanon Philosophy (Exhibit 6-3) states that "As long as he does not accept himself, much of his energies will be used to defend rather than to explore and actualize himself."

Synanon's emphasis on moral values in all aspects of life is quite similar to Jourard's focus (1964) on morality as the basis of emotional health. This emphasis is clearly illustrated in the Synanon Prayer, which is a key document highlighting much of Synanon thought:

The Prayer [2]

Please let me first and always examine myself
Let me be honest and truthful
Let me seek and assume responsibility
Let me understand rather than be understood
Let me trust and have faith in myself and my fellow man
Let me love rather than be loved
Let me give rather than receive

Admitting the validity (truthfulness) of indictments, listening to them, and trying to understand what is being said is the most important part of the game. A person can then make a commitment to the members in a game to change his speech and actions in the future so that he is no longer the kind of person others pictured him to be in the game. A commitment is a guideline for learning new behaviors and is quite appropriate to a social-learning viewpoint since the Camarillo group reinforces new socially suitable behaviors toward others in the token economy program, and later in the community.

The token economy adaptation of the Synanon Game is, as in most forms of behavior therapy, based on the belief that a person is responsible for his asocial and antisocial behaviors. He can also be expected to change unacceptable behaviors, partially because of group pressures in the social learning setting of the game. A patient's first contact with behavioral encountering may be in his reading of the token economy orientation from "Welcome to Unit 231" (pp. 64–68) excerpted below:

[2] Thanks are due Charles Dederich, Chairman of Synanon Foundation, Tomales Bay, Marshall, California, for permission to quote the Synanon Prayer.

Group Encounter Sessions

You can meet with other patients in a group encounter session . . . to discuss your problems and to help you to learn how to handle them better. Mr. Roy Jones . . . is in charge of the group. The group meets every Monday, Wednesday, and Friday from 1:30 to 3:00 in the afternoon. You can also join the *Patient's Group Sessions* on Tuesday, Thursday, and Saturday from 1:30 to 3:00. . . .

The group sessions are a good place to talk about your complaints about anything at all that bothers you. You can learn how to handle things better here in the hospital, and back in your community when you return. You won't be able to talk about your childhood or what other people, like your parents, did to you a long time ago. In these sessions you will be expected to be pretty smart and to learn to talk and act in the hospital so that you can get out sooner. You will also be expected to learn how to talk, act, and look in your community, so that you can stay out of the hospital after you leave it.

Game Relevance to Token Economy Treatment

The Synanon Game and every other behavioral treatment form can be considered a social-learning situation, and as such, descriptions of them belong in a token economy manual. The Synanon Game is especially important in Camarillo's program because it is extensively used as a major focus for social learning for the relatively aware psychotic patient. Psychologists, psychiatrists, social workers, and technicians conduct these sessions on each of the three units of the program. There are three sessions a week, each lasting about 1½ hours. The game is being modified to fit the special social training needs and the particular social repertoires typical of the highly unsocialized or asocial patient. The psychotic patient's awareness of his social inadequacies is the most important discussion area for him. Unlike the neurotic person living in his community, the psychotic patient often does not realize which of his behaviors are socially unacceptable to others in his community or even in the hospital. Often, one of the first steps in behavioral treatment is to get the patient to know what his target behaviors are, those behaviors whose change is of interest to the behavioral therapist, *and* to the patient.

The patient learns to recognize his unacceptable target behaviors in the following way. The professional staff members, who are the group leaders, tell the patient what others think of him for his actions. Other patients also tell him what he says and does that frightens or irritates them. In session after session the patient is pressured by the staff and other patients, who, after all, live with him, to recognize how he offends them and to see what he must do to change himself *if* he is to leave the hospital.

There is another major difference in the game for a relatively normal person and a psychotic one. The relatively normal person often needs only loose guidelines to use his new awareness of himself to decrease the likelihood (probability) that some previously frequent and socially undesirable behaviors will occur, and to increase the likelihood that some previously less frequent socially acceptable behaviors will occur. These changes are not too difficult for the normal person, because he generally has a large repertoire of socially acceptable behaviors, and simply must increase the probability that some of them will occur. In contrast, the psychotic person often lacks many fundamental social skills—even saying hello to others may be new to him—which he must learn, perhaps for the first time.

To help the psychotic patient gain these basic social skills, it is often useful to conduct role rehearsal sessions with him right in the encounter sessions. For example, a male patient totally lacking in social skills with females may be asked to initiate a conversation with a female staff member, and try to have her accept a date with him. The purpose of this role rehearsal is to have the patient learn to talk to a woman and to develop a social repertoire of appropriate responses to a woman, so that he is able to establish a relationship with a woman. And this relationship may become sexually gratifying to him in a socially acceptable way.

Self-Assertive Training

An example of social-learning training in the form of self-assertive training is the situation in which a shy patient is given short, self-assertive training sessions during an encounter meeting. He will be asked to choose the person whom he likes least in the group, and to tell that person the things that he dislikes most about him. These short group sessions tend to be more effective for the patient than equivalent individual sessions with a behavior therapist. The patient tends to profit more from self-assertive sessions when fellow patients are present, because their presence allows self-assertive training to have a broad range of social experiences, including many significant elements of the patient's daily life. And because social learning occurs in a setting that has many aspects in common with other areas of the patient's life, the patient may be able to generalize easily his new social learning to other settings.

In addition, these sessions are usually followed up by "homework assignments" that require the patient to repeat the same things that he learns in groups, outside the groups. The patient is usually well motivated to complete these assignments because he knows that he is then likely to gain the social skills that will enable him to get out of the hospital and stay out. His motivation is often increased because he promises his encounter group of fellow patients that he will fulfill his homework assignments.

Starting Encountering Games in Token Economy Programs

The average behaviorally oriented staff should have little difficulty instituting behavioral encounter groups—games in the Synanon fashion—as described here. Prior to beginning operations, there should be a careful reading of the encounter group literature, even nonbehavioral writings, such as Rogers (1970), to gain an understanding of the underlying principles. There should then be a clear agreement among staff members on the purposes of the encounter group, and how they see it fitting into the overall goals of the token economy program. Next an orientation form should be written for patients, so that the staff's ideas on the purposes of the group and the rules for the group can be clearly spelled out and communicated to patients and to other staff members. (Camarillo's orientation form for group encountering is presented in Exhibit 6-2.)

The group should begin with four or five relatively aware and articulate patients. Two staff members, one a technician and the other the staff member with the most knowledge about encountering techniques, should be present regularly. Other staff members should be rotated through the group, staying until they have some understanding of the operations of the group. This usually takes at least a month. In the meantime, additional patients should be added gradually until there are about ten patients in each session. Sessions should last from one to two hours. A debriefing meeting should follow each session so that staff members can discuss their evaluations of the session, and how future sessions might be improved.

After staff members feel comfortable about the group and its procedures, they should be asked to start groups of their own, with assistance from the program's group leader. Occasionally the leader may visit other groups and share his impressions of the other groups' functioning with their leaders. Literature, such as papers describing behavioral group approaches, should be shared and carefully studied, especially for their potential applications to the existing program. Outside experts should be brought in to consult with staff members and to assist with the program, so that the encounter groups continue to grow and develop, instead of becoming stagnant because the ideas and staff members involved do not change.

The point that is constantly stressed in every encounter group meeting is that the purpose of every meeting is to help each patient learn how to get out of the hospital as soon as possible and to stay out of hospitals and jails as much and as long as possible. Stressing this point makes for businesslike meetings because there are few digressions into discussions that are not directly and immediately relevant to helping the patient achieve these goals. In view of the emphasis on these goals, there is usually considerable resentment of any discussion of irrelevant material.

Purposeful discussions generally include such social-learning goals as getting along with other patients, with the hospital staff, and with others in the community after discharge. Discussion may also legitimately include the necessity for taking psychoactive medication after discharge, because failure to take medication is the leading reason for the usual ex-patient's responding inappropriately to others in his community, and then being readmitted to the hospital. Other patients are usually helpful in focusing discussion on suitable areas, and in helping the patient to reduce his inappropriate behaviors in favor of more appropriate ones.

In addition to verbal discussions and behavioral training sessions, the encounter group provides a ready and effective setting for another new treatment technique—the negotiated, written contract between the patient and the staff. And the encounter group is quite useful in checking on the patient's compliance with his contract, as described in the next section.

WRITTEN CONTRACTS

It may seem obvious by now that insight psychotherapy is based on the belief that when a patient understands his unconscious motivations for behaving inappropriately, he can, and does, relatively easily change his actions. Unfortunately, this understanding (insight) is usually not shown in settings other than the psychotherapy treatment room or after psychotherapy is ended, so that generalization usually does not occur (Eysenck, 1952).

Behavior therapy, too, may not produce generalization unless the therapist specifically trains or guides his patient to act appropriately in various settings. An example is the behavioral encounter group, which provides general guidelines for suitable behaviors in other hospital settings and in the community. The encounter group plus homework assignments—if fully and consistently carried out—are likely to aid generalization, but something more specific than either or both together is needed. The negotiated, written contract seems to fulfill this requirement for many reasons, some of them directly related to the motivation created by the manner in which the contract is negotiated between the patient and the staff. A contract also tends to be effective because the patient works closely with the staff in fulfilling its requirements, and is at all times under the close observation of fellow patients, who can come to have an interest in seeing that the patient follows his contract.

The following is a description of writing and negotiating a contract in the Camarillo program. A contract is practically always requested by a patient because he believes accurately that when the staff sign their names to a paper labeled "contract," he has some power over them. After some encouragement by the members of an encounter group telling the patient that a contract is a good thing to have, the patient generally asks the Camarillo program psychologist to give him a contract. When a patient asks for a contract, the psychologist is likely to ask him why he wants it, because only if a patient wants something specific from a contract is he likely to fulfill its requirements of him. A contract tends to be most effective if a patient wishes to leave the hospital, and if the contract has requirements of the patient that, if fulfilled by him, will require that the staff consider him for discharge.

Once the Camarillo psychologist is satisfied that a patient is motivated to obtain and fulfill a contract, the psychologist may ask the patient to write a rough draft of a contract, including what he will do to get what he wants from the token economy staff. The psychologist reads over this rough draft carefully and discusses it thoroughly with the involved staff members, usually the physician, social worker, head charge, and the group nursing leader. These and other interested staff members will then suggest items that they want the patient to fulfill and that they want included in his contract. The psychologist will then make these suggested changes in the patient's contract and present this new version to him. The patient might then agree to the changes or make some counter suggestions. If the patient offers some new ideas, the psychologist will return to the staff and see if these are acceptable to them. If they agree, he types up the contract and has all concerned sign it. A copy is then given to the patient and to all involved staff members. One copy is placed in the patient's hospital folder for permanent reference. A sample contract of "Mr. John Smith" is presented in Exhibit 6-4. Mr. Smith has a history of many years spent in jails and mental hospitals, and is now seeking staff approval to return to court as a first step toward living freely in his community.

EXHIBIT 6-4

Contract for Mr. John Smith

Date:_____

I, _____, John Smith, agree to fulfill the following conditions for 45 days, understanding that if I do fulfill them—faithfully, consistently, and without a break—I will then be considered for discharge by the staff:

1. I will clean the shower and dressing room every day.
2. I will sort laundry every evening.
3. I will keep neat and clean and shave daily.
4. I will help clean Dorm C and help make beds every day.
5. I will help clean in the kitchen every morning.
6. I will help clean up my dorm every morning.
7. I will attend Mr. Jones's encounter group meetings every Monday, Wednesday, and Friday afternoon at 1:30.

_____	_____
John Smith	Physician
_____	_____
Head Charge, Unit 231	Social Worker
_____	_____
Group Leader	Psychologist

Mr. Smith's contract was first negotiated between him and the psychologist, with consultations with the physician to find out how long Mr. Smith would have to show appropriate behavior before he would be considered for staff examination to evaluate his suitability for discharge from the hospital, and for a return to court. In addition, the psychologist carefully discussed Mr. Smith's case with the head charge, and with Smith's group nursing leader, to determine what other changes would have to be made in Mr. Smith's behavior if he were to be considered ready for discharge. The psychiatric social worker was also involved, and made suggestions about the kinds of behavior desired of the patient before he would be considered ready for discharge.

In effect, the psychologist was trying to specify Mr. Smith's current behavior so that the staff could know what to expect of him, and could effectively coordinate their efforts in training him. The staff knew what kinds of changes the patient would have to make in order for them to consider him suitable for discharge from the hospital and likely to be able to remain in his community. The contract then communicates this information directly to Mr Smith, *and* the staff provide him with the training means to fulfill contract stipulations. These training means include encounter groups, group and individual behavior modification sessions, anger training sessions, and especially day-to-day token economy social training. (See Exhibit 6-5 for another example of a written negotiated contract.)

EXHIBIT 6-5

Contract for Mr. Robert Brown

Date:_____

I, _____, Robert Brown, agree that I will fulfill the following conditions as part of my promotion from Dorm C to Dorm B. I understand that this promotion is one step on the way out of the hospital, and that I will not be considered for discharge from the hospital until I am promoted. I understand that I must do all of the following for 14 consecutive days, and if I miss a day that I must start the 14 days all over again.

1. I will work on an outside detail every day.
2. I will attend Mr. Jones's encounter group meetings every Monday, Wednesday, and Friday from 1:30 to 3:00 in the afternoon.
3. I will keep myself clean and neat.
4. I will try to talk more to get along well with other patients and the staff; and not lose control of myself when I get angry.
5. I will attend as many off-unit activities as possible.

Robert Brown	Physician
Head Charge, Unit 231	Social Worker
Group Leader	Psychologist

A contract is most helpful in teaching self-monitoring and self-controlling behavior to a patient who has great difficulty recognizing that he acts very differently from others in his community. A contract is an excellent way of helping the *motivated* person to become more aware of his behavior when he is not under the direct surveillance of others (which is most of the time), and therefore can help him to learn to control his behavior at all times. A meaningful contract can be written with any psychotic patient in a token economy unit provided that:

1. The patient is generally not delusional.
2. He is motivated to fulfill its conditions because it promises him something that he wants, and that the staff are quite capable of giving him.
3. He is able to read and write, and has at least fair intelligence.
4. He has some ability to control his behavior from moment to moment.
5. The unacceptable target behaviors focused on in the contract are those that are not acceptable to the patient's community, have some relevance to his hospitalization, and hamper his being considered dischargeable.
6. All staff members are aware of his contract, and cooperate with the patient and each other to help the patient to fulfill its conditions.

The contract should include:

1. Clear specification of exactly what is behaviorally desired of the patient in the hospital, *and* in his community. (It should require only that he talk, act, and dress in specified ways, and *not* ask that he change inner states, such as attitudes and opinions.)
2. Clear statement of the requirements of the patient and rewards to be given to him, such as the exact time period that he must behave appropriately.
3. Clear specification of penalties for explicitly stated undesirable behaviors.

When all negotiations have been completed, and the contract signed, it should be made as widely known as possible. Typically at Camarillo, each contract is posted publicly, and discussed openly and often in encounter groups. One copy is given to the patient to carry with him at all times, and another copy is placed in his permanent file. The staff should be informed of it, and the patient's responses to it should be discussed in staff meetings and informal conversations. Other patients should know about it, and their assistance be enlisted to help the patient to fulfill its requirements. Peer pressures tend to be far more effective than staff demands. This peer pressure tends to be most helpful when the contract is talked about in encounter groups, where violations may lead to group censure, and successful fulfillment lead to strong positive social approval. Other patients sometimes take the initiative in repeatedly explaining to the patient that he should fulfill the contract for his own good. These patients may tell him, especially with Camarillo staff prompting, that the purpose of the contract is to change his behavior in the hospital *and* in his community, so that he can get out of the hospital and stay out. And it is reasonable to assume that if the patient fulfills his hospital contract, and is given a similar one by a community institution, such as a board-and-care or nursing home, he is also likely to fulfill that contract.

We are now beginning to write short-term, simple contracts covering only one antisocial behavior for one day. We are in the very beginnings of the one-day contract so that it is not possible to detail any procedures or other suggestions. Even with this small amount of experience, the short-term contract seems to show great promise with the relatively aware and uncontrolled patient, and seems to help him to learn how to negotiate and fulfill more complicated, longer-term contracts.

Instituting Written Contracts

Learning to negotiate and write contracts is likely to be one of the easisest and most attractive tasks to most token economy staffs. Every staff member has experience with a written contract for a house, car, apartment, or loan, and the reasonableness of contracts in a token economy program will seem obvious to each staff member. After some discussion of the purpose and procedures in negotiating and writing a contract, one staff member should be asked to volunteer to work with a patient on a contract. The staff member should have a choice of any patient with whom he wishes to work on a contract. The staff member should be careful to consult with other staff members during the process to get their opinions, particularly if one of them is quite knowledgeable about written contracts.

After the first contract is written, there should be careful monitoring by all staff members of the progress of the patient. Does he conform to the requirements of the contract, and how does his behavior seem to compare to what it was prior to writing the contract? Then another staff member should try writing a contract. Contract writing should progress in this fashion until every staff member has at least one contract operating at all times. Every staff meeting should have some time set aside for discussing contracts, and every patient who is talked about should either be evaluated for his progress in his contract or his suitability for having a contract negotiated with him. No patient should have more than one contract, but all relatively aware patients should be offered the opportunity to have one. As new staff members are brought in, they should be trained and encouraged to write contracts with patients.

SUMMARY

Emphasis on new and creative token economy techniques is important because programs must be able to change constantly to meet new and varied patient problems in a quite unstable society. Each patient will be called upon to cope with many social situations in his community, and the situations are not predictable at this point. New techniques will have to be devised on a continuing basis if token economy is to be able to deal with many patient problems. The results of all of these technical changes should be carefully recorded with numerical data so that behavior therapy, unlike traditional insight therapy, knows what behavior change techniques work, how well, and under what conditions.

One new technique is modeling and behavioral rehearsal, which enables a patient to see exactly what kinds of speech and behaviors are being asked of him by the behavior therapist and his fellow patients, any of whom can act as a model. He is then asked to duplicate what he sees, and to perform in these ways in other hospital settings. Then the behavior therapist and fellow patients in the group can monitor his efforts, and reinforce him for correct performances. Role modeling and behavioral-rehearsal can be instituted by having the staff decide what new behaviors they want, and by having them coordinate their efforts. Another new technique is anger training sessions, which attempt to help the physically aggressive patient to learn to respond with words instead of with his fists, and to tolerate more frustration than he was able to previously. In these sessions the patient is verbally attacked, and he is desensitized while being given verbal rather than physical means of responding to his attacker. Many group sessions are needed to accomplish change in this most difficult and important area. Anger training groups can be started by searching the literature, choosing patients carefully for their motivation, and following a systematic, step-by-step procedure. Anger training should be carefully integrated with other aspects of token economy training.

The encounter group, while originating from traditional insight therapy, has much in common with behavior therapy in focusing on the here-and-now of emotions, and in the assumption of responsibility for changing future actions rather than dwelling on past or unconscious problems. Moral questions of appropriate responses to others form the core of encounter groups, and are directly relevant to changing actions in the future. The Synanon Game is heavily used in Camarillo's program, and Synanon's history, especially the game, are described in detail. The Synanon Game Rules, Philosophy, and Prayer are presented.

The substantial differences between neurotics and psychotics have great relevance for adapting an encounter group to a mental hospital setting. The psychotic patient often needs to learn which of his behaviors offend others in his community, since these behaviors may lead to his rehospitalization. He must also be helped in the group to change these actions in the hospital and in his community. The staff and the other patients use the encounter sessions to inform, change, and to provide behavioral rehearsal opportunities for the patient, all designed to help him to be discharged from the hospital, and to remain in his community. Self-assertive training may also be given in the group, with homework assignments for all patients to perform new ways of behaving outside of sessions so that they can master these new social skills.

Starting a new behavioral encounter group in a token economy program requires that staff agree on the purposes of the group, and its integration into the overall token economy program. There should be a written orientation form and rules for the group should be clearly spelled out. Staff members should actively participate in the groups, first by learning about them and then by running their own groups. A debriefing meeting should be held after every group session to enable learning and communication to occur between staff members.

The written negotiated contract is of considerable value to Camarillo's program, for it enables a patient to indicate exactly what he wants from the staff and what he is willing to do to get these things. The staff, in turn, can specify what they expect from the patient, how they will reward him if he fulfills their expectations, and how they will punish him for violations of token economy rules. The conditions under which a contract can and should be written are detailed. Mention is made of the promising potential of the one-day, one-behavior contract.

SUGGESTED READINGS

Role Modeling

These are the two major books on role modeling from a behavioristic viewpoint:

Bandura, A. *Principles of behavior modification.* New York: Holt, Rinehart and Winston, 1969.
Bandura, A. (Ed.). *Psychological modeling.* Chicago, Ill.: Aldine-Atherton, 1971.

These are three important writings on the use of role modeling in group therapy:

Mowrer, O. H., The behavior therapies, with special reference to modeling and imitation. *American Journal of Psychotherapy*, 1966, *20*, 439–461.
Mowrer, O. H. *The new group therapy.* Princeton, N.J.: D. Van Nostrand, 1964.
Ullmann, L. P. Making use of modeling in the therapeutic interview. Paper read at the Association for the Advancement of Behavior Therapy Meeting, San Francisco, 1968. (Mimeograph)

Behavioral Treatment of Sexual Disorders

Bancroft, J. Aversion therapy of homosexuality. *British Journal of Psychiatry*, 1969, *115*, 1417–1431. Obtained only one success from electrical aversive treatment of homosexuals. Discussion of methodological and ethical problems involved.

Barker, J., & Miller, M. Some clinical applications of aversion therapy. In H. Freeman (Ed.), *Progress in behavior therapy*. Bristol, England: Wright & Sons, 1968. Reviews case studies of aversion therapy with sexual deviates, criminals, and obese persons.

Brady, J. P. Brevital-relaxation treatment of frigidity. *Behaviour Research and Therapy*, 1966, *4*, 71–77. Describes use of Brevital to induce relaxation, and reports success.

Evans, D. R. An exploratory study into the treatment of exhibitionism by means of emotive imagery and aversive conditioning. *Canadian Psychologist*, 1967, *8*, 161.

Jackson, B. T. A case of voyeurism treated by counterconditioning. *Behaviour Research and Therapy*, 1969, 7, 133–134.

Lazarus, A. A. The treatment of a sexually inadequate man. In L. P. Ullman & L. Krasner (Eds.), *Case studies in behavior modification*. New York: Holt, Rinehart and Winston, 1965. A 33-year-old impotent man was systematically desensitized so that he became sexually adequate.

Marks, I. M. Aversion therapy. *British Journal of Medical Psychology*, 1968, *41*, 47–52. A review of the use of aversion therapy with sexual deviates.

Marks, I. M., & Gelder, M. G. Transvestism and fetishism: Clinical and psychological changes during faradic aversion. *British Journal of Psychiatry*, 1967, *113*, 711–729.

Wagner, M. K. A case of public masturbation treated by operant conditioning. *Journal of Child Psychology and Psychiatry*, 1968, *9*, 61–67.

CHAPTER 7

Setting Up a New Behavioral Token Economy or Non–Token Economy Program

INTRODUCTION

Chapters 1 to 6 describe programs at Camarillo and elsewhere, and some of the major principles involved in their working well or poorly. The reader is assumed to be quite interested in token economy, usually because he suddenly finds himself working in one. Or perhaps he plans to set one up, and is interested in what should be done to have a successful, effective program. The following discussion is designed for the reader with little or no experience in a program, so that he will be able to organize a new program. If he has a behavioral background, it will be that much easier for him to create a new program, with the guidelines provided here.

There is every reason to believe that a new and good program could be set in a place that is totally different from Camarillo. Instead of being a state mental hospital, it could be a community hospital, and, indeed, it could even be in other than a mental hospital setting, such as a correctional institution. Guidelines are proposed here that should be adaptable to any suitable institutional context so that a good program can be set up.

The steps required for setting up a new program, and how they might be accomplished are discussed in Table 7-1 and in the remainder of this chapter.

The particular formal background, or lack thereof, should not make it impossible for a well-motivated, capable person to set up a new token economy program. While Camarillo's and most programs are based on the work of a psychologist acting as leader and coordinator of the program, other disciplines, or even a non-formally trained person, should be able to organize and operate a token economy program. If the person has no formal training, he will have to work quite hard to learn about behavior therapy in general, and token economy in particular. He will be helped by any mental hospital experience; preferably in a behavioral program. He will probably have to be quite intelligent, articulate, and exceedingly energetic. If he does not have a degree of any kind, he may have difficulty functioning as an authority figure with physicians, technicians, and a psychologist, who might resent his having administrative power. He may then also have to work hard to get higher administration to support the program with extra staff, facilities, and funds.

TABLE 7-1 Outline of Steps for Organization and Operation
of a New Token Economy Program

Step	Procedure for accomplishment
1. Select an organizer-coordinator	Consultations of organizing committee, including higher administration
2. Obtain commitments from higher administration for necessary staff, facilities, and funds	Consultations with higher administration
3. Select a program coordinator	Either elected or appointed by organizing committee higher administration
4. Obtain approval for needed staff, facilities, and funds	Consultations between coordinator and higher administration
5. Select needed staff and facilities	Personnel screening of future staff members and consultation with higher administration
6. Define day-to-day program operations	Coordination of all staff efforts. Program leader works in concert with other staff members

The first goal in organizing a program is to get higher administration—such as the chief administrator, and the highest ranking physician, if these are different persons—to be willing to give strong support in providing priority allocations of staff, facilities, and funds. These administrators should understand the need for choosing good staff, especially at the beginning of the program, and providing time and resources to train staff in behavioral techniques. If higher administration is not supportive of the program, or, even worse, if it is hostile toward it, this in itself may be enough reason to not consider a token economy program at this time. Instead, the persons involved in planning the token economy program, might consider how and when they can get strong support from higher administration, and begin their program then. Other shortages can be overcome— qualified staff, if not available, can be developed, facilities and funds can be stretched—but the lack of adequate support from higher administration makes the program too vulnerable to problems and criticism, so that demoralization of the staff and poor performance are difficult to avoid and overcome.

The question of criticism is especially important at this time, for behavior therapy and token economy are frequently unfairly attacked (as discussed in Ethical, Moral, and Legal Considerations in Chapter 5). This situation may prevail for the next few years. And so, the staff will need a great deal of encouragement and protection from this criticism, if they are to work effectively and feel that they are genuinely appreciated by the persons who count on them. The Camarillo program is particularly favored, because the first hospital administrator had considerable experience with a token economy program and believed in it. The second administrator, while not experienced with token economy, is also quite supportive of it. This is important because of serious financial constraints on all programs, token economy and otherwise, and token economy staff can then understand that they are not being discriminated against in any way.

TRADITIONAL INSIGHT THERAPY APPROACHES

My view in working with new staff members and students is to request that they never use traditional insight approaches in the Camarillo program. There are several reasons for this position. Learning and practicing behavior therapy takes a great deal of effort, and requires discipline, and can easily become confusing to the practitioner if he mixes it with traditional approaches. For example, if while conducting a behavioral encounter session, he uses insight therapy, the thrust and vigor of the session tends to be diluted by discussions of the past, and whether or not the patient is "really" responsible for his actions. If he sometimes uses insight techniques and other times uses behavior techniques, he tends to lose sight of what common principles of treatment are involved. It is far better to be consistent and clear about the goals of treatment, the techniques to be used, and problems involved from a behavioral viewpoint, than to try to change all of these when a patient does not respond to one behavioral approach.

A change can be readily made from one behavioral approach to another one, and there are many advantages to such a change. If a patient proves unresponsive to one form of behavior therapy, the kind of behavioral approach should be changed. The patient gains from this change by generally improving the rate of acquisition of new social skills. The therapist, too, gains by learning how to choose a new set of behavior therapy tasks for a patient, and how to transfer the patient from the old tasks to the new ones. Even when quite effective, a behavior therapy program must be frequently changed to maintain its effectiveness, as suggested in Chapter 5, the section Individual Behavior Modification. In contrast, when all forms of behavior therapy are discarded in favor of traditional approaches, both the therapist and his patient seem to become confused. (For a short, interesting discussion of a few of the disadvantages of mixing behavioral and traditional approaches, see Wolpe, 1971. A contrasting viewpoint is presented by Lazarus, 1971, in his support of technical eclecticism, a mixing of traditional and behavioral approaches.)

FACILITATING AND HANDICAPPING CONDITIONS FOR SUCCESS

There are many reasons for considering characteristics of a successful token economy program, because no one would like to organize or operate a failing program.[1] And there are many reports of token economy programs that do not work and are discontinued. Even at Camarillo there is a failure case due to poor staff motivation, inadequate leadership, and lack of understanding about what a token economy program does and does not do.

Token economy is a new approach to patient treatment, and is continuously dependent on the staff to try innovative behaviorally-oriented ways of working with each patient. For example, a psychiatric technician may be accustomed to caring primarily for the physical needs of the patient, and the technician may not wish to assume the responsibilities of being a behavior modifier–social trainer. The average technician with many years of experience invested in learning traditional approaches is often reluctant to change his approaches at this time in his working career. Traditional programs provide beds, meals, ground privileges, and other needs and pleasures, noncontingently for each patient. In

---

[1] Evaluation of the effectiveness of any token economy program is difficult. Behavior therapy, like traditional therapy, may be successful or unsuccessful for reasons that have nothing to do with treatment. A patient may receive rewards or punishments without any control by the therapist or even his knowledge, and so the outcome of treatment may be due to circumstances not related to treatment. While it is difficult to use outcome to evaluate treatment effects, in the final analysis outcome *must* be the only way that any treatment program can be evaluated. It should be noted that outcome is easier to evaluate for behavior therapy than for traditional therapy because of behavior therapy's emphasis on observable aspects of personality. And the observable—such as speech, actions, and appearance—is far easier to recognize and measure than the unobservable—such as thoughts and emotions.

contrast, a token economy program in not fulfilling these needs and pleasures *unless* a patient earns them often leads to a technician resenting what he sees as unfair treatment of the patient. If the technician does not understand and is unwilling to learn that it is in the best interests of the patient that he earn these program privileges, the technician is a liability in any token economy program and will be quite unhappy there. He is also likely to complain and criticize the program a great deal, which can lower morale. For this reason, any staff member who finds this work distasteful should be transferred, without prejudice, to a preferred program. And all staff members should be aware of the availability of other program assignments if they wish to have them. A staff member should not be forced to work in a token economy setting against his will, because he is then unlikely to believe in it and will probably not be a constructive, useful member of the team.

Since it is better to avoid problems than to have to solve them once they occur, it is wise for the program leader to make all difficult and unpleasant aspects of the program clear *in advance* to all potential staff members. (An excellent description of token economy administrative problems and their handling is provided by Ball, 1969.) This same reasoning should be used in presenting new procedures to the staff. They should be carefully informed in advance of new procedures that may be used to deal with problems, and asked for their input in solving problems. When these solutions are implemented as new procedures, the leader should be careful to communicate to the staff that he is not trying to make their jobs more difficult, but that additional requests are being made of them *only* to improve the effectiveness of the program.

As noted previously, cooperation of high-level administrators is essential if the program is to work (Bugh, 1969), by providing necessary personnel, funds, and facilities. Administrators are most likely to support a new program if one or more such programs are currently functioning successfully, *and* if appropriate staff, funding, and physical facilities are available for a new program. These administrators are unlikely to support a new token economy program if there is none in the hospital, especially if a program has failed, or if no high-level administrator has experience with a successful program.

STAFF SELECTION AND TRAINING

The most important characteristic of a suitable staff member of a new token economy program is motivation to make that program succeed. Second, he should know his job well, be he the psychologist, psychiatrist, technician, social worker, or rehabilitation counselor. It is not necessary for a new staff member to be knowledgeable about behavior therapy in general or token economy in particular. He can be taught on the job. Indeed, an intensive, continuing staff development program should be maintained for all staff members.

The motivation of all staff members *and* their cooperation and compatibility are important in staff selection and training, because the program can only be effective when it covers all of the waking hours of every patient, seven days a week. A single nonconformist staff member, who may be hostile to other staff members, can easily sabotage the best efforts of all of the other members of the team. For example, if most of the staff is trying to reduce the frequency of one antisocial behavior by time-out or aversive techniques, and another staff member is reinforcing that same behavior, it will continue. For this reason, any team member who becomes disenchanted with token economy, for whatever reason, should be helped to find another position in the hospital.

Organizer-Leader Roles

Of all disciplines involved in token economy, the psychologist with behavior therapy training in graduate school, working experience in a token economy program, and research interests is probably the best suited to organize a new token economy program. A technician with a strong background and interest in token economy may be a good choice. A physician might well handle the task, especially if he has experience working in a token economy program. The psychiatric social worker might need more experience and training because graduate school and most field placements in social work are usually psychoanalytically oriented, and this is almost completely the opposite of behavior therapy. A reader who is not well informed about behavior therapy, but has a good traditional therapy background, such as a social worker, should do some extensive preliminary reading before trying to start a token economy program. It is a distinct advantage to have at least a year of mental hospital experience and good theoretical and applied background in behavior therapy before trying to organize a new token economy program.

If a reader lacks experience in a behavioral setting, but knows behavior therapy well, has hospital experience, and is strongly motivated, he should be able to start an effective token economy program. One of the problems that he will have to face is having to know what is happening with every patient at all times of the day or night. (It is quite common in many token economy programs that some staff member, at some unusual time, is doing something with an especially difficult patient that reduces significantly the impact of all of the other efforts of the rest of the staff.) The reader will have to work quite hard on any new token economy program to make it work right. He is likely to find this experience quite rewarding professionally, but it will not be easy.

Assume that the program is about the size of Camarillo's: about 60 patients and about 25 staff members—1 psychologist, 1 psychiatrist or general physician, 20 psychiatric technicians, 1 psychiatric social worker, and 1 rehabilitation counselor. (This personnel roster does not include necessary clerical, janitorial, and culinary support services.) The program organizer must be unusually patient, understanding, and well disciplined because he will not be able to afford himself the luxury of personal conflict with any staff member. The following material describes a few of the responsibilities of each discipline. The organizer, whatever his discipline, is expected to fulfill manager-coordinator responsibilities for the whole team.

One way of choosing a leader might be to have the group decide on a temporary coordinator for a given period of time, say the first 90 days of planning and implementation. At the end of that period the group can then make another decision as to who will serve next and for how long. This procedure has the advantage of involving all of the staff in the selection process so that there is an explicit commitment to work well with whoever becomes coordinator. And the coordinator, in accepting this role, commits himself to work closely with those who elect him. The limited tenure period also enables change to be made in relatively smooth fashion, with an opportunity to save the pride of a coordinator who is not satisfactory to other team members. Necessary leadership changes can thus be made quite easily and relatively soon, before serious damage is done to the program.

Psychologist

This discussion assumes that the psychologist will act as organizer and leader of the new token economy program, as is the case at Camarillo. This is not necessarily the case, however, for there may be members of other disciplines who have the background, motivation, and personal characteristics to do a far better job than the psychologist. Indeed, it may be that in many community or state mental hospitals, it is better if some other member of the team acts as organizer of the program. For example, a psychologist who has great difficulty working closely with others when he must assume responsibility for coordinating all of their efforts should not be either the organizer or the leader of the program.

In general, as noted earlier, a psychologist is the most likely person to be a program organizer-leader because behavior therapy, and advances in it, are based essentially on the work of psychologists. And most psychologists are taught a great deal about behavior therapy in school, which is generally not true of any other discipline. (The key working roles of the psychologist in terms of other staff members' work are discussed in Chapter 2, the section Roles of the Camarillo Psychologist, and in Chapter 1.) It is important that the psychologist, if he acts as leader, be knowledgeable about behavior therapy, because he must be a technical resource person who can provide practical advice on how all other team members can most effectively handle the unusually difficult patient.

The program leader must be able to understand the problems presented to the staff by the patient who is difficult to treat, and to formulate these problems in behavioristic terms. Then he must be able to search the literature to find out how other behavior therapists dealt with this same problem. He must then communicate his findings to other staff members in a practical, useful way so that they can all work together, pooling the suggestions in the literature with their own ideas to work effectively with this patient. All staff members will thus become more competent to treat similar patients efficiently and easily in the future. All of these responsibilities of the team leader involve considerable sophistication in knowing how to use the behavioristic literature, diplomatically communicating his findings to others, and evaluating the results so that all involved can profit from the process. These efforts are vital to a growing, meaningful token economy program that can adapt itself to a wide variety of patient problems and special community conditions so that the unusual, as well as the usual, patient can be discharged from the hospital to *remain* in his community.

The psychologist-leader must be heavily involved in the program, often working closely with the most trying and physically dangerous patient so that the staff do not think of him as a person who tells them what to do, but does nothing very hard or useful himself. He should be a person who daily demonstrates his expertise in a congenial, authoritative, but not authoritarian, way, so that the staff like and trust him. He should be a pleasant person who is reluctant to criticize other staff members, and who is quick to provide them with substantial encouragement to increase their motivation and effectiveness as behavior modifiers. It is a terse, true, and timely watchword for a psychologist in a token economy program: *Reinforce the reinforcers.*

If the psychologist is the leader, it is best that he be strongly motivated before he attempts to set up a new token economy program. He will be in a better position to do so if he has firsthand experience in working in a program, especially as its leader, than if his knowledge is secondhand, obtained through reading, class work, or by visiting other programs. He is likely to be a better leader if he has strong research interests, because this probably means that he is motivated and able to keep up on the literature, reporting the latest developments in token economy. He can therefore keep the rest of the staff abreast of improved techniques in the field.

The psychologist-leader is important as a role model, demonstrating to other staff members effective patient treatment. He should be quite energetic and willing to work long and unusual hours, for example, because he may have to see how patients who are awake are being handled at 2:00 A.M. He should be personally flexible and able to work in settings other than a professional office. The site of a patient's problem is generally the best place to modify the patient's inappropriate social behaviors into more appropriate forms. The psychologist may work in a dayroom or even a bathroom, if these are the places where a patient responds inappropriately to others—a patient can best learn to respond appropriately to others in these places by being trained there. Later, the psychologist can work with his patient in other settings to help him to generalize his improved social strategies to other persons in still other settings. All of these steps are part of the social training process for helping the patient to develop a suitable social repertoire in the hospital for later community living.

The psychologist often teaches (whether he is the leader of the program or not) many aspects of behavior therapy to other staff members as part of their daily working assignments. (All of these work roles are described in Chapter 2, the section Roles of Camarillo Psychiatric Technicians; Chapter 3, the sections In-service Training for Practice, Academic Credits, and Research, and Staff Research Potentialities and Roles; and Chapter 4, the sections Patient Orientation, Patient Assessment, and Evaluation of Reinforcements.) The psychologist should avoid teaching in an abstract, academic way, and should instead focus on what other staff members of all disciplines have to do with every patient, and how they can do these things most easily and effectively. In effect, the psychologist's teachings should concentrate on what other staff members must do on their jobs, and must know to do their jobs well, instead of trying to educate them in behavior therapy for any other reason.

Much of the psychologist's teaching will occur when he acts as a consultant to other staff members to modify target behaviors of a patient of interest to them. Often the psychologist may act as a consultant to the token economy psychiatrist, requesting a change of medication when a patient is not responding suitably to therapy. Typically, the overmedicated patient may be too sedated and not fully responsive to social training sessions. The delusional patient may not be receiving enough of the right kind of medication to reduce his delusions so that he can be aware of the therapist and therapy.

The psychologist often assumes liaison responsibilities with higher administration to obtain support for the program. For example, the hospital administrator may help in providing funding and facilities, and the nursing coordinator can provide satisfactory technicians. The hospital administrator can often authorize the large amounts of printing and photocopying that must be done.

An orientation form, such as the one presented in Chapter 4, is often the responsibility of the psychologist. An orientation form should be given to every patient upon entering the program. The usual patient has no experience with a token economy program, and needs to know what is expected of him and what he can expect of the staff. If he has no previous experience in a mental hospital and is quite fearful, the orientation form may help to reduce his fears by informing him that no unreasonable demands will be made of him.

The role of the psychologist as team coordinator is illustrated in the writing of the orientation form, which provides a pattern that can be useful in writing other materials for a program. The psychologist may ask the social worker, head charge, psychiatrist, and rehabilitation counselor to write a description of their work as might be seen from the patient's point of view. Typically, the psychologist asks the head charge what token economy rules he would like each patient to know about, and what privileges are available to each patient. Then the psychologist puts all of this information together and has each staff member read it. The psychologist revises the form according to suggestions made by other team members, so that the staff can agree on what the patient can expect of them, and what they want from him, as noted above. In effect, the orientation form is a first general contract between the staff and a new patient, so that the patient can begin new social learning in the program (Ulmer, 1970b).

Psychiatric Technicians (Nurses)

The day-to-day work of modifying a patient's behavior is primarily the responsibility of psychiatric technicians (nurses). The effect of technicians working with a given patient is generally far more important than that of a psychologist, even when the psychologist works intensively twice a day, seven days a week with the same patient. For no matter how much time a psychologist may spend with a patient, most of the patient's time will be spent with technicians and reinforcements will come from technicians. For this reason, technicians can make or break any token economy program. For a full discussion of this issue in an ongoing program, see Chapter 2, the section Roles of Camarillo Psychiatric Technicians and Chapter 3, the section Training of Psychiatric Technicians.

It is especially important that the head charge of all technicians be enthusiastic about a new token economy program, for he must select staff for the program, most of whom are likely to have no experience in a behavior therapy treatment setting. If a charge is enthusiastic about the program, he is likely to select and train his staff behavioristically and suitably for the program. If the charge is neutral or even worse, hostile to token economy, there is no realistic likelihood of success for the program. It is not necessary that the charge be knowledgeable about token economy, but it is essential that he have some commitment to his work—above and beyond getting a paycheck—and that he be motivated to learn and grow in his job. And it is particularly important that the program leader work closely with the charge to have him supervise his staff carefully so that they work behavioristically, rather than traditionally. Another problem to be avoided is having technicians simply warehouse every patient by caring for his physical needs, but not working to prepare each patient to return to community living.

The leader may suggest readings to the charge and his staff, such as token economy manuals, papers, and books. (These references are listed in the Suggested Readings at the ends of the chapters and in the General References, Behavioral and Token Economy Bibliographies and Token Economy Manuals, and Selected Journals Publishing Behaviorally Oriented Research at the end of this book.) Technicians may not do this reading because they are too busy or dislike reading. The leader should work closely with the charge and other technicians to help them to treat effectively the patient who is particularly difficult or dangerous. In this way the program leader can constantly communicate to technicians new ways of dealing with old problems of every patient who is not progressing in the program. This innovative role of the leader is vital in a new program, and can only be accomplished with involved and motivated staff who wish to improve their skills.

Psychiatrists and Other Hospital Physicians

Traditionally the clinical psychiatrist is psychoanalytically oriented and, therefore, unsuitable to function as a token economy organizer or leader. This situation is rapidly changing, with the development of more psychiatric interest in behavioral techniques and an occasional psychiatrist becoming fully committed to behavioral therapy (as described in Training of Psychiatric Residents in Chapter 3.) The nonbehavioral psychiatrist can work quite well on a behavioral team if he fully supports its principles, as is the case in the Camarillo program. A few token economy programs—both successful and unsuccessful ones—are founded by psychiatrists.

By custom, a psychiatrist is the administrative leader of any kind of mental hospital program. This practice is definitely changing, but it is reasonable to assume that for the foreseeable future a physician will be the head of the usual token economy program in a state or community mental hospital. The psychiatrist should be supportive of, if not knowledgeable about, behavior therapy and token economy, if the program is to succeed. If he is oriented toward traditional insight psychotherapy, he can easily subvert the morale and motivation of other staff members. If the physician supports the program, he can use his medical expertise to assist the program considerably. The physician prescribes all psychoactive drugs, and these are so central to token economy treatment that it is important that the physician understand exactly what the social problems and goals of therapy are with each patient, and that he be sympathetic to these goals.

If the team leader is not the psychiatrist, it is essential that the leader work closely with the psychiatrist, because he is generally the final authority in determining when a patient will be discharged from the hospital. (For this reason, the physician is always a signatory to a contract, as shown in Exhibits 6-4 and 6-5.) When discharge is involved in any contract, the psychologist, the team leader, and the chief staff negotiator of the contract must carefully discuss with the physician the behavioral changes that will have to be shown by the patient before the physician will consider discharging him. Typically, the Camarillo psychologist and the psychiatrist come to clear agreement on which kinds of socially appropriate behaviors should be shown by a patient, and especially which should not, before the psychiatrist will sign a contract committing himself to *considering* a patient for discharge. ("Considering" a patient for discharge means that the staff will evaluate him, and does *not* mean that he will automatically be discharged if he fulfills his contract. The difference between considering and discharging is important, because the staff are then honestly appropriately able to determine whether the patient is now showing some new and unpredictable socially unacceptable behaviors that contraindicate discharge. If this is the case, the patient can be retained in the hospital without the staff losing his confidence and that of other patients in the program.) If the psychologist and the psychiatrist have a good relationship, as is definitely the case in Camarillo, the issues themselves can be discussed easily and directly without underlying personal antagonisms, and an amicable agreement is usually quickly reached.

Psychiatric Social Workers

The Camarillo social worker functions full time on a unit of about 60 patients, although this may not be the case in other programs. While much of the social work training is traditionally psychoanalytic, this situation is changing rapidly—as is the case for clinical psychiatry—and behavioral approaches are increasingly being taught. Whatever a social worker's background, if he is willing to learn, and to commit himself to, behavior therapy, he can become a distinct asset to the program. It is important to discuss carefully with any prospective social work staff member the need to follow consistently behavioristic assessment and treatment principles. If the potential staff member does not agree, then as with any other potential staff member who does not wish to be part of the token economy program, it is much better for all concerned if the social worker does not join the staff. It is much easier, more efficient, and certainly fairer to discuss job requirements honestly, fully, and forthrightly in advance, than to be "diplomatic and devious" and create many problems later on.

There are many problems that are predictable if a social worker is not behaviorally oriented. If the social worker is committed to insight rather than behavior therapy, the "behavioral" encounter group is likely to discuss unconscious motivation rather than overt behavior. This same kind of problem is also likely to arise in writing contracts if the social worker believes that unconscious factors must be considered rather than overt behavior. It is becoming increasingly easier to find a behaviorally trained social worker because of the changes now taking place in social work training programs which are placing greater emphasis on behavior therapy and less on traditional therapy. This behavioristic influence is beginning to penetrate social work practice, so that sometimes the psychoanalytically involved social worker becomes interested in learning behavior therapy. And such a person can become quite valuable in a new token economy program.

ORGANIZING AND OPERATING A NEW CANTEEN

The importance of the canteen can hardly be overemphasized, because it provides much of the motivation for each patient to change his old, socially inappropriate ways of behaving for new, more socially acceptable ones. Funding of the canteen is therefore necessary, and if neither higher administration nor other sources can provide a dependable source of money for the canteen, serious consideration should be given to dropping all immediate plans for having a token economy program. The cost of the canteen is about 5¢ per day per patient, and about $1.50 per month per patient. In a program of about 65 patients, the overall cost will be approximately $100 per month.

The daily Camarillo operations, procedures, and problems are discussed in Chapter 4, the section The Token Economy Canteen, which should be carefully reread at this point. The goal of this present section is to provide some general guidelines for setting up an effective token economy canteen in a setting that may be quite different from Camarillo's. Some of the problems are likely to be similar whatever the setting. An occasional patient can be expected to steal, so that some relatively dependable procedure must be developed to thwart stealing. A large variety of desirable goods must be available in the canteen to give value to tokens, and they must be changed from time to time so that the patient does not get bored with canteen goods. A large supply of tokens must be obtained to start the program, with additional tokens constantly added to compensate for about 10 percent of them lost monthly. A record-keeping system is needed so that every patient and staff member can learn at any time how many tokens a patient has on his carry-around card, how much he earns with each effort, and the number of tokens he has in his bank account.

What the tokens are made of makes little difference. They can be wooden or plastic, and of any colors. They need not be fancy in any way. All that counts is that the less expensive they are the better, and the best situation is to have someone donate them to the program. The token carry-around card (Figure 4-1) provides the patient and the staff with a dependable record of how many tokens the patient earns and spends each day. The card is in his name, carried with him at all times, and all transactions must be signed by a staff member, so that stealing can be virtually eliminated.

The token carry-around card is then brought by the patient to the canteen, where the bank account cards are kept in a small box. Each patient's bank balance is then available during any canteen transaction. When a patient accumulates enough tokens on his token carry-around card, they can be transferred to his bank account card (Figure 4-2). And when he is promoted to a higher dorm, or needs tokens for daily living, these transactions can be noted on both his bank account card and carry-around card.

Purchases for the canteen should be made through large wholesale or discount outlets where damaged, out-of-fashion, or other less than first-rate goods are available. The cost is likely to be between one-tenth and one-fifth of what is charged in regular retail stores. Cigarettes are a prime example of possible savings. Cigarette papers and tobacco in large cans can be bought. These provide cigarettes at about one-fifth the cost of ready-made ones. Money savings are essential today because all levels of government have few funds to supply, and token economy, being more expensive to run than traditional programs, must cut costs wherever possible. (Token economy is a tremendous saver of hospital costs in getting chronic and short-term patients out much sooner than is the case in traditional programs, but a new token economy program will probably have to answer many challenging questions about set-up and operational costs *before* it can justify its existence on the basis of effectiveness of treatment.)

The best place for the canteen may be a small room reserved for its goods, papers, and with a counter over which to conduct business with each patient. Times can be set up in the early afternoon and just after dinner each evening so that every patient can get to the canteen to take care of business. (Even if a patient is working away from the program during the day, he can then still get to the canteen in the evening.) Each patient stands in line, and when he comes to the counter, he conducts business with the technician, asking for what he wants, such as pointing to the kind of candy he prefers. The canteen and canteen time should not be the place to pay any patient for his work. (Camarillo's procedure is a poor one of sometimes paying a patient in the canteen line. He is asked what work he does, and is then reinforced for it. But since this occurs some hours after the desired act, the effectiveness of the reinforcement is reduced. Furthermore, in order to pay the patient, the staff member is dependent on the patient's accuracy and honesty in reporting his work, and the patient is generally not very dependable. This procedure is only used when there are serious staff shortages. It is much better to pay a patient at the time he completes a desired act by recording right then and there additional tokens on his token carry-around card.)

SETTING UP A NEW BEHAVIORAL NON-TOKEN ECONOMY PROGRAM

After carefully reading over this material, a reader may feel that he would like to set up a new behavioral program, but not a token economy one, at least not at this time. (For example, the funds and staff time may not be available for a canteen, tokens, and a banking system.) He may feel that too much work is involved or that conditions in his institution are not suitable to having a token economy program, but that a behavioral program is definitely of interest to him, and would work well in his institution. He may also feel that a behavioral non-token economy program is a good first step toward having a token economy program. The staff can learn behavioral techniques, and when they have them well in hand, they can be taught the next steps necessary for having a token economy program.

Any of these views can be quite sensible and appropriate to a setting other than Camarillo's. There is no reason to organize and operate a program—token economy, behavioral, or any other—that does not help patients adequately, is frustrating to the staff and the community, does not really do what it is supposed to do, and is, therefore, a failing program. And token economy programs do occasionally fail—even at Camarillo—and are simply eliminated. No one wants to go through such an unpleasant experience. For this reason, some of the necessary guidelines on how to have a successful behavioral non-token economy program are presented here.

A Personal-Professional Note

I have avoided being associated with any unsuccessful program. When I became assistant program director of a behavior therapy program, I had administrative responsibilities for five units of about 75 patients each, only one of which was token economy. The staff took the initiative in asking me not to change the non–token economy programs into token economy ones. I promised not to do that, and to ask higher administration in Camarillo not to force token economy programs on those units. All of this was done. At the same time I worked to change the operations of these program from traditional insight to behavior therapy approaches. I worked closely with the psychologists and other staff members on these units to help them to understand the behavioral techniques that they would need to work with their patients. On these units behavioral encountering, written contracts, and other techniques were begun by informing the staff of these new social training procedures, and how they might be used. The staff's cooperation, interest, and involvement was sought. The staff was not ordered to do anything, and the changeover from traditional to behavioral treatment was essentially successful. This was an example of using positive reinforcement techniques with the staff, emphasizing the need to reinforce the reinforcers, and avoiding the use of negative reinforcement and aversive techniques with colleagues—and, perhaps above all, listening carefully and thoughtfully to what the staff said, responding as suitably as I could, and being truthful with them.

A sample problem and how it was solved will illustrate how traditionally oriented staff can be taught to use behavioral approaches, in a way that is a pleasant and good learning experience for all concerned. Camarillo's Behavior Modification Program was faced with the problem of setting up a procedure for the objective assessment of patients, and predictions about their changed behaviors and numbers of discharges from the program. (The Department of Mental Hygiene, the California agency administering Camarillo and all other California mental hospitals, required that all programs write a complete program statement, including such aspects of the program as changed behaviors and numbers of discharges.)

Objective personality assessment procedures had to be devised, taught to all staff members, and included in all write-ups on patients in their individual folders. The individual patient assessment procedure (see Appendix D) was taught to all staff members, and this required focusing on objective, apparent aspects of behavior, such as speech, behavior, and appearance. The staff were taught to avoid discussing inferential, unobservable aspects of behavior, such as attitudes and emotions. The staff learned the techniques well, seemed comfortable in the process, and seemed to extend the techniques to other areas of patient care.

Once the individual assessment procedure was learned, the results were included in a formal written statement describing the overall functioning of the program (see Appendix E).

Staff Orientation

Another way of training traditional staff in behavioral approaches was to provide them with a program statement describing the functioning and purposes of the program. This statement, which helped to orient them to the program, is presented in Exhibit 7-1.

EXHIBIT 7-1

Camarillo State Hospital Behavior Modification Program Statement: Brief Form

Raymond A. Ulmer
Assistant Program Director

The CSH Behavior Modification Program includes a psychiatrist-program director, psychologist-assistant program director, nursing coordinator, 6 psychiatric social workers, 3 rehabilitation counselors, another psychologist, 3 additional physicians, and some 100 additional staff, including psychiatric technicians, hospital, janitorial, and clerical workers. There are some 300 patients in 2 male and 3 female units.

The CSH Behavior Modification Program is based upon behavioral principles as developed in the animal laboratory, and human experimental and treatment facilities in universities, clinics, and hospitals. Behavior therapy is a systematic set of social learning principles based upon the belief that man is a social learning and mislearning animal. All men—normal, deviant, as well as abnormal—learn, mislearn, and unlearn according to similar learning principles. They learn appropriate and inappropriate ways of responding to others in their communities. All men develop social repertoires that are sets of social skills shown in speech, actions, and appearances, and with these social repertoires they interact with others in their communities, with staffs of community mental health centers, and with other patients and staff here at the hospital. When social repertoires are signally inappropriate and disturbing or considered dangerous by others in their communities, persons may be sent from their communities to mental hospitals.

Our behavioral training program is based upon the use of social learning principles so that patients' inappropriate social repertoires will be changed to more appropriate ones that will enable them, upon discharge from the hospital, to remain in their communities without signally disrupting others by speech, actions, or self-destructive or dangerous behavior to others. Our program, in effect, is a social training program of last resort for the person in his community who is markedly unacceptable to others in his community. Our program's staff of psychologists, psychiatrists, psychiatric social workers, and nurses are social trainers using behavioral principles as the bases of our training program.

To implement our social training roles, we have instituted staff development programs to help all members of our social training team to understand fully and to implement effectively social learning principles in changing the inappropriate social repertoires of our patients. We are developing orientation material for patients on every unit so that new patients will know from the moment of their entrance into our behavioral program, exactly what staff expects of them, and specifically what treatment (in both senses of this word) staff will provide for patients. Orientation material given to patients enables treatment to begin at once, for behavior therapy only begins when patients have some awareness of what their lives are likely to be like in the hospital. And during an L.P.S. (Lanterman-Petris-Short) era when short-term hospital stays of only days or weeks are common, treatment should begin immediately upon admission.

We are developing behaviorally oriented group encounter sessions on every one of our five units, so that relatively intact patients can meet with staff three times each week, and with other patients in leaderless groups on three other days. We are developing intensive individual and group behavioral social training programs for deeply regressed patients, so that we are returning patients to the community who have been hospitalized for 20 to 40 consecutive years. We are involved in behaviorally oriented individual sessions to help our patients recognize their socially inappropriate speech, actions, and appearances that are likely to keep them in the hospital longer, and, after discharge, to return them to the hospital. In these sessions we attempt to change antisocial and asocial speech, actions, and appearances into forms more acceptable to others in the community.

All of these actions of our behavioral modification staff are built upon the traditional roles of psychologist, psychiatrist, and nurse. From these customary roles we are developing behavioral guidelines for staff to conceptualize the social meanings of hospitalization and treatment, and the goals of return and permanent residence in the community. We have been working together less than three and one-half years, and our team approach seems to be moving definitely and appropriately in the right behavioral directions.

It is worthwhile to make explicit the advantages of a behavioral non-token economy program. If this program succeeds, it is relatively easy to institute such things as tokens and a canteen, and have a token economy program. If this program fails, a token economy program would also probably fail, and this way a great deal less time and effort are invested and lost in the process. The staff can be involved in the planning and implementing process at all times so that the chances of success are far greater than if the changes are ordered from above without full input and interest from the staff.

The Twelve Steps

The twelve steps that should be taken to institute a behavioral non-token economy program are:

1. A staff member assumes the responsibilities as organizer.
2. The organizer meets with other staff members to plan a behavioral non-token economy program.
3. The organizer involves higher administration in all steps from planning through implementation.
4. The organizer and the staff plan specific changes, with time deadlines.
5. The organizer writes an orientation form for staff members.
6. The organizer writes an objective procedure for patient assessment.
7. The organizer writes a general program statement.
8. The organizer and the staff elect a program leader.
9. All staff set up procedures for changing program operations as the program operates.
10. Selection procedures for new staff members are set up.
11. In-service training for all staff members of all disciplines are set up.
12. Training programs for all students of all disciplines such as nursing, psychology, medicine, and social work, are set up.

SUMMARY

Almost any motivated, knowledgeable, and energetic person can organize a new token economy program *if* he has higher administration support for needed staff, facilities, and funds, *and* he acquires the background to plan a new program. If he has formal academic background, and mental hospital experience, especially in a behavioral program, organizing a program will be much easier for him than if he does not have these advantages. A table of steps for the organization and operation of a new program is presented. The patient, the program, and the therapist all seem to profit by consistently using some form of behavior therapy in the treatment program, instead of switching to traditional insight therapy when a behavioral approach does not produce results.

When beginning a new program, all staff members should be motivated to work to try to improve it. Involvement of higher administration is essential in providing staff, facilities, and funding, and supporting the staff against unjustified criticism. Program organizer-leader roles require considerable effort and tact to make the program work effectively. A given psychologist may make a poor team leader if he cannot work closely with others or if he has any personal problems that make him unsuited to responsible managerial roles. The ideal situation may be to have a psychologist whose personality is suited to being a good team leader, who is motivated to work with the difficult and dangerous patient, and who has the technical ability to read the literature and learn how others work with such a patient and then is able to communicate these research findings to other staff members.

The procedure for writing an orientation form and its purposes illustrate the significance of the organizer-leader role for the psychologist or whoever functions in that capacity. Much sensitivity is needed for the feelings of the fearful patient and for the concerns of all other staff members. The head charge and his nursing staff are vital in any program, since they work so closely so much of the time with every patient that they can make or break any token economy program. The head charge should be motivated to select qualified staff and to supervise them well.

The psychiatrist or other physician in a token economy program is extremely important because he handles all physical problems and is almost automatically the administrative leader in many areas in any medical setting. He must have a good working relationship with the organizer-leader, whether this leader is the psychologist or any other staff member, in order for the program to work smoothly. The social worker is usually psychoanalytically oriented, but social workers with behavioral interests are becoming more numerous, and this may make it easier for new programs to hire a behavioristically oriented social worker.

The canteen is a vital part of the whole program and costs about $100 per month for about 65 patients. Suggestions are given on how to cut these costs, operate the canteen, and make the canteen most contributory to the overall effectiveness of the program.

SUGGESTED READINGS

Theory and Practice of Behaviorism and Behavior Therapy

Bergin, A. E., & Suinn, R. M. Individual psychotherapy and behavior therapy. In M. R. Rosensweig & L. W. Porter (Eds.), *Annual review of psychology* (Vol. 26). Palo Alto, Calif.: Annual Reviews, 1975. A report of some new technical advances in behavior therapy that will require a good technical background.

Diebert, A. N. & Harmon, A. J. *New tools for changing behavior.* New York: Holt, Rinehart and Winston, 1965. This is a self-teaching book on the theory and practice of behavior therapy.

Kanfer, F. H., & Phillips, J. S. *Learning foundations of behavior therapy.* New York: Wiley, 1970. This book provides a great deal of basic information about behavior therapy, and especially some new developments that describe the human organism as more than a responding mechanism to immediate stimulation.

Liberman, R. L. *Behavior therapy: A short course of self-instruction.* New York: Pergamon Press, 1972. This is an excellent self-teaching manual with a good annotated bibliography.

Schaefer, H. H., & Martin, P. L. *Behavioral therapy.* New York: McGraw-Hill, 1969. An excellent, readable introduction providing substantial basic information on the practice of behavior therapy in a mental hospital setting and some of its problems.

The following two books provide good general descriptions of behavior therapy approaches, and how these can be used to change specific kinds of disordered personalities.

Ullmann, L. P., & Krasner, L. *Case studies in behavior modification.* New York: Holt, Rinehart and Winston, 1965.

Yates, A. J. *Behavior therapy.* New York: Wiley, 1970.

Evaluation of Effectiveness of Token Economy Programs

Allen, D. J., & Magaro, P. A. Measures of change in token economy programs. *Behavior Research and Therapy,* 1971, *9*(4), 311–318.

Atthowe, J. M., Jr., & Krasner, L. Preliminary report on the application of contingent reinforcement procedures (token economy) on a "chronic" psychiatric ward. *Journal of Abnormal Psychology,* 1968, *73,* 37–43.

Ayllon, T., & Azrin, N. The measurement and reinforcement of behavior of psychotics. *Journal of Experimental Analysis of Behavior,* 1965, *8,* 375–383.

Kazdin, A. E. Methodological and assessment considerations in evaluating reinforcement programs in applied settings. *Journal of Applied Behavior Analysis,* 1975, *6,* 517–531.

Liberman, R. *A view of behavior modification projects in California. Behaviour Research and Therapy,* 1968, *6,* 331–341.

Lloyd, K. E., & Abel, L. Performance on a token-economy psychiatric ward: A two-year summary. *Behaviour Research and Therapy,* 1970, *8,* 1–9.

Appendixes

A Proposed Integration of Independent Mental Health Facilities into Behaviorally Oriented Social Training Programs

Raymond A. Ulmer and **Cyril M. Franks**

Drew Postgraduate Medical School and *Psychological Clinic, Rutgers University*
Martin Luther King, Jr.
Memorial Hospital

Summary—Traditional insight psychotherapy and the medical model have little relevance to mental health facilities viewed as essentially social training institutions for disturbed and disturbing persons with limited social competence. If training for community living is indeed the major function of so-called mental health facilities, it would be as well to change their name to *behavioral, social training programs.* An integrated four-level training program is suggested: Level I. Out-patient Clinics; Level II. Day Treatment Centers; Level III. Half-way Houses; and Level IV. State and Community Mental (Psychiatric) Hospitals.

Within the larger outlines of today's social thought a significant mental health revolution is occurring and the more traditional viewpoints are beginning to lose professional support. For example, individual long-term psychotherapy, usually psychoanalytic, is selectively appropriate, if at all, and socio-economically feasible only for the upper middle socio-economic class, white person (Ulmer, 1966; Hersch, 1969). The individualistic focus of both traditional dyadic psychotherapy and much of group psychotherapy has little significance for those who view the *community* as the source, exacerbator, and potential alleviator of social deviance (Golann, 1970). The relevance of past experience is increasingly challenged by newer treatment methods which emphasize the here-and-now rather than yesteryear. The concept of the unconscious is losing its significance and insight is no longer regarded as an essential precursor to behavior and

Reprinted with permission of publisher:

Franks, C., & Ulmer, R. A. A proposed integration of independent mental health facilities into behaviorally oriented social training programs. *Psychological Reports,* 1973, *32,* 95–104. © Psychological Reports 1973.

Thanks are due for help with this paper to: Saul C. Kupferman, Dept. of Rehabilitation Counseling, California State College at Los Angeles, and Robert E. Rabe, Dept. of Community Psychiatry, Santa Barbara (California) Mental Health Services.

attitude change (e.g., Eysenck, 1952). In any case, there are too many persons needing help and too few trained therapists to serve them for individual techniques to be effective on any widespread scale. And the often suggested training and use of paraprofessional therapists can still be helpful only to a small number of disadvantaged persons, and even then, only under supervision from a well-organized facility (Ulmer, 1970).

The medical model, with assumptions that primarily biochemical and physiological processes produce socially inappropriate behavior, is unsatisfactory for somewhat different reasons. Proponents of this model believe that, someday, these deviant physiochemical processes will be understood and that treatment will be based upon the application of suitable medical techniques. But, to date, there is no clear evidence that the vast majority of emotional disorders are related primarily to "organic" malfunctioning. Even the rapidly growing field of genetic psychology merely offers the suggestion that heredity may be involved in a predisposition to socially inappropriate speech and actions (Hirsch & Hostetter, 1968). A psychoactive drug enables many a disturbed person to leave the hospital sooner and to stay out longer than he would have done 20 years ago, but he is by no means cured of any "mental illness" by any drug known today. Generally, the socially disturbed person must continue taking his medication daily and indefinitely to maintain himself in his community.

The current inappropriateness of the medical model of mental disease can be illustrated by a condensation of the typical hospitalization sequence. No one is ever involuntarily committed to a mental hospital for being "psychotic, schizophrenic, insane, or emotionally ill, or for suffering from any other disordered mental state." A person is sent to a mental hospital for speaking in ways that are considered actually or potentially dangerous to himself or to others in his community. Socially unacceptable speech and actions are by themselves sufficient reason for hospitalizing virtually anyone. And, by-and-large, speech that is quite deviant, even without being physically threatening, is sufficient reason for a person to be hospitalized. If the person under consideration does not speak or act in ways that disturb those around him, he is not likely to be committed to a psychiatric institution, no matter how inappropriate his thoughts and fantasies. Studies have consistently shown that about one adult of each 10, living in his community, is comparably as socially disturbed as the hospitalized person (Faris & Dunham, 1939; Roe, 1953; Srole, Langner, Michael, Opler & Rennie, 1962). Yet the vast majority of this seriously socially disordered group of 1-in-10 will never be included in the some 2-out-of-100 who will experience hospitalization.

Typically, the asocial and anti-social non-hospitalized person obtains financial support from his work or family and does not draw attention to himself because of economic needs. He is then less likely to provoke community and, especially, professional awareness of his social deviance and hence to invoke hospitalization. A good example of the effects of economic self-sufficiency is provided by Faris and Dunham's Ss who worked steadily, supported themselves, but were quite poorly adjusted socially. These were men, primarily in their 50s and 60s, who had never married, had few friends, and lived reclusive existences in rooming-houses. They showed little competence in forming even minimal friendships, rarely if ever disrupting the lives of others by any inappropriate speech or behavior. Despite their social incompetence and isolation, few were ever involuntarily committed to institutions for emotional reasons since they neither disrupted nor made unacceptable demands upon their community. This is not to belie either the existence or the importance of personal or intrapsychic problems. The emotionally distressed person may be a deeply unhappy human being who feels so unbearably burdened that he requests help from a mental health facility, even to the point of commitment to a mental hospital, but his community will never take the initiative in committing him merely for being distressed.

If he is involuntarily or voluntarily hospitalized, his discharge is rarely related to any meaningful changes in his medical status. Quite the contrary, he will be discharged from the hospital and returned to his community when the staff of the hospital perceives him as speaking and acting more appropriately than he did when he entered the hospital and when they believe that the improved social adaptiveness observed in the hospital will be manifest in the community.

BEHAVIORAL AND SYSTEMS VIEW OF THE DISTURBED PERSON IN HIS COMMUNITY

A community may be defined as an aggregation of mutually interdependent individuals residing in a specified area who commonly maintain primary institutions such as churches and schools (Hinsie & Campbell, 1970). Similarly, Susser (1968) defines a community as an aggregate of people who have collective social ties by virtue of their shared locale for residence, services and work. The ex-patient, back in the community, tends to respond to community residents as he did in the hospital to other patients and staff. Now, if this individual perceives the hospital and community settings as similar, in much the same way as he mastered social situations in the hospital, so will he tend to show increased social competence in his community. In effect, each person has a learned set of social responses in his repertoire for gaining approval, affection, love, money, or other emotional or material benefits from others, and reducing the likelihood of disapproval, rejection, or aggression. The extent of this social repertoire is directly related both to his level of social competence and to his needs. The more social skills he possesses, the more likely he is to be able to satisfy his needs. Within genetic limits, the level of social competence achieved is going to be largely determined by the success or otherwise of his encounters with others.

The behaviorist attempts to understand the social responses of the individual in these terms and thus to bring about change. And to this, if the interactions between a person and others in his community are to be fully understood, he would further add a systems approach. Each person is a member of interlocking systems of small groups such as family, friends, and co-workers interacting with each other. These small groups are the focus of community psychology (Glidewell, 1969) and society-at-large can be considered as merely the background to these small group interactions (Holder, 1969). The individual responds to others in these small face-to-face groups as the interfaces between the person and his systems. Interfaces are social interaction regions in which social forces such as stability and change, order and confusion, affect each person.

The socially disturbed person living in his community may leave his permanent systems for a few hours each week to become a member of temporary treatment groups in outpatient facilities. He may enter a temporary system of his community as a halfway house or other resident treatment group for weeks, months, or even years. Whenever he leaves these temporary treatment systems, he attempts to rejoin the permanent systems that he has left, such as his family, work and church. The other members of these permanent systems may accept him conditionally, find him difficult to cope with because he provokes tension in others, or he may be rejected altogether. If he is perceived by others in these small groups, correctly or otherwise, as less disturbing than he was prior to treatment, then he tends to be more accepted than hitherto.

PROPOSAL: INTEGRATED, BEHAVIORAL, SOCIAL TRAINING PROGRAMS

As noted, there are substantial reasons for considering the medical model—and, by implication, "mental health facilities"—misnamed and their purposes incorrectly stated. Too many mental health facilities have their effectiveness reduced because of their individualistic modes of operation, each seemingly "in business for itself" and showing only tangential cooperation with other community facilities. It is therefore suggested that certain mental health facilities, in the first instance, be renamed *social training programs*. Specific aspects of social training can then be handled by various institutions serving various kinds and levels of social competence (Table A-1).

There are many potential advantages to the training approach proposed. The goal of improved and relatively comfortable social functioning, amenable to

Table A-1   Four Social Training Levels

Social training level	Current title
I	Outpatient clinics
II	Day treatment centers
III	Halfway houses
IV	State and community mental (psychiatric) hospitals

discussion at the beginning of training, is more likely to be achieved. A person enrolled as a "trainee in a social training program" rather than "a patient in a mental hospital" is less likely to be stigmatized by his community. His family and certain significant others in his community systems can be expected to cooperate more with a training program for someone who is considered socially handicapped, than if he is judged "sick, helpless, or morally irresponsible."

Clinics, day treatment centers, halfway houses, and resident hospitals then become training institutions for helping the socially disturbed person to modify his anti-social and asocial speech and behavior (Table A-1). Each institution can be considered a specialized community-oriented social training program for the person with a corresponding level of socially disruptive speech and behavior. Each social training program requires a corresponding level of social competence and has the goal of increasing the trainee's competence to a specified level of improved depth and meaningfulness in his relationships with others.[1]

Level I

The person in the community whose speech and behavior is perceived as only mildly disruptive and non-dangerous to himself or to others, so that he can maintain some mutually gratifying relationships with other persons, can usually remain within his community if he so wishes. Should he become excessively anxious, tense, fearful or phobic, he can then request help to reduce his malaise. Others may suggest to him his need for social assistance, but he is generally under little pressure from his community to seek help unless his behavior bothers others. If he so decides, he can then be enrolled as a trainee in a Level I Social Training Program currently labeled an outpatient clinic or mental health center. By means of behavior therapy (Eysenck & Rachman, 1965) or other ways, the goal of a Level I program would be to help the trainee learn more effective social competence and to provide him with psychoactive drugs to reduce his uneasiness while tending to make him more amenable to social training.

Social training sessions, consisting of behavior therapy and related approaches, would consume several hours each week of his time. Ancillary services, such as vocational training, should be available to develop the financial competence necessary for his maintenance even if other social and tension management difficulties continue (Kupferman & Ulmer, 1964). Training could

---

[1] Wishing to present as clear a picture as possible of most socially disordered persons, certain minor categories which differ considerably from the general pattern of disorders are not discussed. For example, persons with transient situational disturbances generally quickly recover their previous levels of social competence with short-term professional attention or often even without assistance, once the crisis situation is over. In like fashion, to present a simple, consistent picture of treatment facilities, this paper does not deal with problems of crisis intervention or substance abuse.

be terminated on a trial basis, of course, when he no longer wishes to continue with either social training or ancillary programs.

Level II

If a trainee does not seem to be profiting from Level I social training, and others in his community—such as his family or the courts—are dissatisfied with his speech and actions, the trainee could be transferred to a Level II program, such as a day treatment center, for more intensive and comprehensive supervision and training throughout working hours each day. Working hours are envisioned as being from 9:00 A.M. to 5:00 P.M. Mondays through Fridays. This level is designed for the person whose level of social competence may be so limited that he cannot function throughout the day without being dangerous or disruptive to himself or to others. He is assumed to be capable and motivated enough to maintain adequately satisfying relationships with his family in the evenings and on weekends and holidays, so that only a complete working day schedule of training and supervision seems needed. Training could emphasize behavior therapy rather than traditional insight psychotherapy, and group rather than dyadic experiences, with medication as indicated. The goal of Level II would be to assist the person to become more able to adapt to others more adequately and comfortably so that he needs either social training at Level I or none at all.

Level III

Level III social training consists of halfway houses for the person who is unable to live either alone or with his family because he needs supervision and training around-the-clock. Typically, he is the recent patient of the traditional mental hospital, and he appears unready to be plunged directly into independent or even family living in his community. Interim social training, supervision, and medication often seems necessary to help him learn to control his speech and behavior so that he is acceptable to others within his community systems. The most probable goal for Level III is the transfer of the trainee to Level II when he achieves adequate social competence to function in his community outside of working hours. For such an individual training and supervision would be required only during the working day. When and if the trainee is transferred to Level II, he is expected to have developed a sufficiently high level of social competence to live either with his family or alone in his community. An occasional Level III trainee could be transferred on a probationary basis to either Level I or even discharged from all training. Whatever his level of placement, the trainee may be told that he can always apply for a higher or a lower level program than the one to which he is assigned. If he is discharged from training he can always re-apply for assistance, leaving the professional staff to decide which program seems most appropriate for him at the time.

Level IV

A Level IV trainee, resident of a "mental hospital," is unable to cope with others in his community because he appears to them, correctly or otherwise, as disruptive or dangerous. Feeling that he cannot live in his community and meet the demands that others place upon him, he may take the initiative in enrolling himself. Others in his community, such as members of his family or the courts, may feel that he is unsuitable for community living, and hence place him in a mental hospital. Typically he is able to spend weekends or holidays with his family, but after that he becomes too disruptive in their lives to remain with them. Level IV training is designed to help the person assume responsibility for the effects of his actions on himself and on others in his community. The difference between this and other programs is that, at Level IV, the person's social competence is far less at the beginning and generally only somewhat higher at the end of even very successful training than for the other levels.

Regardless of its location within or without the community, a Level IV residence hospital should always be considered as a community facility, a kind of "last resort" within the community because the socially disturbed and disturbing person needs to be taken out of direct physical and social contact with others. And the community, especially the courts, has substantial power in determining whether he will be enrolled, and when and under what circumstances he will return to his community. The community wields considerable financial, juridicial, and social influence on the administration of every so-called state mental hospital. Hopefully, Level IV training will help the trainee to develop a level of social competence in which he can be entrusted to fulfill relatively constructive roles in his community. And the community, never the staff of any program, determines the characteristics of socially constructive roles.

ETHICS OF BEHAVIORALLY ORIENTED TRAINING

The programs presented here can be accused of being incompatible with genuine concern for the dignity and integrity of man. The argument can also be made that the essential problem is more than one of social incompetence. But whether or not a person should adjust and conform to the "sickness" or "healthiness" or society-at-large are irrelevant issues for a person who is currently identified as a mental hospital patient. The Level IV trainee, for example, demonstrates an inability to conform, a social incompetence, since he does not seem to have within his social repertoire the means of adjusting to others. He should not be confused with the community resident who has a history of relative success in his work and personal life, who can and does decide how and when, and for what reasons, he will or will not conform to his community. Knowing in advance the penalties which he may incur, he is in a position to elect to pay the price of radical non-conformity if he so chooses. The ideal goal of social training is to enable the Level IV trainee to develop a sufficiently enlarged social repertoire to include as many social choices as the typical community resident. Noteworthy in this context is the fact that inadvertently, because of their unpleasant aspects, social training programs sometimes *stimulate* socialization. Hospitalization may be disliked so much that involuntary commitment can sometimes result in a far greater effort to adapt to his community than hitherto—if only to avoid recommitment.

The epitome of aloof, detached, and culture-freeing psychotherapy is supposedly classical psychoanalysis, and the analyst is expected not to impose his values and beliefs upon the analysand (Freud, 1963; Alexander, 1950). But Lindner (1962), a prolific writer in the area of psychoanalysis, has indicted psychoanalytic treatment as indoctrinating the analysand into the values and beliefs of his middle-class psychoanalyst rather than freeing him. Most students of traditional insight psychotherapy agree that analytic, existential, and even non-directive approaches are seriously biased by the middle-class values of most psychotherapists. Behavioral techniques are no less, and probably no more, culture-free than traditonal techniques, and cultural adaptation is the goal of both traditional and behavioral procedures (Franks, 1967; London, 1964).

Behavioral techniques are alleged by some to be degrading and dehumanizing. But the behaviorally treated subject always has the option of refusing social training. The behavior therapist knows that when he does not motivate his subject adequately, behavior therapy may fail. When his subject wants to work with the behavior therapist, and this motivation is maintained, social competence will tend to improve and be retained with suitable behavioral treatment. For these reasons, the knowledgeable and competent behavior therapist makes every effort to understand the uniqueness of his subject and tries to establish a warm, human relationship with him.

POTENTIAL STAFF TRAINING AND RESEARCH ADVANTAGES OF AN INTEGRATED PROGRAM

Program integration offers substantial possibilities for better integration of staff training and research. The current fragmented approach handicaps the transfer of a person and information about him from one institution to another. Thus, rather than transfer a socially disturbed person to another institution, many mental health workers prefer to wait until they believe that he can maintain himself in his community. The proposed four-level approach would facilitate sending a person from one training level institution to another because the procedures for transfer could be clearly specified, with the goals of training limited, so that the involved professionals could feel a sense of accomplishment with each transfer. Another advantage of the proposed integrated program is that comprehensive information describing each socially disturbed person could be readily provided through a central clearing office. One of the frequent difficulties in providing service to the community as well as research data, is the lack of adequate information. Characteristically, the anti-social or asocial person is known to many community institutions, helping agencies, hospitals, and even jails. If the person is unable or unwilling to reveal this information, the newly contacted institution must set up treatment programs with inadequate or misleading information. All too often, this can result in a repetition of programs which have been tried and found wanting elsewhere.

The institution which has comprehensive information about a person readily available can provide far more effective service, and save considerable replication, expense and effort in staff time. Data could be kept in a central computer-run file, available only with the consent of the individual concerned or his legal representative. Should he leave the community, this information could readily be transferred to the new setting with the explicit consent of all concerned. Training of staff members would also be facilitated by this system, each staff member being provided with a more complete history and follow-up file on each socially disturbed person with whom he worked than under existing conditions.

The proposed approach could provide a scaffolding on which to build richly varied supervised training experiences for the paraprofessional, pre-professional and post-graduate student alike. Each student and staff member would have the opportunity to integrate his experiences with trainees at all four levels. The integrated program might be especially useful in community psychology internships and post-doctoral fellowships which now provide experiences which are difficult for the staff trainee to conceptualize into meaningful wholes (Singer & Bard, 1970). Another advantage lies in the reduction of administrative and staff training costs.

Other training advantages accrue to both staff and the socially disturbed person whenever solutions to problems at one training level, can be applied to problems at another level. For example, the effective use of psychiatric consultation presents many staff-training problems (Ulmer & Kupferman, 1970). Problems encountered at one training level in using psychiatric consultation are likely to be found in similar form at other training levels. Solutions to these problems at one level should provide helpful guidelines for using consultation at other training levels.

Another example may help to detail the suggestion that program integration assists the solution of problems from one training level to another. Early token-economy studies, such as those of Ayllon and Azrin (1968), were completed before the length of hospitalization was shortened dramatically by the extensive use of psychoactive drugs and legal changes such as California's Lanterman-Petris-Short (LPS) Mental Health Act of 1969. (The LPS Act shortens involuntary commitment drastically because, after three days, a psychiatrist must appear in court to obtain legal permission to keep a person who wishes to leave a hospital. There are many legal obstacles written into the LPS Act making extended involuntary commitment most difficult.) Because of the greatly reduced period of institutionalization, token-economy approaches have had to be adapted to be maximally effective within short periods of time. Token economies, in combination with psychoactive drugs, seem helpful in quickly transforming anti-social speech and actions into more socially acceptable forms. Various forms of token-economy approaches are probably quite effective at Level III, and even possibly Level II, provided experienced personnel from Level IV token economies act as organizers and consultants to staff at other levels (Ulmer, 1971).

The proposed integrated procedures may also facilitate program evaluation. Program evaluators might use the central computer office to obtain substantial history, current training, and follow-up information on each trainee. Information describing the trainee might then be used by cooperating members from different training levels to evaluate their joint or individual programs. A typical program evaluation might study the effectiveness of differing kinds and levels of training for various combinations of social competencies and demographic variables such as being Black or Brown. Perhaps most important of all, considering today's tight funding market, program evaluation grants, like staff-training moneys, might be facilitated for integrated, behaviorally oriented social training programs.

REFERENCES

Alexander, F. *The scope of psychoanalysis.* New York: Basic Books, 1950.

Ayllon, T., & Azrin, N. H. *The token economy: A motivational system for therapy and rehabilitation.* New York: Appleton-Century-Crofts, 1968.

Eysenck, H. J. The effects of psychotherapy. *Journal of Consulting Psychology,* 1952, *16,* 319–324.

Eysenck, H. J., & Rachman, S. *The causes and cures of neurosis.* San Diego, Calif.: Knapp, 1965.

Faris, R. E. L., & Dunham, H. W. *Mental disorders in urban areas.* Chicago: University of Chicago Press, 1939.

Franks, C. M. Behavior modification: Perspectives in cross-cultural research. Paper presented at XIth Interamerican Congress of Psychology, Mexico City, 1967.

Freud, S. *New introductory lectures on psychoanalysis* (Reprint). New York: Norton, 1963.

Glidewell, J. D. New psychosocial competence, social change and tension management. In J. W. Carter (Ed.), *Research contributions from psychology to community mental health.* New York: Behavioral Publications, 1969, pp. 100–110.

Golann, S. E. Community psychology and mental health: An analysis of strategies and a survey of training. In I. Iscoe & C. D. Spielberger (Eds.), *Community psychology: Perspectives in training and research.* New York: Appleton-Century-Crofts, 1970, pp. 33–59.

Hersch, C. Mental health services and the poor. In A. J. Bindman & A. D. Spiegel (Eds.), *Perspectives in community and mental health.* Chicago: Aldine, 1969, pp. 476–489.

Hinsie, L. E., & Campbell, R. J. *Psychiatric dictionary.* New York: Oxford University Press, 1970.

Hirsch, J., & Hostetter, R. C. Behavior genetics. In P. London & D. Rosenhan (Eds.), *Foundations of abnormal psychology.* New York: Holt, Rinehart and Winston, 1968, pp. 28–60.

Holder, H. D. Mental health and the search for new organizational strategies. *Archives of General Psychiatry,* 1969, *20,* 709–717.

Kupferman, S. C., & Ulmer, R. A. An experimental total-push program for emotionally disturbed adolescents. *Journal of Personnel and Guidance,* 1964, *62,* 894–899.

Lindner, R. *Prescription for rebellion.* New York: Evergreen, 1962.

London, P. *The modes and morals of psychotherapy.* New York: Holt, Rinehart and Winston, 1964.

Roe, A. A psychological study of eminent psychologists and anthropologists, and a comparison with biological and physical scientists. *Psychological Monographs,* 1953, *67*(2, Whole No. 352).

Singer, J. L., & Bard, M. T. Psychological foundations of a community-oriented clinical psychology training program. In I. Iscoe & C. D. Spielberger (Eds.), *Community psychology: Perspectives in training and research.* New York: Appleton-Century-Crofts, 1970, pp. 125–141.

Srole, L., Langner, T. S., Michael, S. T., Opler, M. K., & Rennie, T. A. *Mental health in the metropolis: The midtown Manhattan study.* New York: McGraw-Hill, 1962.

Susser, M. *Community psychiatry: Epidemiologic and social themes.* New York: Random House, 1968.

Szasz, T. The myth of mental illness. *American Psychologist,* 1960, *15,* 113–118.

Ulmer, R. A. Psychologists' reactions and views of the Watts riots. Paper presented at Western Psychological Association Convention, San Diego, Calif., 1966.

Ulmer, R. A. The University of Southern California Mental Health counselling aide program for training paraprofessional psychotherapists. Paper presented at Western Psychological Association Convention, Los Angeles, April, 1970.

Ulmer, R. A. Behavioristic community psychology. Paper presented at Western Psychological Association Convention, San Francisco, 1971.

Ulmer, R. A. & Kupferman, S. C. An empirical study of the process and outcome of psychiatric consultation. *Journal of Clinical Psychology,* 1970, *26,* 323–326.

An Application and Modification of the Minimal Social Behavior Scale (MSBS): A Short Objective, Empirical, Reliable Measure of Personality Functioning

Raymond A. Ulmer   and   **Edwin O. Timmons**

Martin Luther King, Jr. Hospital and   *Louisiana State University*

Charles R. Drew Postgraduate Medical School

In 1957 Farina, Arenberg, and Guskin published the standardized interview described and reproduced below which they called the "Minimal Social Behavior Scale (MSBS)." The MSBS was developed as an attempt to objectively, empirically, and reliably measure interpersonal behavior of chronic psychotic patients. The MSBS is designed to produce a highly structured interview in which the *E*'s verbal and expressive behavior is clearly ritualized. This rigor is designed to reproduce a standardized stimulus compound for every interview almost independently of interviewer variables: professional background, educational level, clinical ability, etc. In effect, the MSBS maintains a constant *S* for the S-R interview interaction between *E* and *S*. This enables the examiner to

The first two paragraphs of this appendix are reprinted from *Journal of Consulting Psychology*, 1966, *30*(1), 86. Copyright 1966 by the American Psychological Association. Reprinted by permission.

This study was presented at the 1964 APA Convention in Los Angeles, and was part of the drug evaluation project of Tulane University Medical School, Department of Psychiatry, and included the following: Drs. Robert W. Heath, Melvin P. Bishop, and Donald Gallant. The authors wish to express their appreciation to the above persons and to the Louisiana State Department of Hospitals.

A children's form of this Scale was developed by Raymond A. Ulmer, Camarillo State Hospital, and Martha Lieberman of the University of California at Los Angeles: "The Children's Minimal Social Behavior Scale (CMSBS): A Short, Objective, Measure of Personality Functioning (10-Yr Level)." This was presented at the California State Psychological Association Convention, San Diego, Jan. 1967. The Children's scale was published by Psychological Reports in 1968, and a free copy can be obtained by writing to Dr. Ulmer. Free Arabic, French, German, Greek, and Spanish versions of both the children's and the adult's forms of the Minimal Social Behavior Scales can be obtained by writing to Dr. Raymond A. Ulmer, Department of Psychiatry and Human Behavior, Drew Postgraduate Medical School, 1621 East 120th Street, Los Angeles, California, 90059.

attribute differences in Ss' responses to factors within an individual S, since the behavior of the examiner remains standardized. The scale has a simple "go, no-go" scoring procedure yielding extremely high reliability for both test-retest and rater reliability analysis. The MSBS appears useful for research and clinical applications with regressed Ss because of its reliability, objectivity, and economy.

An experiment was performed to test the construct validity of the MSBS to behavioral changes and the effects of drugs on 27 male and 28 female institutionalized chronic psychotic patients. Ss had no drugs for sixty days prior to the start of experimentation. The study lasted ten weeks, and each S was double-blind tested prior to the beginning and during the final week of medication. Of the 55 Ss, 13 were given Trifluoperazine, 14 Butaperazine, 14 were on placebo, and 14 were controls from the same wards as the drug patients. [Ulmer] saw each S in random order during each of the evaluation periods.

RESULTS

MSBS scores changed consistently for each of the four groups in the experiment as reported in Table B-1. It will be noted that of the 14 Ss who were given Butaperazine, the known drug, 11 showed an increase in MSBS scores from pre- and post-medication testing, 3 showed a lower score, and none remained at the same level. The largest decrease in scoring was 2 points, and the largest increase was 16. The mean change of these 14 S was +5.57 scale points. The consistency of the effect is significant, yielding a probability of less than .03. Of the 13 Trifluoperazine Ss, 10 attained higher scores, one a lower score, and 2 remained at the same level as before medication. The mean change was somewhat less than for the Butaperazine Ss, being on the average of +3.31 scale points. This ranged from loss of one to a gain of 12 points during the experimental treatment. This consistency of effect on the 13 patients was found to be significant with a p of less than .02.

Table B-1 MSBS Changes for Drug, Placebo, and Control Groups

	Butaperazine	Trifluoperazine	Placebo	Control
No. Ss scoring higher	11	10	7	5
No. Ss scoring lower	3	1	5	6
No. Ss showing no changes	0	2	2	3
Mean change	+5.57	+3.31	+1.22	−0.79
Range	−2 to +16	−1 to +12	−12 to +11	−13 to +8

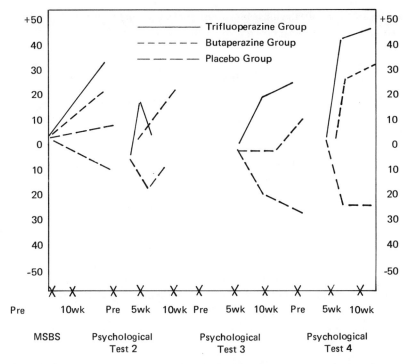

Figure B-1 Mean percent change on MSBS–Psychological Test 2, Psychological Test 3, and Psychological Test 4 for five- and ten-week periods.

The placebo and the control groups present strikingly different pictures. Of the 14 placebo Ss, 7 improved their scores, 5 received lower scores, and the range of change was from −12 to +11. In the control group, 5 gained higher scores, 6 lower scores, and 3 showed no change. The mean change for the control Ss was −0.79 scale points with a range from −13 to a gain of 8. Neither the placebo nor the control groups even approached the accepted levels of significance.

In partial summary of the data of Table B-1, the MSBS scores changed more for the two active drug groups than for the nonactive drug group and the control group. Furthermore, the range or variance of the change scores was greater in the nonactive groups. This suggests that the scale is validly measuring the effects of drugs and not extraneous factors; and that the MSBS does have construct validity in presenting the E as a constant stimulus compound.

Figure B-1 shows that there is a close correspondence among all of the psychological tests used, with Trifluoperazine generally being most effective, Butaperazine next, and the placebo group being least effective. Since only the MSBS utilized a control group for this experiment, there are no comparative data for these 14 Ss. One characteristic of the MSBS differed from all of the other measures used: the placebo group showed a slight gain on the MSBS as compared to a slight loss on each of the other psychological tests.

DISCUSSION

The authors believe that this very quick, approximately five-minute highly reliable behavioral scale yielded very promising results. The strongest advantage of the MSBS appears to be its objectivity and simplicity of evaluation procedure, which suggests that non-professional personnel could be taught to administer the MSBS, and obtain results highly similar to those obtained by any other examiner. The term "minimal" merits serious attention since the original version of the scale is probably most effective with seriously deteriorated mental hospital patients or the intellectually handicapped. This form is probably less effective with Ss currently functioning at average range intellectual ability or better, or when memory factors are likely to be operative, e.g., when the test is re-administered in less than a month.

The addition of a time factor is designed to reduce these limitations by increasing the ceiling since studies now in progress suggest that few Ss, even intellectually gifted ones, can reach the ceiling. Furthermore, sensitivity is likely to be greater since the range will change from zero to 32 to a new range of zero to 64.

SUMMARY

The MSBS appears an objective, empirical, reliable measure of behavior and behavioral changes. For example, analysis of the data of this study showed that both active drug groups gained significantly on the MSBS, while the placebo group showed a small "Hawthorne Effect," and the controls, a small decrement. Agreement with the other psychological tests was high. The authors believe that the MSBS is well worth the addition of a time factor as a means of raising the ceiling and enlarging the range, which should increase the sensitivity of the instrument to behavioral changes. Even without the time factor added, the earlier version of the MSBS appears a highly objective and reliable instrument for the measurement of human behavior.

Additionally, since substantially the same kinds of behavior are of interest in many treatment programs such as those involving other drugs, rehabilitation, special education, psychotherapy, operant conditioning, vocational training, etc., the MSBS should be applicable in a wide variety of settings.

REFERENCE

Farina, A., Arenberg, D., & Guskin, S. A scale for measuring minimal social behavior. *Journal of Consulting Psychology*, 1957, *21*, 265–268.

Minimal Social Behavior Scale (MSBS): A Short Objective Measure of Personality Functioning

(modified by)

Raymond A. Ulmer
Drew Postgraduate Medical School

and

Edwin O. Timmons
Louisiana State University

[The following is a complete revision of the scoring blank of the MSBS, and is reproduced in full to describe both the actions of the E and the scoring method. This modified version of the scale has a time factor added which the authors believe will increase the ceiling and sensitivity beyond that of the original version which was used in this study. Time scores can be obtained by following the testing and scoring instructions included in this modified MSBS version.]

Name or Code No. of S:_____ Time Score:_____

Date of Testing:_____ Performance Score:_____

Purpose of Testing: Time Score +
                          Performance Score = Total Score:_____

Identification of S: Time Score = ___128___
(Group, Age, Sex, etc.)   (Sum in seconds for items
                                          $18 + 21 + 22 + 23$) up to
                                          31 seconds/item

Previous or Subsequent MSBS: Total Score = Time Score +
                                          Performance Score:

Behavioral Comments During Testing:

Background Information:

MSBS Test Items

No additions, modifications or changes of any kind whatsoever should be made in following exactly testing instructions.

1. Patient is brought to door and introduced to Examiner. *E* stands up and says, "*Hello, Mr. . . .* " *E* then extends his hand.
   (1) Score + if patient enters and approaches *E*.   _____
   (2) Score + if any discriminable response to greeting.   _____
   (3) Score + if response is verbal and appropriate.   _____
   (4) Score + if patient shakes hand.   _____

2. *E* says, "*Won't you have a seat?*"
   (5) Score + if patient sits without further urging.   _____

3. *E* sits, and says, "*How are you today?*"
   (6) Score + any discriminable response to the question.   _____
   (7) Score + if response is verbal and appropriate.   _____

4. *E* drops a pencil by pushing it off the desk, ostensibly by accident. If patient does not pick up the pencil spontaneously, *E* says, "*Will you please pick up that pencil for me?*"
   (8) Score + if patient picks up pencil at all.   _____
   (9) Score + if patient picks up pencil spontaneously.   _____

5. *E* says, "*Would you mind moving your chair closer?*" While saying, "*I have something I want to show you*," *E* holds in front of patient the drawing of a three-inch square with diagonals.
   (10) Score + if patient moves chair closer to *E*.   _____
   (11) Score + if patient looks at drawing.   _____

6. *E* says, "*Here is a pencil,*" and offers it to patient. *E* then places pad of blank paper before patient and says, "*I would like you to copy this drawing on this paper.*"
   (12) Score + if patient accepts pencil without further urging. _____
   (13) Score + if patient makes any mark on the paper.   _____
   (14) Score + if patient draws any four-sided figure with diagonals.   _____

7. *E* proffers opened pack of cigarettes to patient and says, "*Cigarette?*"
   (15) Score + any response which indicates acceptance or refusal.   _____

8. *E* says, *"How are you getting along?"*
   (16) Score + any recognizable response to the question.   _____
   (17) Score + if response is verbal and appropriate.   _____

9. *E* crumples sheet of paper, tosses it at the waste basket, purposely missing, and says, *"Damn it, missed again!"*
   (18) Score + if patient smiles or laughs in response to exclamation.   _____
   (19) Score +if patient spontaneously picks up paper and deposits it in waste basket.   _____

10. *E* says, *"I have a few questions I would like to ask you. (a) What year is it? (b) What month is it? (c) What day is it? (d) What season is it? (e) Where are you? (f) What is the nearest city? (g) Who are some of the people you know around here? (h) Do you hear voices now? (i) Is anybody making trouble for you?*
    (20) Score + if patient makes any verbal response, irrespective of content, to all of the questions.   _____

11. *E* places magazine in front of patient and says, *"I'll be busy a minute."*
    (21) Score + if patient turns at least one page of magazine.   _____ Time: _____

12. *E* feigns a headache by rubbing his head with his hands, assuming a pained expression and ostensibly attempting to shake off the pain.
    (22) Score + if any verbal response which includes the content of "head" or "pain."   _____ Time: _____

13. *E* places a cigarette in his lips and fumbles for matches. *E* then stands up and pats his pockets. (A book of matches has previously been placed within easy reach of patient.)
    (23) Score + if patient offers or calls attention to the matches or offers a light from own cigarette.   _____

14. *E* rises and extends hand saying, *"Thank you very much, Mr. . . . ."* If necessary, *E* says, *"Go ahead, Mr. . . . ."* motioning toward the door.
    (24) Score + if patient rises from chair.   _____
    (25) Score + if patient opens door and crosses threshold without further urging.   _____

15. Items 26 through 32 are based on the behavior of the patient throughout the interview.

   (26) Score + unless inappropriate grimaces or mannerisms are readily apparent.   _____

   (27) Score + if patient at any time looks E in the eye.   _____

   (28) Score + unless patient obviously appears to avoid E's gaze at any time, or stares at E fixedly.   _____

   (29) Score + unless patient sits in a bizarre position, in constant motion, or is nearly motionless. (Do not confuse with Item 26.)   _____

   (30) Score + unless patient's clothes are obviously disarranged, unbuttoned.   _____

   (31) Score + unless patient is drooling or nasal mucus is visible or food deposits are conspicuous on clothes or face.   _____

   (32) Score + unless patient rises from chair and moves away from E before termination of interview without explanation.   _____

The Children's Minimal Social Behavior Scale (CMSBS): A Short, Objective Measure of Personality Functioning

Raymond A. Ulmer   and   **Martha Lieberman**

Martin Luther King, Jr. Hospital, and   *University of California*

Charles R. Drew Postgraduate Medical School   *at Los Angeles*

Summary—The CMSBS was administered to the following male and female Ss between their ninth and their eleventh birthdays: 32 normals, 17 schizophrenics, and 32 intellectual retardates. Inter-rater reliability and diagnostic power were statistically significant for the protocols of Ss whose IQs ranged from 13 to 139. The CMSBS was shown to be a reliable measure of social responsiveness for practically the whole range of intelligence for the normal schizophrenic, and retarded Ss of this study. Examiners needed little academic background or training, and the test required only 10 minutes to administer. Scoring was simple, and the scale appeared potentially useful where large numbers of children were to be tested.

A need has often been expressed for a reliable, objective, easily administered and scored test of social behavior that would differentiate between normal and emotionally handicapped children. Most attempts to measure children's behavior use some type of rating scales: Haggarty, Olson, and Wickman (1930); Doll (1947); Bower (1961); Cain, Levine, and Elzey (1963). Rating scales generally

Reprinted with permission of publisher from:

Ulmer, R. A., & Lieberman, M. Children's Minimal Social Behavior Scale (CMSBS): a short, objective measure of personality functioning (10-yr. level). *Psychological Reports*, 1968, *22*, 283–286. Copyright Raymond A. Ulmer 1969.

This paper was presented at the meeting of the California State Psychological Association in San Diego in 1967, and the findings reported in this study, not the test itself, were published in *Psychological Reports*, 1968, *22*, 283–286.

An adult version of this scale was reported in the *Journal of Consulting Psychology*, 1966, *30*(1), 86. A full copy including administrating and scoring instructions can be obtained without fee by writing to Dr. Raymond A. Ulmer, Department of Psychiatry and Human Behavior, Drew Postgraduate Medical School, 1621 East 120th Street, Los Angeles, California, 90059.

Thanks are due to the following: Alvah Bittner for statistical assistance, Ralph Mason Dreger, Mandel Sherman, and Wayne Zimmerman for many suggestions. Thanks are also due to the following for providing Ss for this study: Seymour Feshbach, Madeleine Hunter, Richard Key, Richard Metz, Norbert Rieger, and Arthur B. Silverstein.

have used loosely structured test situations in which the examiner evaluates behavior within several categories.

In contrast, the Children's Minimal Social Behavior Scale (CMSBS) attempts to introduce controls for as many environmental and examiner variables as possible by using a highly structured interview in which the examiner's behavior is clearly ritualized. This rigor is designed to reproduce for every interview a standardized situation in which many interviewer variables are controlled. This enables the examiner to attribute differences in S's responses to factors within an individual child. The scale has a simple success-failure scoring procedure designed to yield high inter-examiner reliability. The CMSBS is an adaptation of the Minimal Social Behavior Scale for adults produced by Farina, Arenberg, and Guskin (1957), and modified by Ulmer and Timmons (1964, 1965).

PROCEDURE

The CMSBS consists of 31 items orally presented to S, including ordinary social questions such as asking him how he is getting along. (A complete copy of the CMSBS, including scoring instructions can be obtained from Dr. Raymond A. Ulmer or from the American Documentation Institute). Each S is also given simple tasks, such as copying a square with diagonals drawn from each corner. Additional scores are given when S takes the initiative in making a spontaneous comment during an interview. Each response is scored on a success-failure basis of a point given for success and no deduction for failure. The scale requires about 10 minutes to administer, and an equal amount of time to score. Its simplicity and lack of interpretive requirements enable nonprofessionals without testing experience to learn easily to administer the test and to score the protocols.

The scale yields a total score divided into three separate subtest scores: a motor score for those items that can be passed using only muscular movements, a verbal score for items that require only speech, and a verbal-motor score for items that involve both muscular movement and speech. There is a time score that is the reciprocal of the sum of the number of seconds needed to complete five items. The performance score is the sum of all items passed. The total score is the sum of the time score and the three performance scores: motor, verbal, and verbal-motor scores (see Figure C-1).

All Ss were tested by one examiner, and he and an observer each scored every S's responses independently. The scores of the examiner and the observor were compared using the Pearson product-moment coefficient as a measure of agreement between the two independent examiners' scores for every S. All Ss were between their ninth and eleventh birthdays; none had known sensory or motor handicaps. Four groups were tested: 15 normal males and 17 normal females with Wechsler and Stanford-Binet IQs ranging from 80 to 139; 14 schizophrenic males and 3 schizophrenic females for whom no IQ was available; and 21 hospitalized intellectual retardate males and 11 retardate females with Wechsler and Stanford-Binet IQs ranging from 13 to 63.

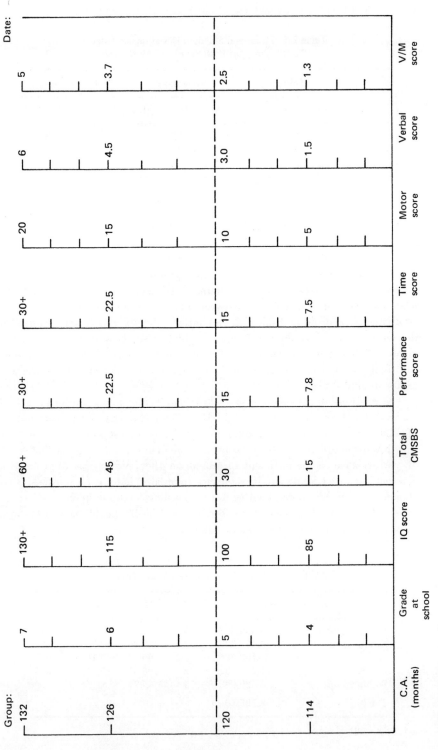

Figure C-1 Behavioralogram.

177

Table C-1 Means and Standard Deviations of Total
CMSBS Scores for Both Sexes and All Groups

	Normals			Retardates			Schizophrenics		
	N	M	SD	N	M	SD	N	M	SD
Males	15	30.51	4.16	21	17.75	9.20	14	13.45	5.78
Females	17	30.53	4.03	11	10.45	7.64	3	12.53	.68
Both sexes	32	30.52	4.09	32	15.25	9.36	17	13.30	5.27

RESULTS AND DISCUSSION

Analysis of variance of total scores, as reported in Table C-1, show that the
CMSBS significantly differentiated the three groups. The data also indicated an
interaction effect between sex and group. This interaction effect appears to be
related to the large differences between the means for the male and female
retardates as reported in Table C-2. In contrast, the sex means were similar for
the normal and schizophrenic groups. The data also show that the CMSBS is
highly reliable. The correlation coefficients ranged from .97 to .99 for subtest
and total scores. This indicates that the two examiners independently scored the
protocols almost identically.

The relationship between various CMSBS and Wechsler and Stanford-Binet IQ
scores differed for all groups. Verbal CMSBS subtest scores showed correlations
of .72 for retardates but only .28 for normals. Time subtest scores correlated .57
with IQs for retardates but only .06 for normals. These results suggest that speed
of performance as defined and measured on the CMSBS was important in
determining both CMSBS and IQ scores for retardates, but not for normals. No S
obtained a CMSBS score at either base or ceiling levels, despite an IQ range
from 13 to 139. This fact suggests that the CMSBS might have usefulness
throughout a wide range of intellectual ability.

Table C-2 Analysis of Variance of CMSBS Total Scores

Source of variation	Sum of squares	df	MS	F	p
Between groups	5,355.59	5			
Groups (population)	3,457.98	2	1,728.99	37.81	.005[*]
Sex	100.28	1	100.28	2.19	N.S.
G × S	1,797.33	2	898.67	19.65	.005[*]
Within groups	3,429.99	75	45.73		
Total	8,785.50				

[*]$p < .01$.

Additional information was obtained from a phi coefficient item analysis, which revealed that six items were especially contributive in adding to the diagnostic power of the CMSBS. This was well beyond the .005 level of p for numbers of items because less than 2 of 31 items would be expected to reach significance by chance alone. These six items also showed much higher correlations than were necessary to reach significance. For example, Item 15 had a phi of 1.00, which revealed that schizophrenics and normals were consistently differentiable by their reactions to Item 15, "How are you getting along? The schizophrenic Ss of this study consistently failed to answer verbally and appropriately, and normal Ss always answered correctly. Items 6, 14, and 26 were almost as effective with phi coefficients of .96, .91, and .91. Item 31 with a phi of 1.00 consistently differentiated retardates and normals because retardates always refused at least one request made by E. Item 31 required that Ss comply with every request of E throughout testing. Items 13 and 15 were particularly helpful in differentiating normals from retardates (phi coefficients were .85 and .80). Items 20, 21, and 29 were slightly contaminated because abnormal Ss passed them somewhat more often than normals.)

REFERENCES

Bower, B. M. A process for in-school screening of children with emotional handicaps. Sacramento, Calif.: State Department of Education, 1961.

Cain, L. F., Levine, S., & Elzey, F. F. *Cain-Levine competency scales.* Palo Alto, Calif.: Consulting Psychology Press, 1963.

Doll, E. A. *Vineland Social Maturity Scale.* Minneapolis, Minn.: Educational Test Bureau, 1947.

Farina, A., Arenberg, D., & Guskin, S. A scale for measuring minimal social behavior. *Journal of Consulting Psychology*, 1957, *21*, 265–268.

Haggerty, M. E., Olson, W. C., & Wickman, I. K. *Haggerty-Olson-Wickman Behavior Rating.* Yonkers-On-Hudson, N.Y.: World Book, 1930.

Ulmer, R. A., & Timmons, E. O. The Minimal Social Behavior Scale (MSBS): A short, objective, empirical, reliable measure of personality functioning. Paper read at meeting of the American Psychological Association, Los Angeles, Calif., 1964.

Ulmer, R. A., & Timmons, E. O. An application and modification of the Minimal Social Behavior Scale (MSBS): A short, objective, empirical, reliable measure of personality functioning. *Journal of Consulting Psychology*, 1966, *30*, 86.

**Children's Minimal Social Behavior Scale (CMSBS):
A Short, Objective, Reliable Measure
of Personality Functioning**

Raymond A. Ulmer
Drew Postgraduate Medical School

and

Martha Lieberman
University of California at Los Angeles

A. *Identifying Data*

1. Name or Code Name of S.   10. Behavioral Comments on Testing:
2. Birthdate:
3. Chronological Age:
4. Sex: 11. Background Information:
5. Date of Testing:
6. Name of Examiner:
7. Research Group: 12. Previous Test Data:
8. Grade in School:
9. Place of Testing:

B. *Test Data*

1. Time Score = _____186_____

No. of seconds up to limit of 31 seconds for each of
the following items: 7, 12, 16, 17, 19, 22

2. Motor Score = Sum of + ratings for all of the following items: 1, 4,
7, 8, 9, 10, 11, 12, 13, 17, 19, 20, 21, 24, 25, 26, 27,
28, 30

3. Verbal Score = Sum of + ratings for all of the following items: 2, 3,
5, 6, 14, 15, 18, 22, 29

4. Verbal-Motor Score = Sum of + ratings for the following items: 16,
23, 31

5. Performance Score = Sum of Motor + Verbal-Motor Scores +
Verbal Scores

6. Total Score = Performance + Time Scores

C. *Materials Needed*

Pad of paper, pencils, individually wrapped attractive pieces of candy
and gum, gold-colored box 13 × 13 × 13 cm, stop watch, wastepaper
basket, geometrical figure measuring 3 in × 3 in patterned as follows:

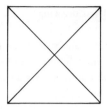

D. *Instructions*

The examiner is to follow the exact wording and directions of the scale. He is not to add other instructions, nor to present additional tasks, nor to explain any further his requests to his subject under any circumstances. The examiner should be very careful not to provide cues to his subjects by his facial expressions, gestures, or posture, but to remain carefully bland except for Item 22.

Please note the examiner is to follow directions and not add to or modify the sequence of items as outlined or to introduce different wording.

TEST ITEMS

I. Child is brought to the door and introduced to the examiner (*E*). *E* stands up and says, *"Hello, . . ."*
   (1) Score + if *S* enters and approaches *E*.   _____
   (2) Score + if any discriminable response to greeting, not necessarily verbal.   _____
   (3) Score + if response is verbal and appropriate.   _____

II. *E* says, *"Won't you have a seat?"*
   (4) Score + if *S* sits down without further urging.   _____

III. *E* sits and says, *"How are you?"*
   (5) Score + any discriminable response to this question.   _____
   (6) Score + if response is verbal and appropriate.   _____

IV. *E* drops a pencil by pushing it off the desk, ostensibly by accident. If *S* does not pick up the pencil spontaneously, *E* says *"Will you please pick up the pencil for me?"*
   (7) Score + if *S* picks up the pencil at all.   _____ Time: _____
   (8) Score + if *S* picks up pencil spontaneously.   _____

V. *E* says, *"Would you mind moving your chair closer? I have something that I want to show to you."* *E* holds a drawing of a 3-inch square with diagonals in front of *S*.
   (9) Score + if *S* moves chair closer to *E*.   _____

(10) Score + if S looks at drawing.   _____

VI. E says, "*Here is a pencil,*" and offers one to S. E then
   places a pad of blank paper before S and says, "*I would
   like you to copy this drawing on this paper.*" (Start
   timing immediately after saying, "on this paper," and
   stop timing when S makes any mark on the paper.)
   (11) Score + if S accepts pencil without further
         encouragement.   _____
   (12) Score + if S makes any mark on this paper.___ Time: _____
   (13) Score + if S draws any four-sided figure with
         diagonals.   _____

VII. E asks, "*How are you getting along?*"
   (14) Score + any recognizable response to this question. _____
   (15) Score + if response is verbal and appropriate.   _____

VIII. E crumbles a sheet of paper, tosses it at the wastebasket,
   and purposely misses. E then says, "*Darn it, missed again.*"
   (16) Score + if S smiles or laughs in response to
         exclamation.   _____Time:_____
   (17) Score + if S spontaneously picks up paper and
         deposits it in wastepaper basket.   _____ Time: _____

IX. E says, "*I have a few questions that I would like to ask
   you.*"
   (a) "*What year is it?*"
   (b) "*What month is it?*"
   (c) "*What day is it?*"
   (d) "*Is there somebody that you really don't like?*"
   (18) Score + if S makes any verbal response, irrespective of
         content to all of the questions.   _____

X. E places an empty gold-colored box in front of S and says,
   "*I'll be busy a minute.*" (Start timing and stop when S
   looks in the direction of the box.)
   (19) Score + if S looks in the general direction of the
         box.   _____ Time: _____

XI. E stands up and then clutches knee and pretends to have a
   severe pain. (Start timing immediately.)
   (22) Score + for any verbal response which includes the
         concept of "leg," "knee," etc., or "pain" or
         "cramp."   _____ Time: _____

XII. *E* places a stick of gum and a piece of candy on the table. *E* says, *"Would you like to have one?"*
  (23) Score + for any response which indicates acceptance or refusal.   _____

XIII. *E* rises and says, *"Thank you very much."* If necessary, *E* says, *"Go ahead,"* motioning toward the door.
  (24) Score + if *S* rises from the chair.   _____
  (25) Score + if *S* opens the door and crosses the threshold without further urging.   _____

XIV. Items 26 through 31 are based upon *S*'s behavior throughout the interview.
  (26) Score + unless inappropriate grimaces or mannerisms are readily apparent.   _____
  (27) Score + if *S* looks *E* in the eye at any time.   _____
  (28) Score + unless *S* obviously appears to avoid *E*'s gaze at any time or stares at *E* fixedly.   _____
  (29) Score + if *S* makes a spontaneous comment during the examination. (He has said something to *E* without being asked a direct question.)   _____
  (30) Score + unless *S* rises from chair and moves away from *E* before termination of interview, without any explanation.   _____
  (31) Score + unless *S* refuses any request.   _____

Revised Form for Rating Individual Patient Personality Functioning and Changes with Residence in Camarillo State Hospital's Behavior Modification Program

Raymond A. Ulmer

I. INTRODUCTION

This booklet is designed to be used by every member of the Behavior Modification Team to rate every patient in the program. Team members include psychiatrists, psychiatric social workers, psychiatric technicians, psychologists, and rehabilitation counselors.

Section I is this Introduction. Section II, General Instructions, can help you to get an overall picture of what this booklet can do to assist you in your job. Section III, Raters, tells which member of the team should rate which section. Section IV, Scheduling of Ratings, tells you when each patient should be rated. Section V is Steps on the Mental Health Status Scale and Their Meanings. This scale is used throughout this booklet, and it is carefully defined so that you can rate each patient easily and accurately. Section VI, Scale of Severity of Social Incapacity in the Community and Hospital, indicates how disturbing the patient's behavior was to others in his social environment before hospitalization. Section VII, Presenting Problem(s) of the Patient Living in His Community, notes the particular problem behavior that the patient shows in his community. Section VIII, Primary Treatment Plan and Progress of Patient, tells how to write about treatment and responses to treatment of the particular kinds of inappropriate behaviors that the patient shows in the hospital, keep him from being discharged, and if shown in his community, are likely to result in rehospitalization. Section IX, Secondary Problems, describes other disturbing behaviors of the patient, and treatment plans designed to change his inappropriate behaviors into more appropriate speech and actions that are acceptable to hospital staff and to others in the patient's community.

Thanks are due for some of the materials used in this paper to John Streifel, James Fossum, and Layle Weeks.

Much of this material was presented at a meeting of Western Psychological Association Convention, Anaheim, California, April 1973.

II. GENERAL INSTRUCTIONS

This is a form designed to help every member of the Behavior Modification Team to assess every patient on admission to the unit, and to set up a treatment plan for him. This form is written to make your work easier rather than giving you extra paper work to do. You will be able to describe your patient's problem behaviors, rate their intensity, and rate their frequency. His primary inappropriate behaviors are the reasons that you and other staff members do not feel that he is now ready to leave the hospital. You can use this form to set up a treatment plan for his inappropriate behaviors. This treatment plan can be known to, and followed by all of, the Behavior Modification Team members: psychiatric technicians, psychologists, psychiatrists, social workers, and rehabilitation counselors. This form should indicate what every staff member knows about a patient, what will be done to get him out of the hospital as soon as possible, and how treatment is designed to keep him out of the hospital as long as possible.

Besides these instructions, Dr. Ulmer, Assistant Program Director, Mrs. Marion Sisson, Nursing Coordinator, and Dr. John Streifel, Staff Psychologist, will be glad to work with you to help you rate your patient.

All staff members who rate a patient will sign their names on the top of the form in Figure D-2. The head charge will sign in orange. The group nursing leader on the day shift will sign in black ink, the afternoon leader in green ink, and the night group leader in red ink. The psychologist will sign in brown ink, with the date opposite his name. The physician will sign in purple, the social worker in blue, and the rehabilitation counselor in yellow.

By using different colors, anyone reading the form can quickly tell the discipline and responsibilities of any rater.

III. RATERS

Each nursing group leader will rate every patient on Sections VIII, IX, and X. Each nurse should carefully study Sections V, VI, and VII so that he clearly understands the meanings of ratings and the kinds of antisocial and asocial behaviors shown by the patient in his community that bring the patient to the hospital, and require behavioral training to help the patient to remain in his community, free of rehospitalization. The social worker will rate Sections V, VI, and VII. The physician, rehabilitation counselor, and psychologist can rate any sections in which they are involved. (More than one staff member can rate any section, and it is quite obvious who did the rating from the color of ink used, and the initials following each rating.) The psychologist is responsible for helping every staff member to know when he is to rate each patient, and on what sections.

IV. SCHEDULING OF RATINGS

Each patient will be rated within the first 48 hours of his admission to the unit. He will then be rated two weeks later, two weeks after that, and if he stays long enough, at the same time as the quarterly reports. Each patient will be rated during his last 48 hours in the hospital.

V. STEPS ON THE MENTAL HEALTH STATUS SCALE AND THEIR MEANINGS

Each patient will be rated on the Mental Health Status Scale (Table D-1) on the nine steps, (1) Major social disability to (9) Ready for discharge. Each one of the nine steps will be defined in a practical way so that you can observe your patient, read his record, and decide how you should rate him. You should *only* rate your patient on what you (or other nurses) can see or hear that he does or says that is not right in getting along in the hospital. For example, you can simply report the unsuitable speech of the patient who curses or speaks of his being a billionaire, takes off his clothes in public, or hits others. You should *not* rate your patient on anything about him that you or other nurses cannot hear or see, such as that he is schizophrenic, mentally retarded, or has a bad attitude toward something. Writing and talking only about what you can hear or see a patient saying or doing is the behavioristic way of looking at patients, and it is the only useful way of thinking about your patient for treatment in a behavioristic program.

VI. SCALE OF SEVERITY OF SOCIAL INCAPACITY IN THE COMMUNITY AND HOSPITAL

This scale indicates the severity of the patient's social handicap in his community (to be rated by the social worker), and in the hospital (to be rated by nurses and other involved staff members.)

1	2	3	4	5	6	7	8	9
Severely impaired social functioning		Disabled social functioning		Conditionally unacceptable social functioning		Minor defect(s) in social functioning		Generally acceptable social functioning

VII. PRESENTING PROBLEM(S) OF THE PATIENT LIVING IN HIS COMMUNITY

This rating (Figure D-1) refers only to the behavior of the patient in his community that brought him to the hospital. This rating should not refer to the

Table D-1 Mental Health Status Scale

Step	Severity of disability	Frequency shown	Ways disability shown
1	Major social disability (a)	Daily or weekly incidents	May be physically dangerous or exceedingly obnoxious to staff or other patients, because of antisocial or asocial actions or delusional speech. Or may avoid practically all contact with other patients or staff.
2	Major social disability (b)	At least once each month	Same as above
3	Major social disability (c)	Less than once a month	Same as above
4	Minor social disability (a)	Rarely speaks on his own initiative, once a week or even less often	Does not communicate with staff or other patients except nonverbally through the simplest of actions, such as going to the cafeteria and eating meals.
5	Minor social disability (b)	Speaks on his own initiative once every few days	Same as above
6	Minor social disability (c)	Daily or weekly	Expresses inappropriate fears, anxieties, or phobias.
7	Minor social disability (d)	Less than once each week	Same as above
8	Minor social disability (e)	Daily or weekly	Expresses inappropriate complaints with hospital regimen. Minor friction with staff and other patients.
9	Ready for discharge	*No patient age 65 years or older is ever to be rated ready for discharge, as this can jeopardize his government support.*	Appears to be functioning appropriately enough with staff and other patients to be sent to a nursing home, board-and-care home, halfway house, or other community facility, or to his home. This category is to be used if a patient seems dischargeable, even if he is under a court hold, conservatorship, or has secondary problems.

patient's behavior in the hospital. When the patient comes into the hospital, the social worker will rate the patient once on his community behavior. The social worker will check off the one community behavior that brings the patient into the hospital, and its severity of incapacity. The social worker will initial and date his rating.

Presenting Problem	Severity of Social Incapacity in Community								
	1	2	3	4	5	6	7	8	9
A. Physical condition									
B. Drug abuse									
C. Alcohol abuse									
D. Dangerous to self									
E. Dangerous to others									
F. Unacceptable sexual behaviors									
G. Other socially unacceptable behaviors:									
H. Transient life crisis									
I. Legal offender									

Figure D-1 Presenting problem of patient.

VIII. PRIMARY TREATMENT PLAN AND PROGRESS OF PATIENT

This is to be rated by the group nursing leader, his alternate, and other involved staff members.

The primary problem of the patient is the kind of speech and behavior shown by him in the hospital that make you feel that he is not ready to leave the hospital. You should *only* rate your patient on what you or other staff members can hear or see a patient saying or doing that does not help him to get along with others in the hospital. You should *not* describe your patient on anything that you or other staff members cannot hear or see, such as that he is schizophrenic, mentally retarded, or has a bad attitude toward something. Describing only what you can hear or see a patient saying or doing is the behavioristic way of looking at patients, and it is the only useful way of thinking about a patient for treatment in a behavioristic program.

Here are some sample suitable behavioristic phrases for describing a patient:

Hits other patients or staff members.
Sits without talking to anyone for long periods of time.
Does not talk to other patients or staff members.
Does not dress himself, shave, or take showers.
Does not talk sensibly or according to the situation that he's in.
Does not dress appropriately, or cleanly.
Takes off clothes in day room or other unsuitable places.
Bangs or slams doors or windows.
Lies in bed most of the time.

Makes sexual advances toward other patients or staff members.
Runs away from the hospital.
Continuously asks for cigarettes from other patients or staff members.
Flips cigarette ashes about.
Continuously asks for medication or drugs to relieve headache or pain.
Sings continuously.
Steals from other patients or staff members.
Walks about at night.
Repetitively complains about "physical illnesses."
Does not keep locker clean.

Primary Hospital Problem (including frequency shown):

Treatment Objective:

Treatment Plan:

Rating of Patient's Functioning in the Hospital (using the Mental Health Status Scale Steps):

Dates of Rating	1	2	3	4	5	6	7	8	9

Comments and Plan Changes:

Addressograph Plate for Patient's Name:

Figure D-2 Primary treatment plan and progress of patient.

Secondary Problem (1)(including frequency shown):

Objective:

Plan:

Comments and Plan Changes:

Date	Mental Health Status Scale Steps								
	1	2	3	4	5	6	7	8	9

Secondary Problem (2)(including frequency shown):

Objective:

Plan

Comments and Plan Changes:

Date	Mental Health Status Scale Steps								
	1	2	3	4	5	6	7	8	9

Figure D-3   Secondary problems of patient.

The inappropriate behaviors should be reduced, eliminated, or be supplanted by more socially appropriate behaviors, and that is the goal of every treatment plan (Figure D-2). For example, if you list a patient's primary problem as taking off his clothes in public, then the treatment objective should be reducing the frequency—or eliminating entirely—his taking off his clothes in public. The treatment plan includes everything done for the patient by the staff, whether or not it seems directly related to changing his behavior. Almost everything being done for the patient—outside of satisfying his physical needs, such as feeding him—should be written in the treatment plan: token economy training, medication, industrial therapy, and recreational therapy.

Under Comments and Plan Changes, note any changes in the patient's behavior that is in the direction of—or directly away from—the treatment objective, and try to relate these changes to any specific aspects of the treatment plan. Then make suggestions about increasing those aspects of the treatment plan that seem to be modifying the patient's behavior in a desirable direction, and about decreasing or changing those aspects of the treatment plan that do not seem productive.

IX. SECONDARY PROBLEMS

The usual patient shows more than one problem behavior in the hospital that is disturbing to staff, and helps to keep him in the hospital. After you have listed the primary problem, all of the other problems that the patient presents to staff are to be noted as secondary problems. List each secondary problem separately in the form in Figure D-3 in the same way that you did with the primary problem. When and if the patient's behavior changes so that the primary problem seems pretty much under his and the staff's control, a secondary problem may be the behavior that is keeping him in the hospital, and the secondary problem should then be listed as the primary problem, with the previous primary problem listed as a secondary problem or dropped.

The Second Camarillo State Hospital Behavior Modification Program Evaluative and Predictive Statement, April 1972

Raymond A. Ulmer
Assistant Program Director

DESCRIPTION

William R. Purmort, M.D., is Acting Program Director, Raymond A. Ulmer, Ph.D., is Acting Assistant Program Director, Mrs. Marion Sisson is Acting Nursing Coordinator, and Roy Jones acts as Chief of Psychiatric Social Services. Besides Dr. Purmort, there are four other physicians. Besides Dr. Ulmer, there are two other psychologists. In addition to Mrs. Sisson there are about one hundred other nursing personnel, and there are three rehabilitation counselors. Mr. Jones has two full-time social workers and one half-time social worker.

The CSH Behavior Modification Program is based on the belief that for all practical diagnostic and treatment purposes each patient's speech, actions, and appearance are his personality. This program is designed to change his speech, actions, and appearance so that he is more acceptable to his community after hospitalization than he was before. This program, which is social training of the last resort for the community, is designed to change antisocial and asocial repertoires into forms more acceptable to others in the community.

Behavioristic treatment uses social-learning principles of the scientific laboratory to change patterns of behavior. Each behavioristic staff member is part of the social change agent treatment team, and he has behavior modification team responsibilities in addition to his usual obligations of being a psychiatrist, psychiatric social worker, psychiatric technician, psychologist, or rehabilitation counselor. Insight, as in traditional evocative psychotherapy, is not used; instead, each patient is taught to respond more appropriately to others than he did prior to hospitalization.

Thanks are due for help with this paper to William R. Purmort, M.D., Marion Sisson, Roy Jones, Dave Freehauf, Esther Hudson, John Streifel, and Bruce Hulett.

BACKGROUND

The Behavior Modification Program is the outgrowth of four major revolutions in mental hospitalization in the 50 years from 1922 to 1972, each of which was described in the first CSH Behavior Modification Evaluation (Ulmer, 1971a). These four major revolutions in hospitalization were responses to the advent of neo-behaviorism, psychoactive medication, community psychiatry and psychology, and socio-legal innovations of the late 1960s and early 1970s.

A behavioral treatment program is based on the view that no one is ever involuntarily committed to a mental hospital for being "psychotic, schizophrenic, insane, or emotionally ill, or for suffering from any other disordered mental state" (Ulmer & Franks, 1973). A person is generally sent to a mental hospital for speaking in ways that are considered, correctly or otherwise, potentially dangerous to himself or to others in his community. Socially unacceptable speech and actions are by themselves sufficient reason for hospitalizing virtually anyone. If the person under consideration does not speak or act in ways that disturb others around him, he is not likely to be committed to a psychiatric institution, no matter how inappropriate his thoughts and fantasies. The community will *only* take the initiative in committing a person involuntarily to a mental hospital if he speaks, acts, or dresses in ways that disturb others in his community. This is not to belie either the existence or the importance of personal or intrapsychic problems. The emotionally disturbed person may be a deeply unhappy human being who feels so unbearably burdened that he requests help from a mental hospital, but his community will never take the initiative in committing him simply because he is distressed.

In parallel fashion, the CSH Behavior Modification Program position is that when a person is involuntarily committed, his discharge is rarely related to deep emotional changes. Quite the contrary, he will be discharged and returned to his community when his treatment staff, correctly or otherwise, perceives him as speaking, acting, and dressing in ways that are more appropriate to those of others in his community than when he entered the hospital, *and* when staff believes that his more socially appropriate repertoire is likely to be maintained by him in his community.

Patient Entry and Release

Patient turnover rate for January through April of 1972, period for this paper, is shown in Table E-1. Patient census for this period has been about 300 in total for the five units of the program, two male and three female. There has been considerable contact with the community, with Dr. Ulmer meeting directly with staff of Community Services Division of North Hollywood to explain the CSH Behavior Modification Program; and Roy Jones, Acting Chief Psychiatric Social Worker and his social workers making contact with many community agencies for the placement of patients, and to obtain financial aid for them, such as Aid to the Totally Disabled (ATD). These community agencies include:

Table E-1 Entry and Discharge Number for Behavior
Modification Program January–April 1972

Month of 1972	Patient entry	Patient release
January	61	42
February	21	39
March	59	53
April (estimated)	84	40
Total	225	144
Average	56	44

Short-Doyle Clinics in Los Angeles County, California State Community Services Branches primarily throughout Los Angeles County, Los Angeles County Conservator's Office, and private agencies such as Reiss-Davis Clinic for Child Guidance. In addition, many board-and-care and nursing homes throughout Los Angeles County have been contacted for placement of Los Angeles County patients.

Procedure for Release

This is probably similar to that of most CSH programs. Voluntary patients can, of course, leave at any time that they choose, and generally they stay for periods of days or weeks. Involuntary patients tend to stay for months or years, although most patients under the Lanterman-Petris-Short (LPS) Act tend to stay for days or weeks only. Involuntary patients consist of three categories: court holds, conservator patients, and LPS patients. Court holds are kept at CSH until the unit physician deems patients to be emotionally competent to stand trial for a criminal charge, usually a felony. The physician's decision is determined by the patient's behavior in the hospital as reported to him by his unit staff, and his judgment of a patient from interviewing him. Court holds usually stay for periods of months, with longer stays for patients accused of more serious offenses, such as physical or sexual assault, especially when repeated, and when patients have mental hospitalization histories. Court hold patients charged with relatively trivial offenses, such as loitering or not paying for a restaurant meal, tend to remain in the hospital for weeks rather than months, unless they have prison or hospitalization records. Most court holds come from Los Angeles County directly or indirectly through Atascadero Hospital for the Criminally Insane. Those from Atascadero have been there for relatively long periods of time, sometimes years, and are sent to Camarillo for "treatment" and eventually return to the courts or their communities.

Once patients are hospitalized, the behavioristic, social-learning approach seems especially suitable for helping them to learn to act appropriately in their communities so that they can be discharged from the hospital, and become able to "pass" for normals, thus remaining free of hospitalization. Release criteria for involuntary patients are:

1. Speech that is similar to that of others in the community, and not objectionable to others.
2. Actions approximating those of others.
3. Appearance essentially like that of many other community members.

While about 45 patients per month have left for the past year of the program, this figure is likely to rise to some 50 to 60 patients per month in fiscal 1973. This increased discharge rate will probably be due to alleviation of past shortages of physicians, and current shortages of social workers and psychologists. And with the patient population likely to increase from an average of about 300 per month to 325 per month, more patients are likely to leave as a response to the turnover of this higher, essentially transient patient population.

PATIENT DEFICITS

Patient deficits are describable as antisocial or asocial repertoires in the community leading to involuntary or even voluntary hospitalization. The following inappropriate repertoires are then rated according to the form in Appendix D. These repertoires are: A. Physical condition (associated with inappropriate behaviors); B. Drug abuse; C. Alcohol abuse; D. Dangerous to self; E. Dangerous to others; F. Unacceptable sexual behaviors; G. Other socially unacceptable behaviors; H. Transient Life Crisis; I. Legal offender.

Degree of disability is operationally described in the 9 steps in the Mental Health Status Scale in the Patient Assessment Form. While the characteristics of patients are defined and operationally described in a theoretical sense, the reality of patient admission is determined by admission policies. The criteria used by Admissions for selection to the Behavior Modification Program are reported in Table E-2.

The kinds of patients to be treated in this program are those with inappropriate community behaviors, except for those whose primary diagnostic problem is drug or alcohol abuse, mental retardation, or neurological impairment. Patients with primary diagnoses of alcohol or drug abuse or mental retardation are not to be accepted in the Behavior Modification Program primarily because there are specialized CSH programs for these patients. When these patients are inadvertently sent to the Behavior Modification Program, they are then routed to the specific programs for these problem areas. Neurologically impaired patients are unsuitable for behavior modification because they are unlikely to respond well to behavior therapy.

Priorities of treatment will be partially determined on the basis of the degree of awareness of a patient, with the most aware receiving the most rapid and intensive treatment. For example, the quite aware patient who is relatively

Table E-2   CHS Admissions Unit Guidelines for Assigning Patients
to the Behavior Modification Program

Categories of patient study	Specific patient characteristics
Major general impression	Socially offensive, abnormal, illegal or antisocial speech
Behavior	Asocial or antisocial speech that attracts community attention by being disruptive and distracting to others
Affect	Inappropriate affect
Social	Interpersonal friction because of offensive manner toward others
Vocational	Work problems although may be skilled
Age	18½ through 61
Etiology	Functional
Length of stay	At least 2 weeks
Unsuitable patient categories	(1) Primary alcoholism, (2) Primary drug abuse, (3) Mental retardation, and (4) Organicity contributing to antisocial behavior

young and is experiencing his first hospitalization will generally be sent to a behavioral encounter group within the first 48 hours of his entrance into the program. A new patient is generally seen by the unit psychologist or social worker fairly soon after his entry into the program, and since encounter groups meet from two to six times each week on various units of the program, he can be quickly seen in one of these groups.

A patient who is expected to be in the hospital for only a short period of time, such as 72 hours or 14 days, will be given priority consideration. His first contact with the psychologist, social worker, and the physician will probably occur within the first 24 hours of hospitalization. Treatment must begin quickly for the short-term patient or else he will leave the hospital after simply sitting on the unit throughout most of his hospital stay. Lower priority for starting treatment is usually given to the patient from Atascadero State Hospital since he is likely to be in the hospital for some months. Lower priority for starting treatment is usually given to the long-term patient with 20 or more years of hospitalization.

In effect, the greater the deficit and severity of social disability of the patient, the lower the priority of his treatment. While this procedure may have an element of injustice, it should also be recognized that the short-term patient with an essentially good social repertoire can be relatively quickly and easily assisted to function well enough to be returned to his community. If this relatively well functioning patient is given a small investment of staff time, he generally returns rapidly to his community, and there is a quick and substantive return for staff efforts. In contrast, the patient with 20 and more years of continuous hospitalization requires hundreds of hours of behavioral training to be able to leave the hospital, and there is a slow and slight return for staff efforts.

Currently, there is considerable effort being made in the program to balance these priorities by having social work and psychology students work intensively with the chronic patient. Students work under the close supervision of senior staff, so that both student and chronic patient benefit from the treatment relationship.

PROGRAM GOALS

Program goals are directly involved with staff training as described in the section Resources. A major goal of the program is to develop an increasingly effective, interdisciplinary behavior modification team. Greater numbers of interdisciplinary meetings are set up for this purpose, so that program members can communicate better, work more effectively, and learn more from each other.

It is planned to enlarge the program to include more divergent kinds of treatment techniques where these overlap with behavior therapy, such as psychodrama, and Sullivan-Berne Transactional Analysis.

OBJECTIVES

The objectives of patient treatment in a behavior modification program can be stated in clear, although simplistic, fashion: treatment is designed to change antisocial and asocial behaviors into socially acceptable enough forms to enable the former patient to remain in his community. Since personality is considered to be observable aspects of speech, actions, and appearance, the behavioristic program is designed to change personality, as so defined, into forms more compatible with those of others in the patient's community. The greater the degree of his deficit, especially when associated with long-term hospitalization, the greater the need for extensive treatment. Often, the long-term patient can best be treated, behaviorally trained, for life in a board-and-care or nursing home, rather than for living alone or with his family in his community. The specifics of these general program approaches are detailed below.

It is predicted that about 700 patients will enter the program in fiscal 1973 and remain an average of about a month in the program. This month's residency includes entry population prior to July 1, 1972, as well as those entering during the subsequent fiscal year. When the patient has a poor physical condition associated with inappropriate social repertoires, this program will provide him with medical care, comparable to a kind he would receive in his community mental health facility, and behavioral training for his specific behavioral deficit. (The kinds of activities given patients including specific treatment modalities are discussed in the section Activities.) It is, of course, hoped that the patient will function well enough so that discharge is indicated. For example, whatever his current disability, it is hoped that he will move at least two steps on the Mental Health Status Scale in each 60-day period, or less, of his hospital stay.

For some special kinds of patients, the movement is far greater and more rapid in a relatively short period of time. Typically, the drug-abusing patient functions quite well in the hospital within a few weeks, as soon as the last traces of his psychomimetic (psychosis mimicking such as LSD) drug are gone from his body. In like fashion, the alcoholic patient generally behaves quite normally in the hospital once he dries out, and if he does not drink, which is the usual case during his hospital stay or visits away from the hospital. Drug and alcohol patients then, if they are not transferred to the appropriate CSH program, are likely to remain in the program about a month or less, and to show sufficient improvement on the Mental Health Status Scale to warrant discharge from the hospital. These categories represent some 100 patients over the period July 1, 1972, to June 30, 1973.

There will be about 200 patients considered dangerous to others during fiscal 1973. Of these about 100 are likely to move an average of two points, and about 100, an average of three points, on the Mental Health Status Scale. While the average patient in this category will spend six months in the hospital, often this will be due to legal complications in his commitment and discharge that may be only indirectly related to his progress in treatment.

There will be about 50 patients with behaviors considered dangerous to themselves, such as suicidogenic patients or those with self-mutilating behaviors. These are likely to gain an average of two points on the scale, and to be considered suitable for discharge within 90 days of their entrance into the hospital.

There will be about 50 patients with sexually unacceptable behaviors, and they will remain an average of nine months during fiscal 1973. During this time they are likely to gain some two points on the Mental Health Status Scale, so that they may be considered for discharge, or return to the courts, in an average of nine months.

Other forms of socially unacceptable behavior will account for some 500 patients, and the average patient will spend about a month in the program, and gain some two points on the scale.

Some 100 patients will come into the program with transient life crises, and, on the average, stay 14 days, gain two points on the scale, and be ready for discharge.

The above discussion is focused on the entry population, and the predictive increases can be quite optimistic for this group. In contrast, the starting population is more likely to consist of chronic patients or those with repeated hospitalization episodes, and this group, is likely to improve less and remain in the hospital longer than the patients entering during fiscal 1973. In effect, the starting population patients, with similar community behavioral problems leading to hospital entrance, are likely to improve less and stay longer than comparable entry population patients.

PATIENT ACTIVITIES

The Behavior Modification Program uses the following patient activities: (1) group behavioral encountering, (2) written, negotiated contracts, (3) individual behavior therapy, (4) group behavior therapy, (5) token economy treatment, (6) unit industrial therapy, (7) psychoactive medication, (8) vocational rehabilitation, (9) recreational therapy, (10) music therapy, and (11) miscellaneous activities.

1. *Group behavioral encountering* differs considerably from group psychotherapy on many counts. Behavioral encountering focuses on the here-and-now of experience without discussions of the past, especially those long past such as early childhood experiences. By contrast, group psychotherapy (therapy) often focuses on the past, especially early childhood experiences. In addition, behavioral encountering, unlike behavior therapy, does not allow philosophical discussions of unconscious functions or dreams, or work toward insightful understanding of emotional conflicts. Instead, encountering emphasizes observable aspects of personality, considers all persons responsible, and capable of becoming even more reliable members of their communities. The behavioral encounter group tries to help its members recognize how they appear to others, how their speech, actions, and manner have led to their being hospitalized or jailed, and what they must do to prevent that from recurring in the future.

Behavioral encountering is solution-focused, not discussion-oriented. The basic purpose of every session is repeated in every session: this group meets to help all members to learn how to get out of the hospital as soon as possible, and to stay out of hospitals and jails as long as possible. Obviously, group encountering is appropriate for the most intact and aware patient, and is designed to help him to develop greater self-awareness of how he differs from others in his community. The group helps to provide the most intact patient with social-learning experiences that are designed to change his behavior so that he becomes more like others who live in his community. The group uses role playing to help a patient see in vivid, enacted scenes how his behavior differs from others and offends others. He is also advised by group leaders and other patients on what he must say, do, and how he must dress to get along with others in his community. The patient will often be encouraged to make commitments to the group to act more socially appropriately. The patient who does not fulfill these commitments will be criticized in later sessions.

There is an encounter group meeting two or three days each week on every one of the five units of this program. Each group is run by an interdisciplinary team, usually of one psychologist, one social worker, and one psychiatric technician, and there are between 10 and 20 patients in each group. Dr. Ulmer, Assistant Program Director, acts as consultant-trainer for all groups, and meets with group leaders each week, and sits in on their groups from time to time. A new, relatively intact patient who seems suitable to encountering treatment is generally brought into an encounter group within 48 hours of his entrance into the program. About 100 patients, or one-third of the patients in the program, are members of groups. The average patient in each group will be expected to gain about two steps on the scale during his last 90 days in the program.

2. *Written, negotiated contracts* may be concluded between a relatively aware patient and the staff, and these are often discussed in the behavioral encounter groups. A contract is often helpful in modifying the antisocial behavior of patients who are physically or verbally aggressive toward other patients or the staff. The contract informs the patient clearly and explicitly of what kinds of antisocial behavior are to be reduced or eliminated by him, and what will be his rewards for fulfillment of the contract as well as punishments for violation of the contract. The average patient on contract will spend his last 60 days in the program on contract, and during this period he will gain an average of two steps on the scale, so that he is socially functioning far more adequately than previously.

3. *Individual behavior therapy* focuses on behavioristic techniques, such as operant conditioning, to train a patient to function more effectively. The typical patient for individual behavior therapy, especially in a token economy unit, is a chronic, exceedingly long-term patient with 5 to 40 years of continuous hospitalization. He is seen in individual therapy one or two times daily, five to seven times each week for a period of 6 to 12 months. He may be seen in short sessions lasting only 10 to 20 minutes. This chronic patient, typically, has serious social deficits in being unable to conduct the simplest of social conversations, such as identifying himself, the time, date, or location of the hospital. The goal of individual behavior therapy is to help him to acquire rudimentary social skills, which will make him acceptable to a board-and-care or nursing home, and allow him to remain there. He is quite likely to remain in his community free of hospitalization, as has been the consistent experience in Unit 231, a token economy program, where many long-term patients have received individual behavior therapy, have been discharged in the past two years, and none of them have been returned to CSH.

In fiscal 1973, some 20 patients throughout the program are likely to receive individual behavior therapy. The average patient will spend his last 180 days in the hospital in this treatment, and move about two steps on the scale, from Step 5 to Step 7.

4. *Group behavior therapy*, like individual behavior therapy, will be used with the long-term, chronic patient with 5 to 40 years of continuous hospitalization. Group treatment is preferable to individual for those patients who are responsive, because group treatment tends to be more effective more quickly than individual therapy. Group treatment uses role modeling where one

patient helps another patient to learn to respond more socially appropriately by demonstrating suitable behavior that is positively reinforced by the group behavior therapist as well as the rest of the group. In addition, each patient can be taught simple social learning in the group by teaching him to initiate and to respond suitably to simple social conversations with other patients.

During fiscal 1973 some 25 patients are expected to be in group behavior therapy at all times with one group on each of the five units. Throughout the year some 50 patients will receive group behavior therapy, and about one-half of them are likely to gain two points on the scale, and be ready for discharge.

5. *Token economy treatment* is organized behavior therapy over a total mental hospital unit, 231 of the Behavior Modification Program, in this case. Token economy treatment, in combination with the most effective psychoactive drug for all patients on the unit, is the most powerful treatment approach yet devised for long-term patients. Token economy Unit 231 has a long (some seven years) history of discharging long-term patients with 20 to 40 years of continuous hospitalization to nursing and board-and-care homes, and few have ever returned. Some 70 patients are in this program at all times.

Besides the long-term patient, there are many different kinds of problems dealt with in today's token economy program. Newer kinds of patients include the short-term patient, such as the legal offender.

To deal with the short-term patient, substantial innovative changes are being effected in token economy treatment, such as behavioral encountering, group behavior therapy, and contract writing, as described above. None of these approaches are recorded in any token economy program other than CSH's. With these changes token economy treatment seems applicable to almost any kind of short- or long-term patient.

With this mixed patient population it is difficult to make general predictions for fiscal 1973 discharge rates. Instead, a breakdown by categories seems indicated with the average long-term patient gaining one scale step during the year, and each short-term patient, independent of specificity of diagnosis, gaining one step per month. Assuming some one-third of patient population (some 23 patients) to be long-term, and some two-thirds to be short-term (some 47 patients), it is likely that one long-term patient will be ready for discharge for each set of five short-term patients. Ready for discharge and discharge are not synchronous in time because the long-term patient, who is ready for discharge from the hospital may not be quickly or easily placed in a board-and-care or nursing home, since most homes may not consider him a desirable resident. And obtaining financial assistance for him, such as ATD, may be another time-consuming source of delay before discharge. In like fashion, the short-term patient may be on a court hold, which frequently blocks his being dischargeable although he behaves appropriately enough in the hospital for the staff to deem him ready to return to his community.

6. *Unit industrial therapy* is designed as a social/work learning experience for patients, and includes some 40 industrial assignments throughout the hospital.

Patients work about six hours, five days each week, in such work activities as: the Work Activity Center (50 patients), painting (35 patients), garden crew (25 patients), and motor pool (10 patients). Many other assignments use only a few patients, such as: Shop, Boiler Room, Equipment Repair, House of Style, Gym, Rehabilitation Supply, Swimming Pool, and Welding Shop. A total of some 125 work assignments are made each month, by request of the unit physician. These assignments are changed every three months for long-term patients, so that they do not have to work longer on any single job.

Unit industrial therapy is direct treatment for patient deficits shown in inability to work. In a more general sense, all work is social therapy, and is often far more therapeutic than psychotherapy (Kupferman & Ulmer, 1964), and unit industrial therapy can therefore be considered relevant treatment for all forms of patient deficits. During fiscal 1973, the average patient will spend about a month in Unit Industrial Therapy and move about one step on the scale.

7. *Psychoactive medication* is primarily useful for controlling bizarre behavior, such as delusions of a patient, and regulating the rate of his responses to others, as noted above in the section Description, and detailed by Ulmer and Franks (1973). Psychoactive drugs are effective in helping the hyperactive person to respond more slowly, and in energizing the apathetic person so that each extreme rate of response is moved toward a midpoint approximating that of others in his community. The psychoactive drug is given with various forms of treatment offered by the Behavior Modification Program, and the usual patient shows increased ability to respond to treatment with the drug.

By and large almost every patient, with every form of deficit, is likely to be given psychoactive medication in fiscal 1973. And it is reasonable to assume that psychoactive medication has some relevance to every form of patient deficit. During fiscal 1973, the average patient will spend about one month in the program, and gain three steps on the scale and be ready for discharge.

8. *Vocational rehabilitation* is preparation for economic self-sufficiency for a patient after he is discharged from the hospital. Vocational rehabilitation includes interviews, tests, and provision of information so that the patient can be helped to make realistic work choices for the time when he will return to his community. Rehabilitation will provide him with funds and facilities to implement his work choices by helping him to keep a job in his community.

Vocational help seems suitable for any patient with a work problem since permanent gainful employment in the community is an important factor in keeping a patient in his community. The gainfully employed ex-patient in his community is likely to have positive emotions in feeling a sense of personal worth, and reduces, or even relieves, the state from having to subsidize him permanently. The average patient in the program in fiscal 1973 will spend about one month in vocational rehabilitation, and gain about three steps on the scale.

9. *Recreational therapy* focuses on arts and crafts with the 100 most regressed (the lower third of the total population), chronic patients in the program. Most of these have deficits such as being gravely disabled, with

unacceptable sexual or social behavior. These patients enroll in a special recreational setting, something that is often definitely indicated to improve their level of social functioning in all areas. These patients are being taught to increase their attention span, learn hobby skills for post-hospital living, and to increase their motivation to join with others in physical activities. The average chronic patient will spend about one year in recreational therapy and move about one step on the scale.

10. *Music therapy* includes many creative activities, such as arts, music practice and listening rooms, running the CSH radio station, and game rooms. Mr. Freehauf, Acting Rehabilitation Supervisor, is also involved in individual behavior therapy and co-leads a behavioral encounter group. Rehabilitation counselors arrange for special musical entertainments for patients from outside groups such as local bands.

11. *Miscellaneous activities* include the movie theater, gym, swimming pool, bowling alley, and Patient's Library. These are most useful for the relatively aware patient. These facilities seem most helpful to the patient with a behavioral deficit who is hospitalized because he is dangerous to himself or others, shows unacceptable sexual or other social behaviors, and is currently experiencing a transient life crisis. These facilities are used by about 50 patients (about one-sixth of the program population), and this percentage is growing, as there is an increasing number of patients hospitalized with legal charges against them. These patients will spend about a month of fiscal 1973 in the program, move about three steps on the scale, and be considered ready for discharge.

EVALUATION

The personality assessment instrument to be used in this program is the *Individual Patient Assessment and Changes with Residence in Camarillo State Hospital's Behavior Modification Program* (IPAC) (Ulmer, 1972). The IPAC was originated by James Fossum, Chief Program Administrator, and Layle Weeks, Chief, Bureau of Biostatistics, both of the California State Department of Mental Hygiene. The IPAC was modified considerably by Dr. Raymond A. Ulmer, senior psychologist, and Acting Assistant Program Director of the CSH Behavior Modification Program. A revised form of the IPAC is reproduced in Appendix D. Previous objective personality assessments used in the Behavior Modification Program include the children's CMSBS (Ulmer & Lieberman, 1967, 1968; van Doorninck, 1972) and adult's MSBS (Ulmer & Timmons, 1964, 1966) forms of the Minimal Behavior Scale.

Each of the 300 patients in the program is rated on the scale, and rating procedures will be as follows. Every patient will be evaluated on entrance and discharge from the program. If a patient stays more than two weeks, he will be rated at the end of two weeks, and again at the end of two weeks if he stays to the end of the month. If he stays more than three months, he will be rated at the end of two weeks, one month, and two months thereafter. Subsequently, he will be rated every three months to coincide with the quarterly progress reports of medical and nursing personnel.

Throughout fiscal 1973 this is the procedure that will be followed in the program. Dr. Ulmer will be responsible for overall coordination of assessment of all patients in the program. He will work closely with Dr. John Streifel, staff psychologist, to supervise assessment on Units 224 and 225. Dr. Ulmer will work with Mrs. Myrna Carleton, psychology associate, in evaluating patients on Units 227 and 230. On each unit, the psychologist will be the key person responsible for working closely with staff on evaluating and reevaluating patients.

RESOURCES

Dr. William Purmort, psychiatrist, is Acting Program Director, Dr. Raymond A. Ulmer, senior psychologist, is Acting Assistant Program Director, Mrs. Marion Sisson, Assistant Superintendant of Nursing Services, is Nursing Coordinator, and Mr. Roy Jones is Acting Chief of Psychiatric Social Workers. Current staff includes four full-time and two half-time physicians, three psychologists, three full-time and one half-time psychiatric social worker, 97 nurses, and three rehabilitation therapists. Allotments of staff time are reported in Table E-3.

Staff training has been an important part of program activities. Staff development meetings occur twice weekly, with one session attended by all disciplines: physicians, nurses, social workers, rehabilitation counselors, and psychologists. Speakers have been engaged from various parts of the hospital including: Dr. Ira Greenberg, a psychologist from another Camarillo Hospital Program, speaking on psychodrama; Mr. William van Doorninck, a psychologist from the Children's Unit, speaking on behavior modification with children; and Dr. Charles Wallace, formerly of the Mental Retardation Program, speaking on behavior modification with mental retardates. Many of the staff development speakers have been from the Behavior Modification Program, such as Dr. Mary Lou Brenneman, psychiatrist, speaking on transactional analysis, Dr. Raymond Ulmer, psychologist, speaking on behavior modification in theory and practice, and behavioral encountering. Dr. John Streifel, psychologist, speaking on contract writing with mental hospital patients, and Mr. Roy Jones, psychiatric social worker, speaking on behavioral aspects of mental hospital entrance.

Consultants from outside the hospital have been brought in for all CSH programs, such as Dr. Cyril Franks, Director of the Psychological Clinic of Rutgers University, New Brunswick, New Jersey. (Dr. Frank's visit was made possible through the cooperation of Dr. Irwin Hart, Director of Training, and Dr. Robert Moebius, Chief, CSH Department of Professional Education.) Additional consultants will be brought in from academic applied settings.

Current facilities of this program include five units with all attendant equipment and officers, vocational rehabilitation facilities, and use of the gym, swimming pool, movie theater, bowling alley, patient's library, and music center.

Table E-3 Allotments of Staff Times

Activity	Physician $(5)^a$	Psychologist (3)	Nursing (97)	Psychiatric Social worker (3.5)	Rehabilitation therapist (3)
Group behavioral encountering		30^b	50	30	
Written negotiated contracts		10	5	5	
Individual behavior therapy		10	50	10	5
Token economy treatment	15	20	800	20	
Unit industrial therapy			540		
Industrial and occupational therapy			150		45
Psychoactive medication	20		500		
Vocational rehabilitation			115		
Recreational therapy					55
Music therapy					
Referral evaluation	40		50		
Mental and physical evaluations	50		120		
Routine patient care	30		1,000		
Social service workups				50	
Education, staff, and other meetings, court appearances, administrative responsibilities	45	50	500	20	15
Totals	200	120	3,880	135	120

^{a}All figures in parentheses are for numbers of staff members.
^{b}All figures within the body of the table are for numbers of staff hours.

SUMMARY

This program statement reflects considerable progress in CSH's Behavior Modification Program from its inception less than a year ago. The staff has become a well-integrated team, increasingly aware and knowledgeable about behavioral assessment and treatment techniques, and able to use innovative approaches, such as group behavioral encountering and contract writing. The spirit of behavioristic practices and involvement has spread to physicians and nursing and rehabilitation personnel, from a core of psychologists who were knowledgeable about behavior therapy to a group of social workers who were sympathetic to behavioristic views and practices.

The results of staff training are showing increasing rewards in improved patient functioning, and enthusiasm of the staff to try new objective approaches, such as the Individual Patient Assessment Form.

REFERENCES

Kupferman, S. C., & Ulmer, R. A., An experimental total-push program for emotionally disturbed adolescents. *Journal of Personnel and Guidance*, 1964, *62*, 894–899.

Ulmer, R. A. The token economy mental hospital society: An American operant, subcultural society for cross-cultural studies. *International Journal of Psychology.* 1970, *5*, 293–305.

Ulmer, R. A. Preliminary Camarillo State Hospital Behavior Modification Program evaluation: August through December 1971. Camarillo State Hospital and Mental Health Center, Camarillo, Calif.: 1971. (a)

Ulmer, R. A. Relationships between objective personality test scores, schizophrenics' history and behavior in a mental hospital token economy ward. *Psychological Reports*, 1971, *29*, 307–312. (b)

Ulmer, R. A. Individual patient assessment and changes with residence in Camarillo State Hospital's Behavior Modification Program. Camarillo State Hospital and Mental Health Center, Camarillo, Calif.: 1972.

Ulmer, R. A., & Franks, C. M. A proposed integration of independent mental health facilities into behaviorally oriented social training programs. *Psychological Reports*, 1973, *32*, 95–104.

Ulmer, R. A., & Lieberman, M. The Children's Minimal Social Behavior Scale (CMSBS): A short, objective measure of personality functioning. Paper presented at California State Psychological Association Convenction, San Diego, Calif., 1967.

Ulmer, R. A., & Lieberman, M. The Children's Minimal Social Behavior Scale (CMSBS): A short, objective measure of personality functioning. *Psychological Reports*, 1968, *22*, 263–286.

Ulmer, R. A., & Timmons, E. O. The Minimal Social Behavior Scale (MSBS): A short, objective measure of personality functioning. Paper presented at the American Psychological Association Convention, Los Angeles, 1964.

Ulmer, R. A., & Timmons, E. O. An application and modification of the Minimal Social Behavior Scale (MSBS). *Jounral of Consulting Psychology*, 1966, *30*, 96.

van Doorninck, W. The assessment of adaptive behavior of male psychiatric inpatients in a token economy treatment setting. Doctoral dissertation at the University of Denver, Denver, Colorado, 1972.

References

GENERAL REFERENCES

Agras, W. S. (Ed.). *Behavior modification: Principles and clinical applications.* Boston: Little, Brown, 1972.

Alberti, R. E., & Emmons, M. L. *Your perfect right: Guide to assertive behavior.* San Luis Obispo, Calif: Impact, 1970.

Allen, B. V. Behavior modification of study habits of "educationally disadvantaged" students. Paper presented at meeting of California State Psychological Association, San Francisco, January 1966.

Allen, D. J., & Magaro, P. A. Measures of change in token economy programs. *Behaviour Research and Therapy,* 1971, *9*(4), 311-318.

American Psychiatric Association. *Diagnostic and statistical manual of mental disorders* (2nd ed.). Washington, D.C.: Author, 1968.

American Psychiatric Association. *Task Force Report 5: Behavior therapy in psychiatry.* Washington, D.C.: Author, 1973.

American Psychological Association. *Casebook on ethical standards of psychologists.* Washington, D.C.: Author, 1967.

American Psychological Association. *Casebook on ethical standards of psychologists.* Washington, D.C.: Author, 1970.

American Psychological Association. *Ethical principles in the conduct of research with human participants.* Washington, D.C.: Author, 1973.

Anderson, D. P., Morrow, J. E., & Scheisinger, R. The effects of token reinforcers on the behavior problems of institutionalized female retardates. Paper presented at meeting of Western Psychological Association, San Francisco, May 1967.

Atthowe, J. M., Jr. Behavior therapy with chronic schizophrenics and the brain damaged. Paper presented at meeting of California State Psychological Association, San Francisco, January 1966. (a)

Atthowe, J. M., Jr. The token economy: Its utility and limitations. Paper presented at meeting of Western Psychological Association, Long Beach, Calif., May 1966. (b)

Atthowe, J. M., Jr. Ward 113 research and service program: Staff orientation and procedure manual for administering the token-incentive program. VA Hospital, Menlo Park Division, California, 1967.

Atthowe, J. M., Jr., & Krasner, L. The systematic application of contingent reinforcement procedures (token economy) in a large social setting. A psychiatric ward. Paper presented at American Psychological Association meeting, Chicago, Ill., September 1965.

Atthowe, J. M. Jr., & Krasner, L. Preliminary report on the application of contingent reinforcement procedures (token economy) on a "chronic" psychiatric ward. *Journal of Abnormal Psychology*, 1968, *73*, 37-43.

Aumack, L. Manual for the Patient Activity Checklist. Technical Report No. 68-2, September 1968. VA Hospital, Danville, Ill.

Aumack, L. The Patient Activity Checklist: An instrument and an approach for measuring behavior. *Journal of Clinical Psychology*, 1969, *25*(2), 134-137.

Ayllon, T. Intensive treatment of psychotic behaviour by stimulus satiation and food reinforcement. *Behaviour Research and Therapy*, 1963, *1*, 53-61.

Ayllon, T., & Azrin, N. H. The measurement and reinforcement of behavior of psychotics. *Journal of Experimental Analysis of Behavior*, 1965, *8*, 357-383.

Ayllon, T., & Azrin, N. H. Reinforcer sampling: A technique for increasing the behavior of mental patients. *Journal of Applied Behavior Analysis*, 1968, *1*, 13-20. (a)

Ayllon, T., & Azrin, N. H. *The token economy: A motivational system for therapy and rehabilitation.* New York: Appleton-Century-Crofts, 1968. (b)

Ayllon, T., & Haughton, E. Modification of symptomatic verbal behavior of mental patients. *Journal of Behavior Research and Therapy*, 1964, *2*, 87-97.

Ayllon, T., & Michael, J. The psychiatric nurse as a behavioral engineer. *Journal of the Experimental Analysis of Behavior*, 1959, *2*, 323.

Ayllon, T., & Roberts, M. D. The token economy now. In W. S. Agras (Ed.), *Behavior modification: Principles and clinical applications.* New York: Little, Brown, 1972.

Baer, D. M., Wolf, M. M., & Risley, T. R. Some current dimensions of applied behavior analysis. *Journal of Applied Behavioral Analysis*, 1968, *1*, 91-97.

Ball, T. S. (Ed.). *The establishment and administration of operant conditioning programs in a state hospital for the retarded.* Sacramento, Calif.: Bureau of Research, California Department of Mental Hygiene, 1969. (Research Symposium No. 4)

Bandura, A. Behavioral psychotherapy. *Scientific American*, March 1967, *21*(6), 78-86.

Bandura, A. *Principles of behavior modification.* New York: Holt, Rinehart and Winston, 1969.

Bandura, A. (Ed.). *Psychological modeling.* Chicago: Aldine-Atherton, 1971.

Beal, E., Slettin, I. W., Ognjanov, V., & Hughes, D. D. Nursing care approaches for operant reinforcement with psychiatric patients. *Journal of Psychiatric Nursing*, 1969, *7*, 157-159.

Bennett, P. S., & Maley, R. F. Modification of interactive behaviors in chronic mental patients. *Journal of Applied Behavior Analysis*, 1973, *6*(4), 609-620.

Bergin, A. E., & Suinn, R. M. Individual psychotherapy and behavior therapy. In M. R. Rosenzweig & L. W. Porter (Eds.), *Annual review of psychology* (Vol. 26). Palo Alto, Calif.: Annual Reviews, 1975.

Birky, J. B., Chambliss, J. E., & Wasden, R. A comparison of residents discharged from a token economy and two traditional programs. *Behavior Therapy*, 1971, 2, 46–51.

Boren, J., & Colman, A. Some reinforcement principles within a psychiatric ward for delinquent soldiers. *Journal of Applied Behavioral Analysis*, 1970, 3, 29–37.

Bricker, W. A. Introduction to behavior modification. In *Peabody Papers in human development*. Nashville, Tenn.: Department of Psychology, Peabody College for Teachers, 1968.

Brockhoff, L. A. Ward 106 token program, incentives and costs—A manual for patients. Unpublished manuscript. VA Hospital, Menlo Park Division, California, 1966.

Bruce, M. Tokens for recovery. *American Journal of Nursing*, 1966, 66, 1799–1802.

Bugh, V. Medical director's point of view on operant conditioning programs in a state hospital for the retarded. In T. S. Ball (Ed.), *The establishment and administration of operant conditioning programs in a state hospital for the retarded*. Sacramento, Calif.: Bureau of Research, California Department of Mental Hygiene, 1969, pp. 13–15.

Bugle, C., Cross, W., & Parsons, R. Token system for ward C-2 east. Paper presented at Rehabilitation Department seminar at Chicago State Hospital, Chicago, February 1967.

Burdock, E. E. & Hardesty, A. S. *The structured clinical interview (SCI)*. New York: Springer, 1969.

Buros, O. K. *Personality tests and reviews*. Highland Park, N.J.: Gryphon Press, 1970.

Carlson, C. G., Hersen, M., & Eisler, R. M. Token economy programs in the treatment of hospitalized adult psychiatric patients. *Journal of Nervous and Mental Disease*, 1972, 155(3), 192–204.

Chaplin, J. P. *Dictionary of psychology*. New York: Dell, 1968.

Chase, J. D. Token economy programs in the Veterans Administration. (Report of a survey conducted in 1969.) Veterans Administration, Washington, D.C., 1970.

Cleckley, H. *The mask of sanity*. St. Louis, Mo.: Mosby, 1964.

Cloa, M. D. Behavior modification treatment in a day hospital. Paper presented at meeting of the American Psychological Association, Washington, D.C., September 1967.

Cohen, R., Florin, I., Grusche, A., Meyer-Osterkamp, S., & Sell, H. The introduction of a token economy in a psychiatric ward with extremely withdrawn chronic schizophrenics. *Behaviour Research and Therapy*, 1972, 10(1), 69–74.

Colman, A. D. *The planned environment in psychiatric treatment: A manual for ward design.* Springfield, Ill.: C. C Thomas, 1971.

Colman, A. D., & Baker, S. L., Jr. Utilization of an operant conditioning model for the treatment of character and behavior disorders in a military setting. *American Journal of Psychiatry,* 1969, *125,* 1395–1403.

Colman, A. D., & Boren, J. J. An information system for measuring patient behavior and its use by staff. *Journal of Applied Behavior Analysis,* 1969, *2,* 207–214.

Cowles, J. T. Food-tokens as incentives for learning by chimpanzees. *Comprehensive Psychology Monograph,* 1937, *14*(71, Whole No. 287).

Curran, J. P., Jourd, S., & Whitman, N. *Evolution and evaluation of a treatment program on a closed psychiatric unit.* Unpublished manuscript. Anoka State Hospital, Minnesota, 1967.

Davis, T. S. Six-month follow-up of hospital patients after termination of token economy program. *Newsletter for Research in Mental Health and Behavioral Sciences,* 1973, *15*(3), 2–9.

Davison, G. C. Behavior modification for rehabilitation: Concepts, possibilities and cautions. In G. R. Leslie (Ed.), *Behavior modification in rehabilitation facilities.* Hot Springs, Ark.: Arkansas Rehabilitation Research and Training Center, 1968.

Davison, G. C. Appraisal of behavior modification techniques with adults in institutional settings. In C. M. Franks (Ed.), *Behavior therapy: Appraisal and status.* New York: McGraw-Hill, 1969.

Department of Health, Education and Welfare. Instruction Sheet for Public Health Service 398. Washington, D.C., 1969; revised March 1970.

Ellsworth, J. R. A token economy system innovated and conducted by nonprofessional hospital personnel. Paper presented at 8th Annual Research Meeting, Department of Institutions, University of Washington, Seattle, November 1967.

Ellsworth, J. R. Reinforcement therapy with chronic patients. *Hospital and Community Psychiatry,* 1969, *20,* 36–38

Endore, G. S. *Synanon.* Garden City, N.Y.: Doubleday, 1968.

English, H. B., & English, A. C. *A comprehensive dictionary of psychological and psychoanalytical terms.* New York: Longmans, Green, 1958.

Eysenck, H. J. The effects of psychotherapy: An evaluation. *Journal of Consulting Psychology,* 1952, *16,* 319–323.

Eysenck, H. J. *Uses and abuses of psychology.* New York: Pelican Books, 1954.

Eysenck, H. J. *Sense and nonsense in psychology.* New York: Pelican Books, 1957.

Eysenck, H. J. *Behavior therapy and the neuroses.* New York: Pergamon Press, 1960.

Eysenck, H. J. The effects of psychotherapy. In H. J. Eysenck (Ed.), *Handbook of abnormal psychology: An experimental approach.* New York: Basic Books, 1961.

Eysenck, H. J. *Experiments in behavior therapy.* New York: Pergamon Press, 1964.

Eysenck, H. J. *Fact and fiction in psychology.* New York: Pelican Books, 1965.

Farina, A., Arenberg, D., & Guskin, S. A scale for measuring minimal social behavior. *Journal of Consulting Psychology,* 1957, *21,* 265–268.

Faris, R. E. L., & Dunham, H. W. *Mental disorders in urban areas.* Chicago: University of Chicago Press, 1939.

Fernandez, J. Token economies: Prosthetic or therapeutic environments? Paper presented at Fourth Annual Southern California Conference on Behavior Modification, Los Angeles, October 1972.

Fernandez, J., Fischer, I., & Ryan, E. Behaviour modification using token reinforcement. *Irish Journal of Psychology,* 1973, *ii*(1), 34–56.

Fernandez, J., Fischer, I., & Ryan, E. The token economy: A living-learning environment. *British Journal of Psychiatry,* 1973, *122,* 453–455.

Ferster, C. B. *Interim progress report. Linwood Project.* Linwood, Md.: Institute of Behavioral Research, 1965.

Ferster, C. B., & Skinner, B. F. *Schedules of reinforcement.* New York: Appleton-Century-Crofts, 1957.

Ferster, C. M. *Behavior principles.* New York: Appleton-Century-Crofts, 1968.

Fethke, G. C. The relevance of economic theory and technology to token reinforcement systems: A comment. *Behaviour Research and Therapy,* 1972, *10*(2), 191–192.

Forehand, R., Mulhern, T. J., & Rickard, H. D. The effects of a token economy in a therapeutic camp. Unpublished manuscript. University of Alabama, Alabama, 1967.

Franks, C. M. *Behavior therapy: Appraisal and status.* New York: McGraw-Hill, 1969.

Franks, C. M., & Wilson, G. T. (Eds.). *Annual review of behavior therapy, 1973.* New York: Brunner/Mazel, 1973.

Frazier, T. W. Training institutional staff in behavior modification principles and techniques. In R. D. Rubin, H. Fensterheim, J. D. Henderson, & L. P. Ullman (Eds.), *Advances in behavior therapy.* New York: Academic Press, 1972.

Gates, J. J. Overspending (stealing) in a token economy. *Behavior Therapy,* 1972, *3*(1), 152–153.

Gelfand, D. M., Gelfand, S., & Dobson, W. R. Unprogrammed reinforcement of patients' behavior in a mental hospital. *Behaviour Research and Therapy,* 1967, *5,* 201–207.

Gericke, O. L. Practical use of operant conditioning procedures in a mental hospital. *Psychiatric Studies and Projects,* 1965, *3*(5), 1–10.

Glicksman, M., Ottomanelli, G., & Cutler, R. The earn-your-way credit system: Use of a token economy in narcotic rehabilitation. *International Journal of the Addictions.* 1971 *6*(3), 525–531.

Goldfried, M. R., & D'Zurilla, T. J. A behavioral-analytic model of assessing competence. In C. D. Spielberger (Ed.), *Current topics in clinical and community psychology.* New York: Academic Press, 1969.

Goldfried, M. R., & Pomeranz, D. M. Role of assessment in behavior modification. *Psychological Reports*, 1968, *23*, 75-87.

Gorham, D. R., & Green, L. W. Effect of operant conditioning techniques on chronic schizophrenics. *Psychological Reports*, 1970, 27, 223-234.

Gripp, R. F., & Magaro, P. A. A token economy program evaluation with untreated control ward comparisons. *Behaviour Research and Therapy*, 1971, *9*, 137-149.

Guralnick, D. B. (Ed.). *Webster's new world dictionary.* New York: World, 1970.

Guyett, I. Behavior modification using resocialization and token economy for the rehabilitation of chronic schizophrenic patients. Paper presented at Quarterly Meeting of State Psychologists of Pennsylvania, Dixmont State Hospital, Pennsylvania, October 1968.

Hall, J., & Baker, R. Token economy systems: Breakdown and control. *Behaviour Research and Therapy*, 1973, *11*(3), 253-263.

Hallsten, E. A., & Fletcher, S. *Toward the systematic use of rewards.* Galesburg State Research Hospital, Galesburg, Ill., 1966.

Hartlage, L. C. Subprofessional therapists' use of reinforcers versus traditional psychotherapeutic techniques with schizophrenics. *Journal of Consulting and Clinical Psychology*, 1970, *34*, 181-183.

Hastorf, A. H. The "reinforcement" of individual actions in a group situation. In L. Krasner, & L. Ullmann (Eds.), *Research in behavior modification.* New York: Holt, Rinehart and Winston, 1965.

Heap, R. F., Boblitt, W. E., Moor, C. H., & Hord, J. E. Behavior-milieu therapy with chronic neuropsychiatric patients. *Journal of Abnormal Psychology*, 1970, *76*, 349-354.

Henderson, J. D. The use of dual reinforcement in an intensive treatment system. In R. D. Rubin & C. M. Franks (Eds.), *Advances in behavior therapy, 1968.* New York: Academic Press, 1969.

Henderson J. D. A community-based operant learning environment. I: Overview. In R. Rubin, H. Fensterheim, A. Lazarus, & C. Franks (Eds.), *Advances in behavior therapy.* New York: Academic Press, 1971.

Henderson, J. D., & Scoles, P. E. Conditioning techniques in a community-based operant environment for psychotic men. *Behavior Therapy*, 1970, *1*, 245-251.

Hersen, M., Eisler, R. M., Alford, G. S., & Agras, W. S. Effects of token economy on neurotic depression: An experimental analysis, *Behavior Therapy*, 1973, *4*, 392-397.

Hersen, M. H., Eisler, R. M., Smith, B. S., & Agras, W. S. A token reinforcement ward for young psychiatric patients. *American Journal of Psychiatry*, 1972, *129*(2), 228-233.

Hibbert, R. F., & Henderson, J. D. A community-based operant learning environment. III: Behavior change. In R. Rubin, H. Fensterheim, A. Lazarus, & C. Franks (Eds.), *Advances in behavior therapy.* New York: Academic Press, 1971.

Higgs, W. J. Effects of cross environmental changes upon behavior of schizophrenics. *Journal of Abnormal Psychology*, 1970, 76, 421–422.

Hinsie, L. E., & Campbell, R. J. *Psychiatric dictionary* (4th ed.). New York: Oxford University Press, 1970.

Holland, J., & Skinner, B. F. *The analysis of behavior.* New York: McGraw-Hill, 1961.

Holmes, D. S. *Reviews of research in behavior pathology.* New York: Wiley, 1968.

Honig, W. K. *Operant behavior: Areas of research and application.* Appleton-Century-Crofts, 1966.

Horn, J., & Black, W. A. M. The effect of token reinforcement on verbal participation in a social activity with long stay psychiatric patients. *Australian and New Zealand Journal of Psychiatry*, 1973, 7, 185–188.

Inglis, J. *The scientific study of abnormal behavior.* Chicago, Ill.: Aldine-Atherton, 1966.

Insalaco, C., & Shea, R. J. *Behavior modification: An annotated bibliography 1965–1969.* Columbia, S.C.: Department of Psychology, University of South Carolina, 1970.

Isaacs, W., Thomas, J., & Goldiamond, I. Applications of operant conditioning to reinstating verbal behavior in psychotics. *Journal of Speech and Hearing Disorders*, 1960, 25, 8–12.

Jones, R. T., & Kazdin, A. E. Programming response maintenance after withdrawing token reinforcement. *Behavior Therapy*, 1975, 6, 151–153.

Jourard, S. M. *The transparent self.* New York: Van Nostrand Reinhold, 1964.

Kanfer, F. H., & Phillips, J. S. *Learning foundations of behavior therapy.* New York: Wiley, 1970.

Karen, R. L., & Bower, R. C. A behavioral analysis of a social control agency: Synanon: *Journal of Research in Crime and Delinquency.* 1968, 5, 18–34.

Kazdin, A. E. The failure of some patients to respond to the token economy. *Journal of Behaviour Therapy and Experimental Psychiatry*, 1973, 4, 7–14.

Kazdin, A. E. Methodological and assessment considerations in evaluating reinforcement programs in applied settings. *Journal of Applied Behavior Analysis*, 1973, 6, 517–531.

Kazdin, A. E. Role of instruction and reinforcement in behavior changes in token reinforcement programs. *Journal of Educational Psychology.* 1973, 64, 63–71.

Kazdin, A. E., & Bootzin, R. R. The token economy: An evaluative review. *Journal of Applied Behavior Analysis*, 1972, 5, 343–372.

Kazdin, A. E., & Polster, R. *Intermittent token reinforcement and response maintenance in extinction. Behavior Therapy*, 1973, 4, 386–391.

Kelleher, R. T. Chaining and conditioned reinforcement. In W. K. Honig (Ed.), *Operant behavior: Areas of research and application.* New York: Appleton-Century-Crofts, 1966.

Kelleher, R. T., & Gollub, C. R. A review of positive conditioned reinforcement. *Journal of the Experimental Analysis of Behavior.* 1965, *5*, 543–597. (Supplement)

Kelley, K. M., & Henderson, J. D. A community-based operant learning environment. II: Systems and procedures. In R. D. Rubin, H. Fensterheim, A. A. Lazarus, & C. M. Franks (Eds.), *Advances in behavior therapy.* New York: Academic Press, 1971.

Kipphardt, H. *In the matter of J. Robert Oppenheimer.* New York: Hill & Wang, 1968.

Krasner, L. Operant conditioning techniques with adults from the laboratory to "real life" behavior modification. Paper presented at meeting of American Psychological Association, Chicago, September 1965.

Krasner, L. The translation of operant conditioning procedures from the experimental laboratory to the psychotherapeutic interaction. Paper presented at meeting of American Psychological Association, New York, September 1966.

Krasner, L. Applications of token economies: Current status—Future directions. Paper presented at meeting of American Psychological Association, San Francisco, September 1968. (a)

Krasner, L. Assessment of token economy programmes in psychiatric hospitals. In R. Porter (Ed.), *The role of learning in psychotherapy.* Ciba Foundation Symposium. London: Churchill, 1968. (b)

Krasner, L. Token economy as an illustration of operant conditioning procedures with the aged, with youth, and with society. In D. J. Lewis (Ed.), *Learning approaches to therapeutic behavior change.* Chicago, Ill.: Aldine-Atherton, 1970.

Krasner, L. Behavior therapy. In P. H. Mussen & M. R. Rosenzweig (Eds.), *Annual review of psychology* (Vol. 22). Palo Alto, Calif.: Annual Reviews, 1971.

Krasner, L., & Atthowe, J. M., Jr. The token economy as a rehabilitative procedure in a mental hospital setting. In H. C. Rickard (Ed.), *Behavioral intervention in human problems.* New York: Pergamon Press, 1971.

Krasner, L., & Krasner, M. Token economies and other planned environments. In *Seventy-Second Yearbook of the National Society for the Study of Education.* Chicago: University of Chicago Press, 1973.

Krasner, L., & Ullman, L. *Research in behavior modification.* New York: Holt, Rinehart and Winston, 1965.

Kupferman, S. C., & Ulmer, R. A. An experimental total-push program for emotionally disturbed adolescents. *Journal of Personnel and Guidance.* 1964, *62*, 894–899.

Kushner, M. Behavior therapy program at V.A. Hospital, Coral Gables, Florida. *Newsletter, Association for the Advancement of the Behavior Therapies,* February 1967.

Laing, R. D. *The divided self.* Baltimore, Md.: Penguin Books, 1959.

Laing, R. D. *The politics of experience.* New York: Pantheon Press, 1967.

Lawson, R. B., Greene, R. T., Richardson, J. S., McClure, G., & Padina, R. J. Token economy program in a maximum security correctional hospital. *Journal of Nervous and Mental Disease,* 1971, *152,* 199–205.

Layton, M. M. Behavior therapy and its implications for psychiatric nursing. *Perspectives in Psychiatric Care,* 1966, *4,* 38–52.

Lazarus, A. A. *Behavior therapy and beyond.* New York: McGraw-Hill, 1971.

Lazarus, A. A. (Ed.). *Clinical behavior therapy.* New York: Bruner/Mazel, 1972.

Lazarus, A. A., & Davison, G. C. Clinical innovations in research and practice. In A. E. Bergin & S. L. Garfield (Eds.), *Handbook of psychotherapy and behavior change.* New York: Wiley, 1970.

Liberman, R. A view of behavior modification projects in California. *Behavior Research and Therapy,* 1968, *6,* 331–341.

Liberman, R. *Behavior therapy: A short course for self-instruction.* New York: Pergamon Press, 1970.

Liberman, R. P. Behavior modification with chronic mental patients. *Journal of Chronic Diseases,* 1971, *23,* 803–812.

Lindsley, O. R. Operant conditioning methods applied to research in chronic schizophrenia. *Psychiatric Research Reports,* 1956, *5,* 118–139.

Lindsley, O. R. Characteristics of the behavior of chronic psychotics as revealed by free-operant conditioning methods. *Diseases of the Nervous System,* 1960, *21,* 66–78. (Monograph Supplement)

Lindsley, O. R., & Skinner, B. F. A method for the experimental analysis of the behavior of psychotic patients. *American Psychologist,* 1954, *9,* 419–420.

Lloyd, K. E., & Abel, L. Performance on a token-economy psychiatric ward: A two-year summary. *Behavior Research and Therapy,* 1970, *8,* 1–9.

Lloyd, K. E., & Garlington, W. K. Weekly variations in performance on a token economy psychiatric ward. *Behaviour Research and Therapy,* 1968, *6,* 407–410.

London, P. Ethical problems in behavior control. In W. A. Hunt (Ed.), *Human behavior and its control.* Cambridge, Mass.: Schenkman, 1957.

London, P. *Behavior control.* New York: Perennial Library, 1969.

Maley, R. F. Group methods and interpersonal learning on a token economy ward. In A. Jacobs & W. Spradlin (Eds.), *The group as an agent of change.* Chicago: Aldine-Atherton, 1972.

Malott, R. W., & Whaley, D. L. *Elementary principles of behavior* (Vols. I & II). Kalamazoo, Mich: Western Michigan University Press, 1968.

Marks, J., Schalock, R., & Sonoda, B. Reinforcement versus relationship therapy for schizophrenics. In *Proceedings, 75th Annual Convention, American Psychiatric Association,* 1967.

Marks, J., Sonoda, B., Collings, G., Schalock, R., Tibbets, L., & Kreie, P. Comparative therapy study, relationship vs. reinforcement therapy. *Research Ward Study No. 5.* Sacramento, Calif.: California State Department of Mental Hygiene, 1966.

Marlowe, L. *Social psychology: An interdisciplinary approach to human behavior.* Boston: Holbrook Press, 1971.

Matin, P. L., & Farish, D. L. Behavioral control of early morning rising on hospital wards for the mentally ill. *California Mental Health Research Digest,* 1967, *6,* 109–111.

McReynolds, W. T., & Coleman, J. Token economy: Patient and staff changes. *Behaviour Research and Therapy,* 1972, *10*(1), 29–34.

Meichenbaum, D. H. The effects of instruction and reinforcement on thinking and language behavior of schizophrenics. *Behaviour Research and Therapy,* 1969, 7, 101–114.

Melin, G. L., & Gotestam, K. G. A contingency management program on a drug-free unit for intravenous amphetamine addicts. *Journal of Behavior Therapy and Experimental Psychiatry,* 1973, *4*(4), 331–337.

Mertens, G. C., & Fuller, G. B. Conditioning of molar behavior in "regressed" psychotics: 1. An objective measure of personal habit training with "regressed" psychotics. *Journal of Clinical Psychology,* 1963, *19,* 333–337.

Mertens, G. C., Luker, A., & Boltuck, C. *Behavior science, behaviorally taught.* Minneapolis, Minn.: Burgess, 1968.

Meyer, V. The current status of behavior therapy with emphasis on clinical application. Paper presented at Fourth Annual Southern California Conference on Behavior Modification, Los Angeles, October 1972.

Milby, J. B. A system for recording individualized behavioral data in a token program. *Journal of Applied Behavior Analysis,* 1973, *62*(2), 333–338.

Miller, P., & Drennen, W. T. Establishment of social reinforcement as an effective modifier of verbal behavior in chronic psychiatric patients. *Journal of Abnormal Psychology,* 1970, *76*(3), 392–395.

Miller, P. M. The use of behavioral contracting in the treatment of alcoholism: A case report. *Behavior Therapy,* 1972, *3*(4), 593–596.

Mishara, B. L., & Kastenbaum, R. Wine in the treatment of long-term geriatric patients in mental institutions. *Journal of the American Geriatrics Society,* 1974, *22*(2), 88–94.

Montgomery, J., & McBurney, R. D. Problems and pitfalls of establishing an operant conditioning–token economy program. *Mental Hygiene,* 1970, *53*(3), 382–387.

Moreno, J. L. *Psychodrama.* Beacon, N.Y.: Beacon House, 1959.

Mowrer, O. H. *The new group therapy.* Princeton, N.J.: Van Nostrand Reinhold, 1964.

Mowrer, O. H. The behavior therapies with special reference to modeling and imitation. *American Journal of Psychotherapy,* 1966, *20,* 439–461.

O'Leary, K. D., & Drabman, R. Token reinforcement programs in the classroom: A review. In C. M. Franks & G. T. Wilson (Eds.), *Annual review of behavior therapy theory and practice.* New York: Brunner/Mazel, 1973.

Oseas, L. The clinician as organization consultant. Paper presented at meeting of American Psychological Association, Washington, D.C., September 1969.

Panek, D. M. Word association learning by chronic schizophrenics on a token economy ward under conditions of reward and punishment. Paper presented at Western Psychological Association Meeting, San Francisco, May 1967.

Parlour, R. R. The reorganization of the California Department of Mental Hygiene. *American Journal of Psychiatry*, 1972, *128*(11), 1388-1394.

Paul, G. L. Chronic mental patient: Current status—Future directions. *Psychological Bulletin*, 1969, *71*, 81-94.

Pavlov, I. P. *The work of the digestive glands* (2nd English ed.). London: Griffin, 1910.

Perls, F. S. *Gestalt therapy verbatim.* Lafayette, Calif.: Real People's Press, 1969.

Pomeranz, D. M., & Goldfried, M. R. An intake report outline for behavior modification. *Psychological Reports*, 1970, *26*, 447-450.

Pomerleau, O. F., Bobrove, P. H., & Harris, L. C. Some observations on a controlled environment for psychiatric patients. *Journal of Behavior Therapy and Experimental Psychiatry*, 1972, *3*(1), 15-22.

Roberts, C. L., & Perry, R. M. A total token economy. *Mental Retardation*, 1970, *8*(1), 15-18.

Roe, A. A psychological study of eminent psychologists and anthropologists, and a comparison with biological and physical scientists. *Psychological Monographs*, 1953, *67*(2, Whole No. 352).

Rogers, C. R. *Carl Rogers on encounter groups.* New York: Harper & Row, 1970.

Rubin, R., & Franks, C. (Eds.). *Advances in behavior therapy.* New York: Academic Press, 1968-1972.

Ruskin, R. S., & Maley, R. F. Item preference in a token economy ward store. *Journal of Applied Behavior Analysis*, 1972, *5*(3), 373-378.

Schaefer, H. H. Investigations in operant conditioning procedures in a mental hospital. In J. Fisher & R. Harris (Eds.). *Reinforcement theory in psychological treatment—A symposium.* Bureau of Research, California State Department of Mental Hygiene. *Research Monographs*, 1966, No. 8.

Schaefer, H. H., & Martin, P. L. Behavior therapy for "apathy" of hospitalized schizophrenics. *Psychological Reports*, 1966, *19*, 1147-1158.

Schaefer, H. H., & Martin, P. L. *Behavioral therapy.* New York: McGraw-Hill, 1969.

Schalock, R. Behavior modification: Evaluation in a typical psychiatric ward setting. *Psychological Reports*, 1973, *33*(3), 953-954.

Scoles, P. E., & Henderson, J. Effects of token reinforcement on the social performance of psychotic men. Unpublished manuscript. Spruce House, Horizon House, Philadelphia, 1968.

Shean, J. D., & Zeidberg, Z. Token reinforcement therapy: A comparison of matched groups. *Journal of Behavior Therapy and Experimental Psychiatry*, 1971, *2*, 95-105.

Sidman, M. *Tactics of scientific research.* New York: Basic Books, 1960.

Skinner, B. F. *Science and human behavior.* New York: Macmillan, 1953.

Skinner, B. F. Operant behavior. *American Psychologist,* 1963, *18*(2), 503–515.

Skinner, B. F. *Contingencies of reinforcement.* New York: Appleton-Century-Crofts, 1969.

Skinner, B. F. *Beyond freedom and dignity.* New York: Knopf, 1971.

Skinner, B. F. *Cummulative record* (3rd ed.). New York: Appleton-Century-Crofts, 1972.

Sletten, I., Hughes, D., Lamont, R. J., & Ognjanov, V. Work performance in psychiatric patients: Tokens versus money. *Diseases of the Nervous System,* 1968, *29,* 261–264.

Sobell, L. C., Schaefer, H. H., Sobell, M. B., & Kremer, M. E. Food priming: A therapeutic tool to increase the percentage of meals bought by chronic patients. *Behaviour Research and Therapy,* 1970, *8,* 339–345.

Srole, L., Langner, T. S., Michael, S. T., Opler, M. K., & Rennie, T. A. *Mental health in metropolis: The midtown Manhattan study.* New York: McGraw-Hill, 1962.

Steffy, R. A., Hart, J., Crain, M., Torney, D., & Marlett, N. Operant behaviour modification techniques applied to a ward of severely regressed and aggressive patients. *Canadian Psychiatric Association Journal,* 1969, *14,* 59–67.

Steffy, R. A., Torney, D., Hart, J., Craw, M., & Marlett, N. An application of learning techniques to the management and rehabilitation of severely regressed, chronically ill patients: Preliminary findings. Paper presented at meeting of Ontario Psychological Association, Ottawa, Canada, February 1966.

Stein, J. (Ed.). *The Random House dictionary of the English Language.* New York: Random House, 1966.

Suchotliff, L., Greaves, S., Stecker, H., & Berke, R. Critical variables in the token economy. In *Proceedings, 78th Annual Convention, American Psychological Association,* 1970, *5,* 517–518.

Susser, M. *Community psychiatry: Epidemiologic and social themes.* New York: Random House, 1968.

Szasz, T. S. *The myth of mental illness.* New York: Hoeber-Harper, 1961.

Szasz, T. S. *Psychiatric justice.* New York: Macmillan, 1965.

Tanner, B. A., Parrino, J. J., & Daniels, A. C. A token economy with "automated" data collection. *Behavior Therapy,* 1975, *6,* 111–118.

Timmons, E. O., Noblin, D. C., Adams, H. E., & Butler, J. R. Operant conditioning with schizophrenics comparing verbal reinforcers versus psychoanalytic interpretations: Differential extinction effects. *Journal of Personality and Social Psychology,* 1965, *1,* 373–377.

Ullmann, L., & Krasner, L. *Case studies in behavior modification.* New York: Holt, Rinehart and Winston, 1965.

Ullmann, L., & Krasner, L. *A psychological approach to abnormal behavior.* New York: Prentice-Hall, 1969.

Ulmer, R. A. Objective time-dimensional measures of past, present, and future time concepts. Paper presented at 18th International Congress of Psychology, Moscow, 1966. (a)

Ulmer, R. A. Psychologists' reactions and views of the Watts riots. Paper presented at Western Psychological Association Convention, Long Beach, Calif., April 1966. (b)

Ulmer, R. A. Objective time-dimensional measures differentiating between normals and schizophrenics. Paper presented at 11th Interamerican Congress of Psychology, Mexico City, December 1967.

Ulmer, R. A. Culture-fair tests as assessment instruments for educationally and socially disadvantaged Americans. Symposium presented at California State Psychological Association Convention, Santa Barbara, Calif., April 1968.

Ulmer, R. A. Cross-cultural cooperation on research-applied aspects of objective personality assessment problems of children and adults. Paper presented at 12th Interamerican Congress of Psychology, Montevideo, Uruguay, March 1969. (a)

Ulmer, R. A. Cross-cultural research and applied problems of personality assessment. Symposium presented at California State Psychological Association Convention, Newport Beach, Calif., 1969. (b)

Ulmer, R. A. Personality assessment across cultures: Research and applied problems. Symposium presented at Western Psychological Association Convention, Vancouver, Canada, June 1969. (c)

Ulmer, R. A. Community psychology. Symposium presented at California State Psychological Association Convention, Monterey, Calif., January 1970. (a)

Ulmer, R. A. The token economy mental hospital society: An American operant sub-cultural society for cross-cultural studies. *International Journal of Psychology*, 1970, 5, 293–305. (b)

Ulmer, R. A. Training of undergraduates and graduate psychology students in objective personality assessment. Paper presented at California State Psychological Association Convention, Monterey, Calif., January 1970. (c)

Ulmer, R. A. University of Southern California Mental Health counselling aide program for Training Paraprofessional Psychotherapists. Paper presented at Western Psychological Association Convention, Los Angeles, April 1970. (d)

Ulmer, R. A. The behavioristically-oriented viewpoint. Paper presented at California State Psychological Association Convention, San Diego, Calif., January 1971. (a)

Ulmer, R. A. Community psychology in practice and in theory. Symposium presented at Western Psychological Association Convention, San Francisco, April 1971. (b)

Ulmer, R. A. Relationships between objective personality test scores, schizophrenics' history and behavior in a mental hospital token economy ward. *Psychological Reports*, 1971, 29, 307–312. (c)

Ulmer, R. A. The fourth Camarillo State Hospital Behavior Modification Program evaluative statement: August 2, 1972 to September 29, 1972. Unpublished manuscript. Camarillo State Hospital and Mental Health Center, Camarillo, Calif., 1972. (a)

Ulmer, R. A. Individual patient assessment and changes with residence in Camarillo State Hospital's Behavior Modification Program. Unpublished manuscript. Camarillo State Hospital and Mental Health Center, Camarillo, Calif., 1972. (b)

Ulmer, R. A. Community psychology: Objective personality assessment and program evaluation. Paper presented at meeting of Western Psychological Association, Anaheim, Calif., April 1973. (a)

Ulmer, R. A. Revised form for rating individual patient functioning and changes with residence in Camarillo State Hospital's Behavior Modification Program. Paper presented at meeting of Western Psychological Association, Anaheim, Calif., April 1973. (b)

Ulmer, R. A. *A drug abuse program manual: The King Hospital-Drew Postgraduate Medical School Treatment, Training and Research Program.* Los Angeles, Calif.: King Hospital-Drew School, 1974.

Ulmer, R. A. *The drug abuse treatment program at Martin Luther King, Jr. General Hospital: A guide for patients.* Los Angeles, Calif.: King Hospital, 1975.

Ulmer, R. A. Behavior therapy: A promising drug abuse treatment and research approach. *The International Journal of the Addictions,* 1976, *12*(4), in press.

Ulmer, R. A., & Franks, C. M. A proposed integration of independent mental health facilities into behaviorally oriented social training programs. *Psychological Reports,* 1973, *32,* 95–104.

Ulmer, R. A., & Kupferman, S. C. An empirical study of the process and outcome of psychiatric consultation. *Journal of Clinical Psychology,* 1970, *26,* 323–326.

Ulmer, R. A., & Lieberman, M. The Children's Minimal Social Behavior Scale (CMSBS): A short, objective measure of personality functioning. Paper presented at meeting of California State Psychological Association, San Diego, Calif., January 1967.

Ulmer, R. A., & Lieberman, M. The Children's Minimal Social Behavior Scale (CMSBS): A short, objective measure of personality functioning. *Psychological Reports,* 1968, *22,* 283–286.

Ulmer, R. A., & Timmons, E. O. The Minimal Social Behavior Scale (MSBS). Paper presented at meeting of American Psychological Association, Los Angeles, Calif., September 1964.

Ulmer, R. A., & Timmons, E. O. An application and modification of the Minimum Social Behavior Scale (MSBS): A short, objective measure of personality functioning. *Journal of Consulting Psychology,* 1966, *30,* 86.

Ulrich, R., Stachnick, T., & Mabry, J. (Eds.). *Control of human behavior* (2 vols.). Glenview, Ill.: Scott, Foresman, 1966–1969.

Upper, D. A "ticket" system for reducing ward rules violations on a token economy program. Paper presented at meeting of Association for the Advancement of Behavior Therapy, Washington, D.C., September 1971.

van Doorninck, W. The assessment of adaptive behavior of male psychiatric inpatients in a token economy treatment setting. Doctoral dissertation. University of Denver, Denver, Col., 1972.

van Doren, M. (Ed.). *The portable Emerson.* New York: Viking Press, 1946.

Wagner, B. R. Essential features of a behaviorally oriented hospital program. Paper presented at Rehabilitation Department Seminar on Behavior Modification. Chicago State Hospital, Chicago, February 1967.

Watson, J. B. *Psychology from the standpoint of a behaviorist.* Philadelphia: Lippincott, 1919.

Wenrich, W. W. *A primer of behavior modification.* Belmont, Calif.: Brooks/ Cole, 1970.

Wexler, D. B. Token and taboo: Behavior modification, token economies and the law. *Behaviorism,* 1973, *1*(2), 1-24.

White, O. R. *A glossary of behavioral terminology.* Champaign, Ill.: Research Press, 1971.

Wincze, J. P., Leitenberg, H., & Agras, W. S. The effects of token reinforcement and feedback on the delusional verbal behavior of chronic paranoid schizophrenics. *Journal of Applied Behavior Analysis,* 1972, *5*(3), 247-262.

Winkler, R. C. Health and unhealthy economies. *Australian Psychologist,* 1968, *3*, (Abstract)

Winkler, R. C. The conceptual analysis of token systems. *Australian Psychologist,* 1969, *4* (Abstract)

Winkler, R. C. Management of chronic psychiatric patients by a token reinforcement system. *Journal of Applied Behavior Analysis,* 1970, *3*, 47-55.

Winkler, R. C. Reinforcement schedules for individual patients in a token economy. *Behavior Therapy,* 1971, *2*, 534-537. (a)

Winkler, R. C. The relevance of economic theory and technology to token reinforcement systems. *Behaviour Research and Therapy,* 1971, *9*, 81-88. (b)

Winkler, R. C., & Krasner, L. The contribution of economics to token economies. Paper presented at meeting of Eastern Psychological Association, New York, April 1971.

Wolman, B. B. (Ed.). *Dictionary of behavioral science.* New York: Van Nostrand Reinhold, 1973.

Wolpe, J. *The practice of behavior therapy.* New York: Pergamon Press, 1969.

Wolpe, J. The compass of behavior therapy. *Behavior Therapy,* 1971, *2*(3), 403-405.

Wolpe, J., & Lazarus, A. A. *Behavior therapy techniques.* New York: Pergamon Press, 1966.

Yablonsky, L. *The tunnel back: Synanon.* New York: Macmillan, 1965.

Yates, A. J. *Behavior therapy.* New York: Wiley, 1970.

Zimmerman, J. Techniques for sustaining behavior with conditioned reinforcers. *Science,* 1963, *142*, 582-584.

DICTIONARIES

Chaplin, J. P. *Dictionary of psychology.* New York: Dell, 1968. A pocket dictionary providing a few of the core ideas of most general psychological terms.

English, H. B., & English, A. C. *A comprehensive dictionary of psychological and psychoanalytical terms.* New York: Longmans, Green, 1958. An excellent dictionary providing a good description of many psychological terms, unfortunately dated by this time.

Guralnik, D. B. (Ed.). *Webster's new world dictionary.* New York: World, 1970. A standard desk reference dictionary without special psychological emphasis.

Hinsie, L. E., & Campbell, R. J. *Psychiatric dictionary* (4th ed.). New York: Oxford University Press, 1970. An excellent psychiatric-psychological dictionary describing in essay form many of the most widely used terms in clinical work.

Stein, J. (Ed.). *The Random House dictionary of the English language.* New York: Random House, 1966. A large, comprehensive, dictionary, almost unabridged in its scope of many useful terms in psychology and psychiatry.

White, O. R. *A glossary of behavioral terminology.* Champaign, Ill.: Research Press, 1971.

BEHAVIORAL AND TOKEN ECONOMY BIBLIOGRAPHIES AND TOKEN ECONOMY MANUALS

Ball, T. S. The establishment and administration of operant conditioning programs in a state hospital for the retarded. (Research Monograph). Sacramento, Calif.: California State Department of Mental Hygiene, 1969.

Barnard, J. W., & Orlando, R. *Behavior modification: A bibliography.* Nashville, Tenn.: John F. Kennedy Center for Research on Education and Human Development, 1967.

Brown, D. G. *A selected bibliography on behavioral modifications for mental health personnel.* Chevy Chase, Md.: National Institute of Mental Health, 1969.

Insalaco, C., & Shea, R. J. *Behavior modification: An annotated bibliography 1965-69.* Columbia, S.C.: Department of Psychology, University of South Carolina, 1970.

Kazdin, A. E. *The token economy: An annotated bibliography.* Washington, D.C.: Journal Supplement Abstract Services, 1972.

Krasner, L., & Atthowe, J. M., Jr. *Token economy bibliography.* Stony Brook, N.Y.: State University of New York, 1969.

Montgomery, J., & McBurney, R. D. Operant conditioning—token economy. Sacramento, Calif.: California State Department of Mental Hygiene, 1970. (Research Monograph)

Morrow, W. R. *Behavior therapy bibliography: 1950-1969.* Columbia, Mo.: Universiy of Missouri Press, 1971.

Rooney, J. R. Paxton Program: Orientation and procedure manual for a token economy. Unpublished manuscript. Sonoma State Hospital, Eldridge, Calif., 1966.

SELECTED JOURNALS PUBLISHING
BEHAVIORALLY ORIENTED RESEARCH

*Behavior Research and Therapy
*Behavior Therapy
 Journal of Abnormal Psychology
*Journal of Applied Analysis of Behavior
*Journal of Behavior Therapy and Experimental Psychiatry
 Journal of Clinical Psychology
 Journal of Consulting and Clinical Psychology
*Journal of Experimental Analysis of Behavior
 Psychological Bulletin
 Psychological Reports

*Almost exclusively behaviorally oriented.

Author Index

Numbers in italics refer to the pages on which the complete references are cited.

Subject Index

231